THE CRITIC'S MONEY IS ON

STOCK MARKET PRIMER

"The average beginning investor in stocks: read the dailies and weeklies, and try *Stock Market Primer*."
—**Robert Netz**
***New York Times* Investment Columnist**

"Sophisticated but straightforward investing advice."
—***Sylvia Porter's Personal Finance***

"A blue-chip book."
—***St. Louis Post-Dispatch***

"Time-tested, very basic, commonsensical . . . an excellent primer . . . author Claude Rosenberg is very careful to make his explanations as clear as possible. . . . Consider this book a good weapon if you know nothing about the stock market and are considering jumping into it."
—***Houston Post***

"FOUR STARS! A complete, entertaining, and well-written look at the stock market. Highly recommended."
—***Minneapolis Star and Tribune***

"First published in 1962, this is the foremost quick-reference guide. . . . Questions for you to ponder are everywhere. There are informative lists and tables. . . . [and] possible strategies."
—***Changing Times***

The Revised and Updated Edition

STOCK MARKET PRIMER

THE CLASSIC GUIDE
TO INVESTMENT SUCCESS
FOR THE NOVICE
AND THE EXPERT

Claude N. Rosenberg, Jr.

WARNER BOOKS

A Time Warner Company

First Trade Printing: June 1991
10 9 8 7 6 5 4

Book design: H. Roberts
Cover design: Mike Stromberg

Library of Congress Cataloging-in-Publication Data

Rosenberg, Claude N.
    Stock market primer.

    Includes index.
        1. Investments—United States—Handbooks, manuals,
etc. 2. Stocks—United States—Handbooks, manuals,
etc. 3. Stock-exchange—United States—Handbooks,
manuals, etc. 1. Title.
HG4921.R58 1987   332.63'22   87-40163
ISBN 0-446-38718-5

Contents

From Writer to Reader

This book was originally published in 1962 at the "blue chip" price of $12.50. At that time—and every year since—I have heard from countless people who have told me that they consider *Stock Market Primer* the most understandable and worthwhile book they have ever read on the subject of stocks and the market. I hope they are right—and I hope that you, too, find it useful.

The *Primer* is now fully revised. What encourages me most is that the revision entailed almost no change in basic approach. What seemed basic and important twenty-five years ago still holds today. This successful aging gives me confidence that the substance is there and that the reader can gain lasting benefit from its use.

The stock market! One very learned man I know calls it "the greatest dice game in the world." "What," he asks, "makes Exxon worth two points less—or over $1.5 billion less—today than it was yesterday? Has the company really changed by a billion and a half dollars in one day? And then, what makes the same company worth three points more—or over $2.2 billion more—next week?"

Indeed, if you approach the market on this basis, it does appear to be a senior Las Vegas. Yet there is far more to the stock market than these day-to-day fluctuations. From the average investor's viewpoint, it is of much greater importance to know what makes IBM or Abbott Laboratories or XYZ Electronics Company worth double or triple or quadruple or ten times its value of five or ten years ago.

The answer to this is relatively simple. After all, hindsight is *always* 20–20! The important thing is that we can learn from our hindsight.

Anyone connected with investment securities will agree that it is a very *in*exact science. Like many other pursuits, it involves a certain amount of luck. But luck is often enhanced by placing yourself in the right strategic position. Hence, you *can* improve your probabilities. You can *prepare* yourself to take better advantage of luck than the next person and achieve far superior results.

Is there an exact formula that will promise *you* superior results? Well, I know of one. A man I know determined forty years ago that he would retire in forty years with $100,000. Believe it or not, he succeeded. The formula that allowed him to retire after forty years with $100,000 involved four factors:

1. Hard work.
2. Economical living.
3. Occasional saving.
4. The recent death of an uncle who left him $97,000!

I don't know how many of you can depend on such a formula to cushion *your* future. But I do know that there is a serious approach to investing money and achieving success. If this formula were boiled down to its essential elements, it would look something like this:

$$Hindsight + Foresight = Success$$

This book gives you the basic facts you need to know in buying stocks and bonds. It provides the background and foundation for intelligent investing. In essence, it attempts to give you the first part of our formula—hindsight. As to foresight— the *in*exact part of investing—an important portion of this book is devoted to providing you with it so that you will arrive at the right investment decisions for your personal future.

[Note: References in the masculine throughout the book are simply editorial shorthand.]

PART I
An Introduction to Investments

1

Investment Channels

A simple definition of the word "investment" would read: "setting money to work to earn more money." Yet simple definitions are seldom enough, and the case of investments is no exception. A few more words should be added to our definition, namely that "any investment involves risk." And before you argue that certain investments are risk-free (e.g., savings accounts under $100,000, U.S. government bonds), let's take a look at the two basic risks that exist:

1. The risk that you might lose your capital (this is the ordinary risk that you take when you go into business, buy real estate, stocks, etc.).
2. The risk that your investment will not keep up with the purchasing value of the dollar.

The first of these risks is, of course, obvious and always has been. The second risk emanates from *inflation* and the chance that $1 invested today will not buy the same $1 worth of goods and services in the future. Those of us in the investment business have done our best to warn of the declining purchasing power of the dollar and to advise people to provide themselves with a "hedge against inflation." The statistics bear us out. From 1939 to 1959, for example, the purchasing power of the dollar was more than cut in half; the next ten years saw "only" a further 20% deterioration; but the ensuing four years heated up and produced a further 35% inflation, which was followed by staggering cost-of-living increases from 1973 through 1981. Since then, inflation has moderated rather dramatically; but history (and common sense) suggest that purchasing power risk should always be a consideration.

The people who have suffered most from inflation over the years were the most conservative investors—those who concentrated on safety and avoided the forms of investment that involve more risk. Those who preserved cash or who bought future protection through insurance, those who depended on social security or pensions—all were left behind by the soaring cost of living.

Before discussing the different types of investment and how they rank in risks and rewards, let me point out one more "risk" that we in the United States especially are prone to. Some people might call it the risk of "not keeping up with the Joneses"; suffice it to say that our population enjoys a high standard of living and should not be denied such pleasures. Certainly we are accustomed to a steadily increasing standard of living, and we must make our money work to keep us up with this progress. Luxuries turn into necessities as time flies, and we have to make our money grow to buy these new necessities. For example, 30 years ago, a television set was a luxury; today it is virtually a necessity. As one philosopher so aptly put it: More and more we find ourselves pondering how to reconcile our *net income* with our *gross habits*.

WHERE TO INVEST?

Let's look at the various forms of investment and see where they fit in a discussion of risks. In doing this, it's important that you understand the difference between *fixed income* and *equity* investing. In the former, you are a creditor—a lender of money—from which you expect a fixed rate of return and expect no ownership benefits. In contrast, your returns from equity investing in businesses or common stocks or real estate will depend on the relative success or failure of those vehicles. Following are the fixed income and equity vehicles most readily available to investors:

Fixed Income

U.S. and foreign government obligations (bonds, notes, bills, etc.).

Corporate, municipal and other bonds.

Corporate preferred stocks.

Savings deposits and NOW accounts in commercial banks.

Savings deposits in savings and loan associations.

Real estate mortgages.

Equities

Common stocks.

Real estate (ownership).

Following is a brief discussion of each of these investment channels:

FIXED INCOME

U.S. Government and Government Agencies' Obligations

Certainly U.S. government securities do not carry the so-called ordinary risk. You should not have to worry about the government defaulting on its obligations (if you worry about this, then there just isn't any investment suitable for you). Without getting into a detailed discussion of "governments," let's look at the two basic forms of government securities that are of interest to the average investor:

1. Government obligations that can fluctuate in market price.
2. Government obligations that are *not* traded and therefore do not fluctuate in market price.

In the first category are all government securities *with the exception of savings bonds.* Treasury bills (which always come due within one year), Treasury notes (one- to ten-year obligations), and Treasury bonds (issued only for a term of ten years or more) all sell after their issue on a supply-and-demand basis and thus are subject to changes in market price.

Savings bonds, on the other hand, are not transferable and cannot be sold. Instead, holders must turn them in to the government if they want cash and will be paid a fixed amount depending on how long the bonds have been held.

In either case, investors know that they will receive the income they have bargained for, with safety. If held to their maturity dates, government obligations typify investments that do not carry the ordinary risk of losing capital. What these fixed-income securities lack is protection against the rising cost of living; therefore they do carry the second risk mentioned. The table on p. 7 illustrates this risk; considering taxes and the increased cost of living, savings bonds bought in any year from 1935 to 1946 would *not* have kept up with inflation. Savings bonds purchased from 1947 to 1958 (after World War II) did better. Bonds maturing from 1957 through 1968 just barely kept abreast of the rising cost of living for the lowest tax-bracket individual; but, as might be expected, a high-bracket taxpayer would have suffered a loss of purchasing power. And the small after-tax, after-inflation gains made by the low-tax bracket bond owners were hardly sufficient to provide them with an improved standard of living. The 1969–1981 experience was disastrous for investors in both low and high tax brackets.

A respite from this disappointing experience finally occurred over the next five years, which found fixed income securities performing extremely well. As interest rates dropped dramatically, the positive returns on bonds easily outpaced shrinking inflation rates. Nevertheless, history warns us that bonds will not always offer protection against cost-of-living increases—and that the after-tax, real (after inflation) returns are likely to be negative.

RETURN ON 1935-1946 SAVINGS BOND ISSUES AFTER INCOME TAX AND "INFLATION TAX"

Bought for $75 in	Maturity Value of $100 in	Initial (Lowest) Personal Income Tax Rate (%)	Income Tax on $25 Interest	Maturity Value Less Income Tax	"Inflation Tax"—Increase in Cost-of-Living Index over the 10 Years (%)	Amount of "Inflation Tax"	Maturity Value Less Income Tax and "Inflation Tax"	Dollars of Original Investment Lost	Average Annual Rate of Loss (%)
1935	1945	23.0	*	$100.00	35.9	$26.42	$73.58	$1.42	0.19
1936	1946	19.0	*	100.00	44.2	30.65	69.35	5.65	0.75
1937	1947	19.0	*	100.00	55.7	35.77	64.23	10.77	1.44
1938	1948	16.6	*	100.00	70.5	41.35	58.65	16.35	2.18
1939	1949	16.6	*	100.00	71.4	41.66	58.34	16.66	2.22
1940	1950	17.4	*	100.00	71.6	41.72	58.28	16.72	2.23
1941	1951	20.4	$5.10	94.90	76.5	41.13	53.77	21.23	2.83
1942	1952	22.2	5.55	94.45	61.2	35.86	58.59	16.41	2.19
1943	1953	22.2	5.55	94.45	51.3	32.02	62.43	12.57	1.68
1944	1954	20.0	5.00	95.00	47.7	30.68	64.32	10.68	1.42
1945	1955	20.0	5.00	95.00	43.5	28.80	66.20	8.80	1.17
1946	1956	20.0	5.00	95.00	34.0	24.10	70.90	4.10	0.55

* The interest on savings bonds bought from 1935 to 1940 was not subject to federal income tax.

SOURCE: First National City Bank of New York monthly letter, May 1956, p. 57.

Other U.S. Government Bonds

The U.S. government has numerous agencies, such as FNMA, GNMA, FHLB, and others, which issue fixed income securities of varying maturities. Despite obvious government support, investors do not normally rank agency bonds as high as direct Treasury obligations. For this reason, agency bonds usually provide slightly higher income than Treasuries—but not high enough to offset the normal negative after-tax purchasing power results likely to exist in Treasuries.

Corporate, Municipal, and Other Bonds

Bonds are, of course, issued by entities other than the Federal government. Corporations of all sorts, representing practically all industry groups, have bond issues outstanding. Because private enterprises have less financial resources available to pay their debts than the Federal government, investors generally demand higher returns from these bonds than they do from Treasuries. Whether such higher income is sufficient to offset taxes and inflation is hard to generalize.

Cities, counties, states, and their respective agencies issue so-called municipal bonds for a variety of uses. Since these "muni's" are exempt from Federal income taxes and from state income taxes if the bond issuer is from the state of your residency, the calculation of protection of standard of living is simpler. If the interest income is higher than inflation, protection exists—provided of course that there is sufficient creditworthiness of the issuer to pay both interest and repayment of principal at maturity. (I emphasize this here only because investors have a tendency to assume that muni's have no credit risk. The record of muni credits has certainly been a solid one, but there is some additional risk in them versus Federal obligations.)

Savings Deposits and NOW Accounts in Commercial Banks

Here, too we find investments that lack ordinary risk (because of insurance on accounts up to $100,000 in any one bank by an agency of the federal government: the Federal Deposit Insurance Corporation or F.D.I.C.), but we assume the risk, similar to that for savings bonds, that our dollars will not keep up with cost-of-living increases. Savings accounts can only grow through compounding interest, and the interest paid by banks has been historically well below that available from other investments. However, with the banking deregulation acts of 1980, banks have been allowed to compete more aggressively with other investment instruments, and interest on savings accounts has improved a bit. Deregulation also led to the advent of NOW accounts (interest paid on checking accounts). Of course, NOW accounts pay below-average rates and usually require rather sizable minimum account balances.

Money Market Funds

These instruments allow investors to place money in a pot along with other investors. This "pot" is then managed by professionals. Money market funds aim to exceed short-term interest rates by investing in a broad list of short-term fixed income obligations.

Savings Accounts in Savings and Loan Associations

Here, again, we have a "static" investment and we take the chance that inflation may well eat away at our dollars. Savings and loan deposits (also insured up to $100,000 by a federal agency: the Federal Savings and Loan Insurance Corporation or F.S.L.I.C.) pay such a nominal amount more than bank deposits that it is doubtful whether their returns, like the banks', will be sufficient to overcome inflation over the years.

Insurance

Insurance doesn't qualify as either fixed income or equity; in fact, in most cases, it doesn't qualify as an investment at all. Because of its importance to almost everybody, however, it certainly is worthy of discussion. As you can imagine, the countless insurance plans available could fill many volumes. So I will simply summarize a few pertinent points:

1. Insurance with the top companies carries no ordinary risk because of the huge reserves set up for the policy holder.
2. Life insurance should be purchased as *protection*, not as investment. It should protect the family from death, but should not be counted on to accomplish much for you while you're living. (Life insurance has been aptly described as "a plan that keeps you poor all your life so you can *die rich.*")
3. Life insurance and annuities carry the very definite risk of not keeping up with the dollar. In both cases, you are buying a guarantee of a specified number of today's dollars *for a future date.* For example, people who bought annuities in 1939 (or any time thereafter) and protected themselves with what looked like adequate income at that time found themselves far short of a living income fifteen or twenty years later.
4. Universal life is an interest sensitive product that has enabled the life insurance industry to compete in the deregulated financial marketplace and to provide a tax deferred savings plan to policyholders. One advantage to investors is that universal life policies usually offer some flexibility in premium payments, which can be adjusted upwards or downwards within certain limits. The policy really consists of two parts. The first part is the amount of the premium payment that is required to cover the actual cost of death protection and associated expenses. The remainder of the premium represents the savings feature of the policy. These "excess" premium payments earn tax deferred market interest rates, which are competitive with pre-tax yields of

money market mutual funds. Universal life certainly offers a much more attractive investment alternative than traditional life insurance due to both the interest rate sensitivity of the product and the tax deferred status of the savings portion. Like all such products, however, you should understand the special risks and conditions which may exist with any specific policies.

5. Annuities, like life insurance, have their use as a protective device, but they constitute a very poor form of investment. For one thing, they provide no hedge against inflation. Second, they are extremely low-yielding investments. Annuity policies written many years ago assumed that the insurance company would earn a very low 3–5% for the holder; even in the late 1970's and early 1980's, with interest rates skyrocketing, earning assumptions by the insurance writers seldom exceeded 7–8½%—hardly generous. Annuities are a convenient savings medium, but frankly I don't recommend them.* The advent of "variable annuities" (wherein future payments to the policyholder will vary according to the value of an investment portfolio managed by the insurance company) may overcome the weaknesses mentioned.

Preferred Stocks

(To be discussed in Chapter 3.)

Real Estate Mortgages

Mortgages (especially second mortgages) can carry considerable ordinary risk and it is debatable whether they constitute a completely adequate hedge against inflation, al-

---

*The exception is if you live an abnormally long life. In 1960, for example, one of our country's largest insurance companies pointed proudly to the fact that certain (fifteen) policy holders had collected over two and a half times their investments in annuities. These people were all between 99 and 102 years of age, however, and not many of us can count on this kind of life span.

though certainly when they are bought at sizable discounts, the return may be more than sufficient to account for any increased living costs.

EQUITIES

Real Estate

Like insurance, real estate is a broad field that is a study in itself. For the sake of our discussion, ownership of property (whether improved or unimproved) carries the ordinary risks of losing part of your capital, but well-chosen real estate should more than compensate for inflation. I believe that real estate constitutes a wonderful investment vehicle. Just a few attributes of real estate ownership are:

1. Depreciation from a building provides certain tax advantages and enables the owner to receive a tax-free cash "throw-off" to pay off his investment; likewise, the fact that property taxes and interest payments are deductible items in some cases for income tax purposes can be of sizable benefit to the property owner.
2. Rate of return (yield) may or may not be higher than on corporate securities. In 1987, for example, the average going-in returns to real estate purchasers who borrow (mortgage) were about equal to dividend yields on most common stocks but well below yields from bonds and other fixed-income instruments. Returns for the institutional buyer who doesn't borrow will be greater than stocks but about equal to bonds.
3. An investor can borrow more heavily to buy real estate, thereby affording considerable "leverage" (described in Chapter 18).
4. There may be a limited supply of land and/or property in a given area. In a growing region, this creates a very favorable supply–demand relationship—and leads to increasing property values.

5. An owner can trade properties without incurring a capital gains tax.

Unfortunately, real estate is not generally available to the smaller investor (other than home ownership, that is) and it does require management. Faucets leak, pipes occasionally break, and tenants often move. Furthermore, neighborhoods and property values change and real estate, like the stock market (or, for that matter, anything in life), is not a "one-way street." For those not interested in owning property directly, pools and other vehicles such as syndications are available; but these are too often layered with excessive fees and costs.

Common Stocks

Common stocks generally have successfully protected investors against the rising cost of living, although selection here is all-important. Selection, timing, strategies, and philosophy of investing wisely in stocks will all be covered in the pages to follow.

CONCLUSIONS

Not everyone can afford to concentrate solely on ordinary risk investments such as real estate and common stocks. Later on, after we have discussed the stock market, growth stocks, and other topics, we will come to more conclusions on investing, but it is important to point out here that most people should *balance* their investments to include a certain portion of ordinary-risk ventures and a certain portion of ventures that are safe from ordinary risks, even though they do carry the purchasing power risk. Emphasis, however, should decidedly be on equities—on *ownership* forms of investment such as real estate and common stocks. As a matter of fact, aside from the protection of life insurance and cash reserves, investors who are thinking longer term should concentrate almost solely on equities.

2

Forms of Business Organization

Because this book is devoted almost exclusively to *corporate* securities, it seems only proper to distinguish a *corporation* from other forms of business organization.

There are three basic ways of going into business in our country: (1) by yourself (as sole proprietor); (2) in partnership with one or more associates; and (3) by forming a corporation.

SOLE PROPRIETORSHIP

This is the simplest way of going into business. No legal papers are needed, no extra expenses—you have only yourself to blame if things go wrong, and the profit is all yours if you succeed. Tax consequences are the simplest. Whatever you earn you simply report to Uncle Sam and pay the prevailing income tax on this amount.

PARTNERSHIP

This, too, is easy to form. You and I can go into business as partners with only a verbal agreement (but don't ever do it that way). Legal papers are relatively simple, so these expenses are minimal. And there are no extra expenses such as state fees and the like. Taxes are also simple. You and I merely take our agreed portion of the year's profits and report that portion to Internal Revenue and pay our taxes.

There are two distinct disadvantages to a partnership. First, the death of one partner automatically dissolves the partnership, necessitating the drawing up of a new partnership agreement. Of greater significance is the fact that each partner assumes unlimited liability for debts incurred *in the business*. And I mean *unlimited personal liability*. For example, let's assume you and I go into partnership. I buy some heavy machinery and make other expenditures for our business that do not work out. In a short time, we're broke and we owe considerable money. Our creditors press us for the money and bring suit to get it. Nothing is left in the business, but they *can* sue us personally for these debts *because it's a partnership*. Frankly, partner, I haven't a dime. I put all my eggs into the business. Fortunately for our creditors, *you* have other assets. The court can take those assets away from you to pay *our* debts, and there's no limit to how much they can take. They won't take the mattress out from under you, but they will grab almost everything else. So you can see that a partnership is a business marriage. And I don't recommend becoming partners with just anybody, any more than I do your marrying Lucy Vonderkronkle, whom you just met last night after consuming sixteen drinks at the local pub.

CORPORATION

This is a separate entity legally set up for business purposes. A corporation is quite different from a partnership. First of all, it is not as easily set up (it can't possibly be done verbally or in a matter of minutes); establishing a corporation takes legal know-how, and naturally involves the corresponding fees.

Of great importance is the liability limitation from being

incorporated.* You simply can't lose any more money than you put in. The company can go broke and owe millions, but the creditors can't get any more money from the stockholders. The obvious question is: Why in the world doesn't everybody in business incorporate to protect themselves? The answer: *Double taxation.* A stockholder is actually taxed twice in a corporation: first, in the form of a corporate income tax (rates under the new tax law after Dec. 31, 1987, are 15% on corporate income of $50,000 and below, 25% on the next $25,000, and 34% on $75,000 and above), and second, in the normal manner when the stockholder declares to Internal Revenue how much in dividends he received during the year (personal tax rates are 15% up to $29,750 in income and 28% above that with a 5% surcharge for high income persons that is gradually phased out above a certain level).

For example, let's assume you and I are considering the purchase of a business earning $100,000 a year. If we go in as equal *partners* (not incorporating), each of us will report $50,000 in income from the business and Uncle Sam will take over $10,000 in taxes from each of us (15% × $29,750 + 28% × $20,250 = $10,132) leaving us $39,868 apiece, for a total of $79,736 net after taxes for us both. Our effective tax rate in this case is only 20% ($20,264 in taxes/$100,000 in income). If, instead, we incorporate, the $100,000 will be subject first to the corporate tax, which leaves us $77,750 ($100,000 minus the sum of 15% × $50,000 + 25% × $25,000 + 34% × $25,000 which equals $22,250). Then (assuming all earnings are paid out in dividends) we have to declare our share of this—$38,875 each—and pay tax on it. In this case the tax would be about $7,000 each (15% × $29,750 + 28% × $9,125 = $7,018). So we are left with $31,857 each after taxes, for a total of $63,714—or about 80% of what we would have retained as partners. Our effective tax rate if we incorporate would be 36% (a total of $36,250 in taxes/$100,000 in income) versus only about 20% under the partnership form. The following table shows all of this rather clearly:

---

*Assuming stock is nonassessable and that's the only kind of stock under discussion in this book.

	Partnership		Corporation	
Total net income	$100,000		$100,000	
Less corporate income tax	None		22,250	
Balance available for owners	$100,000		$ 77,750	

	Your Share	*My Share*	*Your Share*	*My Share*
	$50,000	$50,000	$38,875	$38,875
Less income tax paid personally	10,132	10,132	7,018	7,018
Income left after all taxes	$39,868	$39,868	$31,857	$31,857

This discussion provides the broad major advantages and disadvantages of partnership versus incorporation. It does not allow for the possibility of stockholders receiving salaries from their corporation (thereby minimizing the effect of double taxation), nor does it discuss certain tax regulations (such as one that allows certain corporations to choose taxation as a partnership). In short, an attorney is the best judge of whether you should incorporate or form a partnership.

Now that we know more about corporations, we can go ahead and talk about the securities they issue.

3

Corporate Securities

To commence business and to remain in business, a corporation needs capital. There are three basic means of obtaining this capital, namely through the sale of bonds, preferred stocks, and/or common stock. Let's take a look at these three and see how they differ from one another.

BONDS

Bonds are issued in exchange for money loaned to a corporation (or to a federal government, state, city, etc.). The *lender* of money *becomes a bondholder and a creditor* of the company. As in any loan, the lender expects to receive a fixed rate of return on his money—called *interest*—and to receive back the full amount of his loan at some future date, called the *maturity date*. Let me emphasize that bondholders are creditors of the company; they have *no ownership* and have nothing to say about the running of the business unless the company gets way behind in interest payments and is forced into bankruptcy or recapitalization. Therefore, bondholders do not share in the success of a growing company, other than knowing that their interest is being better covered by earnings and through more assurance that they will get their original investment back at maturity. Thus, bonds (unless convertible into common stock—discussed in Chapter 11) are bought for their fixed income, which you hope protects your purchasing power. Although publicly traded bonds will fluctuate in price and present capital gain and loss potentials throughout their lives, investors who hold these securities to their maturity simply get back their original principal. And, if inflation climbs above the fixed interest rate on a bond your real return can dwindle to zero or even become negative. Incidentally, the maturity date serves to limit both the loss and gain in market price of a bond over the years. Assuming a bond pays off at maturity, this factor keeps a bond from going down indefinitely or from plunging too far below, or rising very far above, its value at maturity. The longer the maturity, however, the greater the potential fluctuation in interim market price levels. Also, volatility in interest rates produces volatility in price for fixed income securities. In recent years declining interest rates have produced large capital gains for bondholders. Capital losses, however, could be the rule in the future, as they were in the past, if interest rates rise.

Another concern when holding corporate bonds is that, unlike corporate stocks, the market for these securities is not very active. Each day two-thirds of the 3,000 or so issues on the NYSE's bond board don't trade at all. On one recent day the total bond volume was $42 million, less than the action in a single stock like duPont. What does this mean to the bond investor? First, the prices reported in the paper may have very little relation to a bond's value. Second, the thin market leaves a wide and hazardous gulf between bid and ask prices. It doesn't pay to trade unless you have some very special insights. U.S. government bonds, of course, are very liquid; they trade in huge volume and daily price volatility is significantly less than in corporate bonds.

PREFERRED STOCK

The term "preferred" makes this security sound glamorous and attractive. Nothing could be further from the truth! Although a preferred stock ranks ahead of common stock both as to payment of dividends and as to disposition of assets if a company goes out of business, a preferred stock is a "hybrid" security; it carries neither the extreme safety of a bond nor the chance for growth of a common stock. Like a bond, a preferred issue carries a fixed rate of annual payment (called a *dividend* in the case of a preferred stock and *interest* in the case of a bond) and this payment will *not* be increased.* No dividends can be paid on preferreds until all bond interest has been paid. Dividends are usually *cumulative*, meaning that the preferred stockholders are entitled to any omitted payments; that is, if preferred dividends are not earned and subsequently not paid, the corporation still has an obligation to pay all those accrued dividends when its earnings do recover. Naturally, the corporation has to pay off all its accrued dividends (called "arrearages") before it can pay any dividends on the *common stock*.

Like bondholders, preferred stockholders generally have no choice in management of the company (no voting power). Almost all bonds and preferreds have a *call price* (redemption price), which is the price at which the *company* can call in the issues if it chooses. This call price limits any large gains in market price for bonds and preferreds. An investor is not going to pay 115 for an issue that has a call price of 105, because the day after he buys it at 115, the issue could be called at the 105 figure. The bond or preferred that has no call price does not have this disadvantage.

One of the big differences between bonds and preferred stocks is that the latter have *no maturity date*. At least bondholders know they are entitled to a certain sum at maturity. Preferred stockholders have no assurance of getting their investment back. They have to depend on market conditions and could conceivably hold their stock for 100 years and never see it back where it started. At least with a bond investors know that in 10, 20, or so many years they will have their money back. On the other hand, a preferred stock that is bought for its high yield at least guarantees owners a yield for as many years as they desire, with no "interference" from a maturity date.

*Unless it is a "participating" preferred, in which case the preferred holders, after receiving their stipulated regular dividend, then share in the earnings available for the common stock.

COMMON STOCK

Here we come to the actual ownership of a company. Whereas bondholders are lenders of money and holders of preferred stock are in-between investors, common stockholders supply permanent *equity capital* and own the company. They have voting power, elect the board of directors, and thereby indirectly control management of the company. For this privilege, they have last claim on dividends and are the last to collect in case the company goes broke and is forced to liquidate. On the other hand, common stockholders are the ones who benefit if the company is a success. As earnings increase, stockholders should enjoy growing dividends and a higher market price for their corporate security.

CONCLUSIONS

Bonds represent a creditor's interest in a corporation. Bonds generally provide a high degree of safety—a fixed rate of return in good times and bad. This fixed rate, however, means that they are vulnerable to inflation when investors are demanding higher and higher returns.

Preferred stocks represent a very limited form of ownership. They carry ownership risks with very little opportunity for appreciation of capital. Long unpaid preferred dividends are seldom settled satisfactorily and preferred stocks, because they have no maturity date and are not of the same quality as bonds, have greater price instability than bonds, yet they usually provide only slightly higher yield. After this glum discussion you're probably wondering who buys preferred stocks. They are bought mainly by institutional investors, who want the higher return, and they are especially attractive to investing corporations, who get a tax advantage from receiving dividends from another corporation. Individuals, too, occasionally own preferred stocks, but I would generally advise against this, except for an elderly person not interested in growth who needs that "last ounce" of current income. Why, for example, should an individual buy Pacific Gas and Electric preferred with a return around 9% when he can buy the common to yield only 1% less? Pacific Gas and Electric is a stable utility company; its common stock dividend should be safe. Assuming the company is granted sufficient rate increases to bring about higher earnings over the years, dividends will rise, too, and chances are the ultimate return to the common shareholder will exceed that of the preferred holder. True, there is more market risk on the common, but anyone looking more than a few years ahead for the benefits of his investment would be better off with the common stock.

Common stocks represent ownership. If it is growth of capital or a hedge against inflation you are seeking, here is where you are going to get it.

Now, before we learn to distinguish between attractive stocks and those we should leave alone, let's see how corporate securities are bought and sold.

PART II
How the Stock Market Functions

4
How the Stock Market Works

One of the great advantages of owning corporate securities is that they are liquid. By that I don't mean you can drink them. Only that they can be sold at a moment's notice and converted into cash. Contrast that with trying to sell your business or a large piece of property. The best example of this liquidity is that provided by the New York Stock Exchange. Here we have as close to a "perfect market" as there is anywhere for investments.

Open five days a week from 9:30 A.M. to 4:00 P.M. (Eastern time), the New York Stock Exchange enables a buyer in Connecticut to get together with a seller in California in a matter of seconds. The New York exchange is a dynamic communications system. It is a central marketplace connected with multiple offices throughout the world by about a half million miles of telephone and telegraph wire and satellite communications. Many countries, from Argentina to Thailand, have securities exchanges but only two others figure as importantly in the transaction of U.S. securities: the Tokyo and London exchanges, whose business hours (Eastern Standard Time) are 7:00 P.M.–9:00 P.M. and 11:00 P.M.–1:00 A.M. for Tokyo and 4:30 A.M.–10:30 A.M. for London (see next page).

International Trading Clock

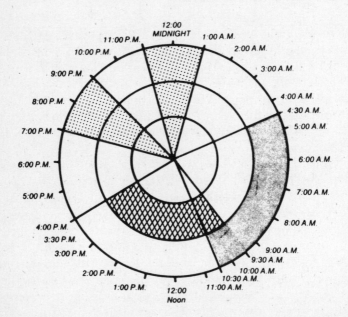

Around the clock trading—where the purchase or sale of any security, foreign or domestic, could take place at any time of the day or night—may eventually develop. Until then, however, New York and the other American exchanges will figure most prominently in transactions by American investors.

From the gallery, the NYSE looks like a wild mass of confusion. But it's the most organized mass of confusion I know of. For those of you who have not seen the New York exchange, picture a floor about two-thirds the size of an ordinary football field. Around the floor are the countless telephone stations that connect about 1,365 stock exchange members with their offices. These are the brokers who are handling orders for their customers. Also stationed around the room are numerous "trading posts," each one manned by specialists. In 1986 the exchange had 410 specialists on the floor.

Each specialist is assigned certain stocks. It is his business to see that a proper market is made in each and every one of these stocks. It is his job to take care of orders to buy and sell for brokers. And it is his job to buy and sell for his own account to assure a good market at all times. In other words, the exchange expects there will always be a buyer for any stock within a close proximity of the last sale that took place in that stock. (The same rule applies for expecting to find a seller within close range of the last buy.) But sometimes there will be no buyer (or seller) from the public, and this is when the specialist must step in and bid to buy (or offer to sell) the stock for his own account. Specialists are closely regulated by the exchange and by the Securities and Exchange Commission (SEC).

Your broker can buy and sell for you and trade on the floor of the exchange because he owns a "seat" on the exchange. The number of seats available is limited and a new broker desiring one must buy it from a present holder, much as you buy a stock from another person. Also like individual stocks, these seats vary in price according to supply and demand. Over the past seventeen years, for example, there has been great variance in the price of New York Stock Exchange seats:

Year	High Price	Low Price
1986	$600,000	$455,000
1985	480,000	310,000
1984	400,000	290,000
1983	425,000	310,000
1982	340,000	190,000
1981	285,000	220,000
1980	275,000	82,000
1979	210,000	82,000
1978	105,000	46,000
1977	95,000	35,000
1976	104,000	40,000
1975	138,000	60,000
1974	105,000	65,000
1973	190,000	72,000
1972	250,000	150,000
1971	300,000	145,000
1970	320,000	130,000

Aside from the seat price, the exchange has certain capital requirements and other standards that must be met by members.

There are a few thousand persons on the floor of the exchange, including stock exchange members, clerks, and employees of the NYSE itself. The clerks must turn over orders to the specialists, while exchange members can choose to turn over orders to the specialists or attempt to transact the orders themselves.

Before learning how an order is transacted on the exchange, let's distinguish between the various orders that can be placed by an investor to buy or sell stocks. The most common order placed is the *market* order, in which the investor is instructing his broker to transact the order *just as soon as he can* and *to buy or sell it at the prevailing market* at that time. The broker is obligated to complete the order when he reaches the specialist's post, regardless of what the stock is selling for at that time. (Remember there may be considerable differences in price between the time a client places his order and the minute or so later when the broker reaches the post.)

There is a distinction between a market order and an order

giving *market discretion*. The client granting discretion is also instructing the broker to complete an order to buy or sell, but in this case the broker does not have to transact at the prevailing price. Instead, the broker can use his judgment on price. Why doesn't everyone use this order instead of a market order? The answer is that you run the risk in giving market discretion that the broker's judgment may prove incorrect. He may elect to wait to buy or sell instead of transacting the order right at the moment, and his waiting may cost you money. When you give a broker discretion, *he is not held* for his error of judgment. Of course, his discretion may prove correct and save you money, but there is no guarantee of this.

A third type of order placed is the *limit* order. Here, you give your broker a price limit *that he cannot exceed* when buying the stock for you (or cannot lower in case you are selling). For example, say you want to buy 100 shares of XYZ Company, which is currently selling at $10, but for which you are not willing to pay over $9. In this case, the broker is prohibited from paying any more than your designated limit of $9 for your intended purchase of 100 shares. When you place such a limit on a stock, you usually have to wait for the stock to reach that level; therefore most limit orders are put in for a period of time and are called *open limit orders*. In the case of this XYZ purchase example, you might instruct your broker to leave the order in for a week, two weeks, a month, or any period of your choice. In the meantime, of course, it is your privilege to change your limit price at any time; for example, you can raise the limit to 9½ or lower it to 8 or 8½ anytime—or you can cancel the order completely. After the designated period of the open order is over, it automatically expires, unless you renew it. You may place a limit order good for only one day, in which case it is called a *day order*.

I insist there is one basic rule for limit orders. *Don't place a limit order only a fraction of a point away from the present price.* If you think a stock deserves to sell either far below or far above its going rate, then it may well pay you to wait for it to reach such a level, but when you are trying to save only a fraction of a point it's a bad gamble. Why? Because the maximum you can save is the fraction you are trying to squeeze out, but you may lose a great deal by not transacting the order "at the market."

For example, assume you are thinking of buying our $10 XYZ stock. If you place your order with a limit of, say 9¾, the very most you can save is ¼ of 1 point or 25 cents a share *if the stock declines to 9¾.* But if the stock does not decline to that level, what can it cost you? There's no limit! The stock may advance from 10 to 20 or 30 or more and you may "lose" a potential doubling or tripling of your money—all for a measly 25 cents a share. The same thing goes for selling a stock. If you think a stock is fully valued and that it should be sold, what can you gain by putting in an order a fraction above the market? Once again, only a few pennies, and if the stock never reaches your fractionally higher level and commences to go down in price, you could lose many points—and this is out-of-pocket loss from not selling it at the market.

A good basic rule of investing or speculating is that you should see a possibility for a good-sized gain from any venture before plunging. *Never risk a lot of dollars to make a few!*

It's a different philosophy if you believe that a stock is overvalued now but that it represents a good buy at considerably lower levels. Here is where limit orders are most valuable, because you get yourself in line early to buy the stock where you think it represents a good buy. You place your limit order and then it's there when the stock reaches that price. The advantage is that you are not influenced by your emotions at that time, whereas were you to wait for the stock to get to that level, chances are the declining nature of the market would cause you to say to yourself, "I think it's going lower yet." And this is probably just the time you *should* be buying!

THE SPECIALIST'S BOOK AND
HOW ORDERS ARE HANDLED

Let's assume you want to buy 100 shares of XYZ Company and you instruct your broker to do so "at the market" for your account. Your broker writes out a tag with these instructions; this tag goes to his order department, which relays it to the floor of the exchange. The broker's partner on the floor receives the order and proceeds directly to the specialist's post where XYZ stock is traded. He asks the specialist what the going price is for XYZ. The very last sale price is easy to determine (it is posted on an electric board at the post), but the *next* sale price is still a mystery. The specialist has a guide to what the next sale will be, because he keeps track of all limit orders for the brokers. Of course he can't keep them in his head, so he utilizes what is known as the *specialist's book* (which is computerized today).

The specialist keeps separate records for each stock he follows, including open orders at various prices. For example, let's set up the specialist's book on XYZ Company:

XYZ COMPANY

Orders to Buy	Broker Placing Order	Date Order Expires	Price of Stock	Orders to Sell	Broker Placing Order	Date Order Expires
100 shs.	Laurel	Feb. 26	9			
200 shs.	Hardy	Mar. 1	9			
100 shs.	Abbott	Mar. 15	9			
100 shs.	Costello	Feb. 12	9			
200 shs.	Lunt	Mar. 15	9⅛			
100 shs.	Fontanne	Feb. 13	9⅛			
100 shs.	Gilbert	Mar. 1	9¼			
100 shs.	Sullivan	Mar. 3	9¼			
500 shs.	Smythe	Mar. 5	9⅜			
	No orders—		9½	—No orders		
			9⅝			
			9¾	100 shs.	Chase	Mar. 20
			9¾	300 shs.	Sanborn	Mar. 1
			9⅞	100 shs.	Crosse	Mar. 3
			9⅞	200 shs.	Bl'ckw'll	Feb. 4

Your broker approaches the specialist and asks for a "quote," which is a request for the highest order to buy (the bid) and the lowest order to sell (the offer). In this case, the quote would be "9⅜ at 9¾," which means that there is someone bidding 9⅜ and no higher, and someone offering stock for sale at 9¾ and no lower. Your broker can also request the "size," meaning the number of shares wanted at 9⅜ and the number for sale at 9¾. In this case, the size would be 500 and 400, meaning 500 shares bid for at 9⅜ and 400 shares offered at 9¾.

Now, if you have given your broker a market order, he is obligated to buy the stock at the lowest offering showing, which would be 9¾. Actually the specialist can help out your broker by "stopping" him at 9¾ (meaning that he will guarantee to sell him 100 shares at 9¾ if there is another purchase at 9¾ by someone else—after all, he is carrying open orders to sell 400 shares at 9¾). In this way, he allows your broker to step in and try to get you a lower price. Let's assume the specialist does "stop" your broker at 9¾. Then your broker will probably step in among the other brokers milling around the XYZ post and call in a loud and clear voice, "9½ for 100 shares," (which means, I'm willing to pay 9½ for 100 shares.). Chances are there are both potential buyers and sellers of XYZ in the crowd who have not entrusted their orders to the specialist. They haven't "tipped their hand" and are waiting to hear new orders for XYZ. When your broker bids 9½, he changes the quote from "9⅜ at 9¾" to "9½ at 9¾." Another broker hears the higher bid and decides he'll offer 100 shares for sale at 9⅝ (remember, if he waits for 9¾, he has to get back in line behind Chase and Sanborn, who are already on the book for 9¾). Your broker is satisfied that he won't do much better than this and yells, "Take it," at the 9⅝ offerer and a sale has taken place.

The specialist has served his function of handling buy and sell orders and of seeing to it that an orderly market exists in his stock at all times.

This bidding and offering goes on all day in front of the post. The result is a continuous market that reflects the supply and demand for the stocks. You would be amazed how efficient the system is, especially if you have watched, as I have, hundreds of thousands of shares of a particular stock being bought and sold in a brief period of time without drastically affecting a change in the price of the stock.

RECORDING OF TRADES
AND THE TRADING SCREEN

Whenever a transaction takes place on the exchange it is recorded immediately and, within a minute, is sent over the wires to appear on the trading screen. Every stock has an abbreviated symbol and the transactions are shown as follows:

XYZ   GM   X

9⅝   2s 80   4s 25.24½

Our previous 100-share trade of XYZ is the first example; whenever a transaction involves 100 shares, no mention is made of *anything but the price*. Whenever more than 100 shares are traded, though, the stock price is preceded by the volume; in GM (General Motors), the "2s" means "200 shares"; in X (USX's, formerly U.S. Steel's, symbol), the "4s 25" means that 400 shares traded in one block at the price of 25, then the "24½" means that the 25 trade was followed by a 100-share transaction at 24½.

There are other peculiarities to this reporting of transactions. I won't list them here—your broker can explain them if you are interested. The main thing is that trends of the market and of individual stocks are reported and published immediately—nothing is hidden from you.

THE CENTRAL MARKET SYSTEM

Thus far you have heard only about the New York Stock Exchange. There is more to come on the American Stock Exchange, regional exchanges, and the over-the-counter markets. These markets may someday be combined, *from a reporting-to-the-public standpoint*, into one reporting body, called the Central Market System. The various mechanisms described here may not be altered, but their combined results may be centralized and communicated to investors through one "tape." In 1987, for example, a consolidated ticker tape exists that includes trades completed on all markets except the OTC market described in Chapter 6. Whether an American Telephone transaction takes place on the Pacific, Philadelphia, or New York exchange, or, as to be explained, in the so-called Third and Fourth markets, the result is flashed for all to see on one centralized recording (and reporting) device—one tape.

Additional facets of the Central Market System are still to be worked out, such as: (a) a composite quote system (so you can find the most reasonable market wherever it is); (b) a consolidated limit order book; (c) centralized trading rules and regulations; and (d) an integrated clearance and settlement system (which, it is hoped, will someday become computerized to the point where the bulky stock certificate will become obsolete).

ODD LOTS

Up to this time we've been talking only about buying and selling stocks in 100-share lots—called round lots. Actually considerable business in stocks is not in round lots but rather in less-than-100-share units—called odd lots.

For many years the various exchanges had specialists who dealt exclusively in odd lots. To take care of the buyer or seller of 39 or 62 or 3 shares of any security, these specialized odd lot dealers guaranteed to sell or buy all the stock necessary to complete odd lot orders—in exchange for a set fee (called the odd lot "differential"). All these transactions were determined by the price of round lots. Thus if you were a buyer of 10 shares of XYZ stock, the odd lot dealer waited for the next 100 shares of XYZ to sell and then executed your order at that price plus the differential, which was either $\frac{1}{8}$ or $\frac{1}{4}$ of a point. If you were a seller of XYZ, the differential would be deducted from your sale price rather than added.

In 1976 the procedure was changed. Odd lots are no longer executed at any set differentials from round lot transaction prices. They are instead executed as separate orders, with the resulting price a competitive one—which could be the same, more, or less than the last sale.

Most important, odd lot purchasers and sellers are assured of good markets for their securities, and at reasonable costs.

Therefore the conclusion on odd lots is as it was in previous *Primer* editions: The fee charged is small and should not be a deterrent to investing in odd lots.

COMMISSIONS

Commission rates were once set by the member firms of stock exchanges, but charges made for buying and selling are now negotiable. Different brokers charge different amounts for different types of transactions, so you simply have to check to determine what your costs will be. This, incidentally, does not imply that you should always deal through the lowest-cost broker; brokers provide varying services and you should expect to pay some premium for these. In addition, you want to be certain that the broker with whom you deal is financially stable. Low cost does not necessarily signify best value.

SHORT SELLING

One of the interesting types of speculation in the stock market and one of the most difficult to comprehend is the "short sale." When a person *buys* a stock, he does so with the obvious hope the stock will go *up* in value. When a person sells a stock "short," he is (usually) *selling something he doesn't now own* with the hope that he will make a profit by buying it back later at a lower price.

Now, don't think yourself dense if you are asking, "How can a person sell something he *doesn't own*?" Let me give you a practical example.

I own a 1955 Chevrolet. You and I are talking one day and I tell you how I just turned down an offer to sell my car for $1,000. You think it's only worth $500, but I'm sentimentally attached to the old buggy and I want to keep it. Well, it so happened that I'm going away tomorrow for a month and leaving my car here. Your eyes light up: If only you could "borrow" my car for the month, find that fool who was willing to pay $1,000 for my car, sell it to him, and then buy a similar car before I return. The result would be a profit of $500 to you:

$1,000 received by you when you sold my car

__500_ paid out to put similar car back in my garage

$ 500 net profit to you

What you have done is sell my car "short." You don't own it, but you've sold it just the same with the idea of replacing it at a lower price in the future.

Actually it's easier to sell short in stocks than in cars. How could you be sure the $500 1955 Chevrolet you put back in my garage would be the same exact color and have the same dented fenders as my original? You couldn't! But in stocks, it's easy. Any 100-share certificate of General Motors is exactly the same as any other. Thus, if you think that the present market price of GM stock is too high and that it will go down, why not sell it now for $80 (your broker will arrange to borrow it for you to deliver to the buyer) and then simply buy it back when it goes lower, say to $60.

Short selling does serve a function. It allows one to speculate that the market is too high and thus has a stabilizing influence. After all, if we had buyers of stocks by a great majority, stocks would quickly become inflated and priced too high. And then we'd be in for a sharp drop someday. Since most investors are conscious of *buying* stocks, short sellers can at least have a restraining influence and keep stocks from becoming overly inflated. And remember that every short seller is a potential buyer later on, and this buying when the market is sinking is also a stabilizing factor.

I don't recommend short selling for the average investor. For one thing, the risks are unlimited. There's no end to how much you can lose. If you sell a stock short at $10, who's to say it won't go to $100 or $1,000, in which cases you would lose 1,000% or 10,000% of your money, if you didn't buy back before.

This possibility is exactly what enters the short seller's mind and often panics him into buying back as quickly as possible when the market is rising. This sudden buying by short sellers (called "short covering") is one reason for occasional rapid upswings in various popular issues.

In contrast, if you *buy* a $10 stock, what is the worst that can happen? That the company will go bankrupt and the stock will be worth nothing, in which case you've "only" lost your original investment (you've lost 100% of your money). And chances are that it will never go to zero; perhaps $2 or $3 or $5 is the lowest you can visualize, even under the worst circumstances.

A second disadvantage to short selling is that you face a negative return on your money. Whereas when you *buy* a stock you normally receive dividends that give you a certain annual return on your money, in a short sale you have to *pay* out dividends as they are declared to the person from whom you borrowed the stock to make the short sale (you never come into contact with the person who owns the stock you are borrowing—your broker handles all this for you, and generally there is no cost to the borrowing).

The third reason for avoiding short selling is psychological. If you have sold short and the market goes down, you're a hero. But it is very frustrating being short when the market is rising. Everyone you know is either buying stock or selling what he already owns. Ninety-nine percent of your friends are happy as a lark when the market is rising. To be losing money while all your friends are reaping the harvest is tough to live with.

A fourth criticism of short selling existed under previous tax law. No matter how long you waited to buy back a stock you had sold short, any gain from the transaction was considered by Internal Revenue *to be a short-term gain, and thus you could never benefit from the then advantageous long-term capital gain tax rate in short selling.*

Short selling is for the real *speculator*, not the *investor*, and if you are one of those highly speculative individuals, remember that risk factor. And recall the old adage:

> *He who sells what isn't his'n*
> *Must eventually buy it back or go to prison.*

If you're short and the stock is rising, you're going to have to put up more money* right along—or eventually buy it back.

---

*Short selling requires original capital, too. In spite of the fact that you receive money from your short sale right away, you are required to put up this amount out of your own pocket (or at least the existing margin requirement; i.e., in 1987, 50% of the total amount). Then when you buy back the stock ("cover the short sale"), you can withdraw your cash plus the profit or minus the loss incurred from the short sale transaction.

So be sure you have ample cash on hand if you decide to become a short seller.

TWO "PROTECTION" ORDERS ON THE STOCK EXCHANGE

We've already discussed limit orders, but there are two other types of limit orders that should be mentioned briefly. These are the stop-sell and stop-buy orders.

Stop-Sell

Suppose you own a stock that is now selling at $60. You think the stock will go considerably higher, but in case you are wrong you want to be sure you sell it at $55, and if the stock retreats *to that level*, your stock will be automatically sold "at the market" after the $55 price is reached (since it becomes a "market order" there is no guarantee your stock will be sold at the $55 figure; you might receive 54½, 54¼, or even less if numerous other stop-sell orders are touched off at the same time as yours). If the stock never retreats to $55, it won't be sold at all. The stop-sell order, therefore, allows you to limit your loss or protect your profit to some extent if it declines.

Stop-Buy

This order is intended mainly for the short seller. If a person sells stock short at $60 and wants to be sure he loses no more than 5 or 6 points, he can place an open stop-buy at $65. Then if and when the stock goes up to $65, his order automatically becomes an order to buy the stock "at the market."

The stop-buy order can also be used to buy stocks as they rise or as they break through technical "resistance points." Some chartists use the stop-buy in this way to accumulate *stocks as they are rising*. The protection features of both the stop-sell and stop-buy orders make them sound very useful. Actually, these orders are most practical for the short-term speculator. They are not as suitable for the long-term investor, who is less concerned with day-to-day fluctuations and who is investing for large, long-range benefits. Stop orders tend to make an account too active (constantly in and out of the market). As I will discuss in Chapter 30 on stock market "trading," considerable trading activity is to the definite detriment of the investor.

5

Regional Stock Exchanges

Chapter 4 dealt with procedures on the New York Stock Exchange. While the NYSE is by far the largest, it is not the only central marketplace for securities. The American Stock Exchange is another, and there are numerous regional exchanges throughout the country, including the Pacific Coast, the Midwest-Philadelphia-Washington, the Boston, and the Cincinnati exchanges. Listing requirements are the strictest on the New York exchange, but these other markets serve an important function and the stocks traded on the other exchanges may equal or even be superior in quality to many issues traded on the New York board.

None of the regional exchanges in the United States opens before the New York exchange; the regionals all coincide their opening hours with that of the "Big Board." Because of differences in time, however, some exchanges are open after others have closed. The Pacific Coast exchange, for example, opens at 6:30 A.M. Pacific time, which is the same as the 9:30 A.M. Eastern time opening of the New York exchange, but the Pacific exchange does not close until 1:30 P.M. Pacific time (equivalent to 4:30 P.M. New York time)—or half an hour after the close of the Big Board. Many times significant news will be released *after* the close of the *New York* exchange but *before* the close of the *Pacific,* and a great deal of activity will take place on the latter exchange. Assume, for example, that XYZ stock closed at 45 on the Big Board and that shortly after the 4:00 P.M. New York closing an important announcement affecting XYZ is made. Provided that XYZ stock is traded on the Pacific exchange, too (many stocks are traded on more than one exchange), a person wanting to buy or sell XYZ can still do so on the Pacific because of the time differential. The idea, of course, is to make the purchase or sale before the news spreads so that you will be ahead of those who hear the news later and are forced to act after you on the Pacific or have to wait until the New York opening the next day. I must point out, however, that it may be dangerous to pay a big premium on the Pacific over the closing price in New York the same day (or, in the case of bad news, to sell well below what the last sale was in New York) because a great deal of "emotional action" takes place on the Pacific after the New York close. Suppose that after XYZ closes at 45 in the East, some good news suddenly appears and a few frantic people put in market orders to buy the stock; perhaps the first order results in a purchase at 45½, the next at 47 or so. Unless your order is the first or second, you might pay a premium of a couple of points over the New York close. My experience has shown that when frantic activity such as this appears on the Pacific after the New York close, the resulting prices are *usually out of kilter enough* that a *person will strike a better price the next day in New York.*

Some confusion exists because prices sometimes vary widely between the New York exchange and any of the regional exchanges in the same stock during the same day. Let's assume you are following the stock of Hercules, Inc., which is listed on both the New York and the Pacific Coast exchanges. You are eager to know what happened to Hercules in today's market and rush to buy the evening newspaper. Frantically you turn to the financial section and look for Hercules in the long list of New York stocks and find the following:

Sls	High	Low	Close	N'Ch
146 Hercules	39	38	38	− ½

Then you notice how the stock traded on the Pacific exchange:

2200 Hercules	38¾	38¼	38¼

Now perhaps the following legitimate questions come to your mind:

Q. Why did Hercules close at 38 in New York and at 38¼ on the Pacific?

A. The closing price on the NYSE was at or near 4:00 P.M. New York time (1:00 Pacific time), while the very last sale that took place in Hercules on the Pacific may have been either before or after the New York close. In other words, the Pacific close may have no relationship in time to the New York.

Q. Was the volume higher on the Pacific than on the NYSE?

A. No. The "146" on the NYSE means 14,600 whereas the 2200 on the Pacific really means 2,200 shares traded.

Q. Hercules never sold as high as 39 on the Pacific. Does that mean that a person could have bought it cheaper there than in New York?

A. No. The volume of trading on the Pacific was small compared to that in New York. It happens that at the time Hercules was selling at 39 in the East, there was no trading at all in the stock on the West Coast.

CONCLUSIONS

Regional exchanges serve a vital function. For one thing, they provide a good market for many stocks—some of which have a local following—that do not qualify or do not wish to qualify for listing on the American or New York stock exchange. Regional exchanges are closely regulated; they have specialists and other conveniences and safeguards that are provided by the larger exchanges. In addition, they provide markets for many stocks that are also listed on the major exchanges—though it is fair to say that the great preponderance of trading exists in New York and thus the best market exists there. Prices of stocks listed on regional exchanges are generally determined by activity and trading in New York. Prices on the local exchanges are arrived at in sympathy with what is going on in that central marketplace.

6

The Unlisted (Over-the-Counter) Market

Though listed stocks include most of our country's largest enterprises, in number alone listed securities are actually a small minority. Of more than 20,000 securities traded in the United States today, less than 3,000 are listed on any exchange. The rest are unlisted, or traded "over-the-counter" (please, not "under-the-counter"!). The fact that a stock is unlisted does not mean that a good market does not exist for it. Take, for example, three companies from the San Francisco Bay Area— Pacific Gas and Electric, Hexcel, and Genentech. An active market exists in all four, yet PG&E is listed on all exchanges, Hexcel is listed on the New York and Midwest exchanges, and Genentech is traded over-the-counter (OTC).

Most of our country's top industrial concerns were traded OTC—and many experienced their greatest appreciation before they were listed. Many blue chip companies are still unlisted (Roadway Services, Betz, Millipore, Farmers Group Insurance). All the bonds of our cities, counties, and states (called municipal bonds) are unlisted, as are almost all U.S. government securities. More than 75% of all corporation bonds and all mutual funds are OTC. And, of course, all new issues start out trading in the unlisted market.

The main differences between listed and unlisted markets are:

1. There is no one central marketplace OTC. Whereas an order to buy stock on the New York exchange goes directly to that one spot, the OTC involves numerous dealers throughout the country who "make a market" in that stock.

2. There is generally a wider "spread" between the bid and ask price OTC than for a stock traded on an exchange (although there are many exceptions: i.e., the spread on Apple Computer, unlisted, is normally narrower than that on Wallace Computer, listed).

3. Large-volume orders to buy or sell are more easily handled on the exchange.

4. An investor can only margin (borrow to buy) a select number of unlisted stocks through his broker. This list of marginable OTC issues is set by the Securities and Exchange Commission. An unlisted stock not on this list must be paid for in full by the buyer; you may be able to borrow from your bank on such a security, but this availability is limited—if you are considering this or any other kind of borrowing on securities, you should check with your broker or banker for up-to-date regulations.

5. Unlisted stocks sometimes do not fluctuate as much as listed ones on an *hour-by-hour basis*.

6. There are no "stop" orders in the over-the-counter market, and short selling is impractical (in fact, it can only be accomplished if you can borrow the stock before the short sale is executed).

Tracing through an actual transaction OTC might clarify a few things. Let's say you want to buy 100 shares of Apple Computer stock. If the stock were listed, the order would go through the procedure explained in Chapter 4 at the Apple post. But Apple is not listed. So your order will go to the OTC department of your broker (usually called the "trading department"). The OTC clerk receives the order and looks on the national quotation sheet, or on an electronic visual display, which shows which brokers throughout the country "make a market" in this stock. Let's assume there are four firms "trading" Apple. The clerk proceeds to get a quote from each of them as follows:

Clerk: "How's Apple?"

Broker B: "25 at 25½." (This means that B is willing to buy at least 100 shares of that stock at the bid price of 25 and stands willing to sell at least 100 shares at 25½.)

Broker C gives his market as: 25⅛ at 25½.

Broker D gives his market as: 25 at 25¼.

Broker E gives his market as: 25⅛ at 25⅝.

The clerk has now checked the market and finds that the lowest offering is 25¼ by Broker D. He calls D back immediately and, if he finds that his market has not changed, he tells D, "Buy 100 from you at 25¼." Actually, the clerk may try to get the stock a little cheaper by bidding 25⅛, but he takes a chance that D may then change his offer. If the clerk decides that 25¼ is a fair price, the transaction is completed and you will be billed at this price plus commission.

Certain firms make a business of "making a market" in OTC securities. They stand ready to buy and sell, and naturally hope to make a good living from the spread that exists between the bid and ask. For example, if a broker can buy and sell the same number of shares without the market changing, he can make good money (in the Apple example, if broker D buys 100 shares from another firm at his bid price of 25 and then sells your broker these 100 shares at 25¼, he makes himself $25). The difficulty is that these OTC dealers can't count on buying and selling the same number of shares each day—and the price is always fluctuating. Take the theoretical case of a firm making a market in the apparel company Liz Claiborne. Let's say he quotes the stock 45 bid, 45½ offered. In the course of the day he buys 500 shares at 45, without selling any at the offer of 45½. The next day more selling comes in on Liz Claiborne and the price drops to 43½ at 44 (that is, the other dealers in that stock have lowered their price to 43½ bid, 44 offered). This dealer naturally has to adjust his market to approximately the same level. Now another broker comes in and buys 500 shares at the current offer price of 44—this is the same 500 that the OTC dealer purchased only yesterday at 45 and thus he lost $1 per share on 500 shares, or $500. As you can see, "making a market" in OTC securities is risky business.

HOW DO UNLISTED SECURITIES
SHOW IN THE NEWSPAPER?

We'll see in Chapter 11 how listed stocks' prices show in the daily papers. Whereas nearly all the stocks listed on the various exchanges show in the paper every day, there would not be room for the many thousands of unlisted securities. Therefore it is normal for the papers to show only the most widely traded unlisted issues and those that have a local following. Many papers print quotations on fifty to one hundred stocks total. *The Wall Street Journal* shows daily prices of a few hundred.

Now, suppose you own one of the many stocks that are not shown in your local newspaper or in *The Wall Street Journal* (or in a long list of weekly quotations shown in *Barron's*). How do you know where your stock is selling? Well, the only way to determine the stock's price is by asking your broker, who can get you a quote at any time.

Let's assume, however, that your unlisted stock or stocks are printed daily. They will show in one of two ways:

Sls	Stock	High	Low	Last	N'Chg
8088	Apple	36⅜	35½	36¼	+ ⅜
1519	Liz Claiborne	46	45½	45¾	. . .

or

Sls	Stock	Bid	Ask	Last	N'Chg
104	The Local S&L	12	11¼	12	. . .
53	Nearby Airways	23	23½	23	− ½

The first format (found in most major newspapers) is the "NASDAQ" (National Association of Securities Dealers Automatic Quotations) presentation. NASDAQ's electronic quotation system provides price information on many OTC stocks (usually the larger, better known unlisted securities), and it shows the high and low prices for the day—as well as the last sale price and the net change in price since the previous day's trading. The second format is more typical of local newspapers; here the results simply show an approximate Bid and Ask price, with no information on the high and low prices reached that day.

You should also know that the published prices for non-NASDAQ unlisted securities will not be exact prices. What appears are the bids and offers quoted by over-the-counter dealers as of approximately 4 P.M. (Eastern Time). These quotations do not represent actual transactions. NASDAQ quotations, however, are prices from actual trades, also as of 4 P.M. (Eastern Time).

CONCLUSIONS

Some of the best money-making opportunities exist in the OTC market because it contains not-so-recognized stocks that may become the blue chips of tomorrow. Many times you will find an OTC stock that is not so well known, that is much more reasonably priced in relation to its earnings, dividends, or book value than a comparable listed security. If and when this OTC stock becomes better known, it may rise in price very rapidly just because it is "catching up" and beginning to sell on the same basis as better-known comparable stocks.

Certain securities in the OTC market do not have a "good market." For these stocks, you have little assurance that you will be able to find a buyer when you want to sell. If you are considering investing in this type of stock (which, incidentally, is the exception), you should realize that you are sacrificing marketability or liquidity.

For the most part, however, you can be sure of reasonable marketability in unlisted stocks. A general rule: If a stock looks very attractive to you, don't let the fact that it is unlisted deter you from buying. Many very interesting situations will present themselves in OTC securities, so don't be prejudiced against them for that reason alone.

7

The "Third" and "Fourth" Markets

For many years a sharp distinction existed between so-called listed (listed on a stock exchange) and unlisted securities. The stock exchanges insisted that a security that had listing privileges on their exchange(s) could only be traded on those exchanges.

At that time, commission rates on those exchanges were fixed; if you wanted to buy American Telephone stock, you had to pay a set commission rate.

Such monopoly was not to persist forever. Certain entrepreneurial brokers recognized a potential opportunity—they were willing to take over-the-counter type positions on American Tel and other listed issues and attempt to effect transactions that would result in lower net costs to their customers than if these buyers and sellers went through exchange member brokers. Thus was born what came to be known as the Third Market.

The exchanges were constantly battling what they considered to be "intruders," but the cost saving potentials were so attractive that the Third Market flourished. Its major thrust was with large institutional-type investors, although some also had profitable business with individual investors. Weeden and Company, Jeffries, and other companies soon became very important market makers; they combined the function of specialist and broker and they transacted large amounts of business.

Later on, another market appeared—this one strictly oriented to institutions. This was labeled the Fourth Market. Without going into great detail, this new competitor offered a clearing house arrangement for such large investors. By paying some minimum fee, the institution (a large bank, insurance company, mutual fund, investment adviser, etc.) would communicate to the Fourth Market broker its desire to buy or sell certain securities. The Fourth Market broker would see if there was a "match" with any of his other customers, and if so, would attempt to arrange a transaction price between the two—with little or no cost to either side for this service. Thus if Bank A had registered an interest in selling General Motors, and if Insurance Company B called in and indicated a buying interest in GM, the Fourth Market broker would communicate with both A and B, to see if they could agree on a price and number of shares, and if they did, arrange for the transaction to take place. The Fourth Market broker might charge a small fee to take care of clearing charges, handling fees, and so forth. Or he might not, taking his compensation instead from some fixed fee agreed to by his customers on an annual basis.

With set brokerage fees no longer the standard rule on the major exchanges, the competitive advantages of both Third and Fourth markets have diminished. Yet they still flourish— they actually handle a significant volume of trading every day.* These markets are also tied in to the Central Market System, so that all transactions—whether they be on the exchanges, in the over-the-counter markets, or in the Third or Fourth markets— appear on the trading screen that was once the exclusive domain of listed securities.

---

*In special instances, the Third and Fourth markets may continue to operate while other exchanges are closed. In the autumn of 1985, for example, the NYSE did not open one morning as the city braced itself for a threatening hurricane. Yet active trading took place for many stocks through the Third and Fourth market system!

PART III
How to Judge the Stock Market and Gauge Where It Is Going

8
The Market and How to Follow It

If nothing else is certain about stocks, one thing is: *The Market will fluctuate*. To be up or to be down, that is the question. While the stock market is looked upon by many as a *thermometer* of business, political, and other conditions, I view it more as a *crystal ball*. Stock investors focus more on forecasting what *will* happen rather than reflecting on what has already occurred. That is why the axiom "Buy stocks when things look at their worst" is so important. When things seem to be at their worst, less sophisticated investors generally reflect their pessimism by selling stocks on a wholesale basis. Smart investors buy these greatly depressed stocks on the theory that if things are at their worst, they can only get better. In the stock market, if you wait until things actually *are* better, you'll be late. By that time, stocks will have risen in value by a goodly amount.

People are always amazed when a company announces higher earnings, a raised dividend, or other good news—only to find its stock go *down* in price. Why does this happen? Because too many holders had already anticipated the good news, bought the stock at low prices before the announcement, and then sold their stock when the news finally broke, forcing the stock down in price. Of course, many times a stock will rise on good news (in fact, this is usually the case), but this does not refute this theory. It only proves that the good news had not been anticipated by the majority of investors and speculators.

The stock market in general is subject to the same "anticipation of news." The market is always trying to *forecast* events. And that is why I say the market is more like a crystal ball than a thermometer. Of course, the crystal ball isn't always crystal clear. People often get optimistic about the near future (and the market rises), only to be proved wrong. For example, the 1956 stock market was rising and anticipating continued good business for some time to come, only to find business slump very rapidly in mid-1957 and 1958. Sometimes the market will get worried about conditions, as it did in 1946–47, only to find that business was not bad when 1948–49 rolled around. The same thing happened with the 1962, 1979, and 1985 markets; no recessions developed. Many, many times, however, the market is correct in its forecasts of things to come. The main thing is that you, as a potential owner of stocks, should always *look ahead* and attempt to forecast, too. But how can *you* forecast complicated economic and political events better than others? The following discussions should aid you in getting the jump. The necessary facts are available—it's a matter of knowing where to find them and how to interpret them.

WHERE TO GET THE FACTS

Many local newspapers will give you most of the facts you need to assess in judging business and the stock market. But the "bible" in our business is *The Wall Street Journal*. This daily (five days a week) publication will keep you current on economic statistics and industry and individual company reports. It also prints feature articles of interest. Countless other publications are valuable supplements to the *Journal*, namely *Barron's* (weekly), *Fortune* (biweekly), *Business Week* magazine (weekly— devoted to all aspects of business, including marketing, finance, labor, advertising), *Magazine of Wall Street* (strictly finance), *Forbes* (a biweekly publication with excellent articles on individual companies and investing in general), *Financial World*, and many others.

In addition, there are some government publications that will give you all the economic facts you can possibly digest, namely the Federal Reserve Board's monthly bulletin and two Department of Commerce publications—*Economic Indicators* (monthly business statistics in chart form) and the *Survey of Current Business.*

Furthermore, if you're willing to spend a few more dollars, there are many investment "services" that will boil down these facts for you and recommend individual issues as well as give advice on the market in general. *Standard & Poor's, Moody's,* and *Value Line* are perhaps the best known of these services, but there are countless others, and the number has been growing in recent years.

Caution about the use of advisory services is certainly in order. The "investment letter" business is easy to enter and many of the writers are no more adept than those seeking advice. As a matter of fact, the overall record of such services has been poor—so poor that astute professionals such as Alan Abelson of *Barron's,* plus others, point to the opinions of advisory letters as being reliable *reverse* indicators.

If the majority are bullish, they contend, look for the market to decline, not advance; and vice versa. There are sound reasons for such cynicism, so be careful here!

One additional word of caution about following the investment recommendations of these services. Many times a widely subscribed service will put out a buy or sell recommendation on a particular stock. When such recommendations are mailed throughout the country and arrive at different locations on different days, there may not be any concentrated orders coming from this recommendation on one day. Many such recommendations are mailed out, however, to arrive in the mail over the weekend. Hundreds of subscribers read their mail on Saturday or Sunday, call their broker and place an order for the opening on Monday morning, and what happens? The stock is subject to a sudden spurt! Perhaps it closed at $30 on Friday, but orders to buy a few thousand shares are placed "at the market" on Monday and it opens at $33, or the stock has a concentrated rise during the whole day because of this recommendation. You should beware of this, because chances are high that when this concentrated buying from the recommendation subsides (which may be only a day or so later), the stock will drop back near its Friday's close. In other words, be discreet with your order—don't become "one of the mob" that rushes to buy the stock all at once. For example, a number of years ago a famed news commentator took to giving investment "tips" on his evening show (which would be in violation of FCC regulations today). These tips were followed by certain listeners and invariably a rash of buy orders would accumulate the next morning and cause the given stock to rise suddenly and sharply. In the great majority of cases these buyers paid inflated prices and it generally took them quite some time to get even on their purchases. Some of us in the securities business used to say, "Whatever Mr. _____ recommends on Sunday night, *don't buy, but instead sell short* on Monday morning." In practice, this was one of the most consistent theories ever in the stock market.

There are countless economic factors you should consider when reading the financial page of your newspaper. Like all statistics, these are only meaningful when compared with like figures for a previous period. Let's take a look at some indicators that tell you how *business in general* is at the moment. Naturally, it takes interpretation (and some guesswork) to shape these factors into a projection of what kind of business lies ahead.

Gross National Product

The GNP tells you the total goods and services produced in this country on an annual basis. Obviously the higher the GNP, the better business in general is. Inflated prices can fool you, however, so investors have learned to focus on *real* GNP— which subtracts inflation from the gross figures.

Employment

Employment figures are, of course, indicative of the state of business. You notice I stress *employment* rather than *unemployment* figures, mainly because the latter can be deceiving. For example, unemployment can rise even though business is booming if an exceptionally large group of eighteen-to-twenty-two-year-olds suddenly enters the labor force. A bumper baby crop eighteen to twenty years ago may have added to the employable list after their schooling—and unemployment figures might well indicate caution about business, despite strong and reassuring employment figures.

Disposable Personal Income

This figure tells you how much money people have to spend, which is basic to good business both currently and in the near future.

Index of Industrial Production

The IIP gives you the amount of general business volume, shown as a percentage of the average that existed in 1977 (given a base of 100). For example, an IIP of 150 means that business volume is 50% higher than the average of the base period.

Bank Deposits

It's always nice to see bank deposits rising along with higher consumer spending. Were deposits to drop substantially, it would be a sign for caution, because people can't draw down from savings forever. Savings provide future business. The burgeoning growth of money market funds has, however, made bank deposits a less reliable indicator of investor savings patterns.

Manufacturers' New Orders, Unfilled Orders, and Inventories

The importance of the first two of these three factors is obvious. *New orders* received by manufacturers build up the amount of *unfilled orders* they have on the books; the larger the unfilled orders, the more assurance you have that business will be good in the time ahead. Not quite so obvious, but of the very utmost importance, are *inventories*, which are the amount of goods already on the shelves of manufacturers.

Despite the old story "Salt," the more goods businessmen have on their shelves, the more cautious they are about buying.*

Businessmen are willing to buy more than they require when they sense booming conditions, but the minute business starts to slip, they cut back on their buying of goods. And if they already have large supplies on hand, they delay buying altogether until their inventories go down to more manageable levels. *When inventories are rising from anything but depressed levels, it is a sign for caution.* At least two of our country's worst recessions since the end of World War II were the direct result of inventory cutbacks—businessmen ceased to buy because their inventories were too high.

Consumer Debt

This is another important indicator. People can only owe so much before they have to slow down their buying on credit. One of several causes of the 1957–1958 recession was the large amount of debt piled up by consumers during the bulging 1955–1956 automobile sales. The public simply saturated themselves and had to hold off purchases of goods—especially those usually sold "on time"—till their debt payments declined. A similar pattern (though more severe) existed in 1980. Again, in 1986, many economists noted the record levels of consumer debt and forecasted a slowdown in consumer spending. Con-

*A customer entered a grocery store and asked, "Have you any salt?" "Salt," replied the grocer, "have I got salt? Take a look!" Behind him were shelves filled with salt. Then he took the customer to the back of the store and showed him more rows of shelves filled with salt. "Have I got salt?" he repeated again and took the customer by the hand to the basement, where he had a roomful of salt. "Have I got salt!!" the grocer kept muttering.

The customer looked at him and said the obvious: "My, but you must sell a lot of salt every year!"

"Salt? Who sells salt?" cried the grocer. "Maybe three cases a year, I sell. But there's a salesman who comes here three times a year, and wow, can he sell salt!!!"

THIS IS DEFINITELY THE EXCEPTION TO OUR ECONOMIC REASONING ABOUT INVENTORIES.

sumer debt alone can be deceiving, however. Some effort should be made to relate it to personal income before reaching any conclusions about whether it is too high or too low.

Imports and Exports

Naturally these are important to the nation. While we encourage foreign trade and the building up of other nations, it is distressing to see an unfavorable balance of trade wherein the United States is importing more than it is selling to others. This was certainly the 1980–1986 U.S. experience, initially due to a sharp rise in the dollar versus the currency of its trading partners. The strong dollar effectively made U.S. goods more expensive relative to foreign goods. It remains to be seen whether the 1985–1986 drop in the dollar will reverse the trade imbalance.

Business Failures

A marked increase in failures is a credit caution signal.

Cost-of-Living Index

The cost-of-living index (CPI) and the producers price index (PPI) indicate how much inflation we are having. Inflation has become an important consideration for investors, whether they be interested in bonds, stocks, real estate, gold, or whatever.

Money Supply

Money supply has become another important forecasting factor. Many investors have become "Fed watchers" (the Federal Reserve Board will be discussed later in this chapter), on the theory that the manipulation of the money supply has a significant bearing on future business conditions and inflation.

Money supply is expressed in such terms as M1, M2, and M3, and a full explanation of its intricacies is beyond the scope of this book. Suffice it to say that the sharply rising money supply is stimulative to the economy *and* it is potentially inflationary (and vice versa).

"MORE SPECIALIZED" FACTORS TO WATCH FOR

The following are additional indicators, most of which have a double meaning to forecasters:

Paperboard Production

Certainly you should watch this statistic if you have an interest in paper stocks. In addition, this happens to be a very sensitive indicator of the trend of business. Why? Because most of what is produced has to be wrapped and shipped. And what is the most important material for this use? Paperboard, of course. Remember, most companies report their earnings every three months. You may not know how a company's business is going in between these quarterly statements. But the paperboard figures appear weekly and can be a good lead indicator of business in general, of an industry trend, or of the stock market in general.

Railroad Carloadings

A similar indicator is railroad carloadings, which is the number of railroad cars being loaded for shipment each week. If you own railroad stocks, here is the best indicator of how the rail business is going. But these figures have added significance, for everything produced must eventually be shipped and railroads and trucks handle most of the manufactured goods in the United States. So when rail shipments decline, they show up *weekly* in the carloading figures. The carloadings are broken down for you by geographical location and by freight classification. A similar "Intercity Trucks Tonnage Index" exists for goods shipped by trucks. Here again, you can stay ahead of quarterly reports by following these important business indicators.

Electric Power Production

This is important for holders of utility stocks, but it also provides a check on overall business conditions. After all, when business is good, more power is used, so these weekly figures give a broad picture of activity.

Automobiles and Building

Figures from these two basic industries are very important. Aside from the huge sums of money paid out in wages to workers in these industries, think of the related industries that are so dependent on them. Auto-truck production has a great effect on steel, glass, chemicals, rubber, aluminum, and other metals, as well as on transportation. Building likewise involves steel, glass, and aluminum and has considerable effect on cement, gypsum, asphalt, lumber, plywood, and so on. Therefore both new car-truck sales and building activity give you insight into overall business conditions, especially into the major industries they involve. Auto-truck production figures are published weekly, while housing starts and other construction figures are generally published on a monthly basis.

London Metal Prices

If you're following nonferrous metal stocks (copper, zinc, lead, etc.), keep a close eye on London metal prices. Prices overseas eventually have an effect domestically. Incidentally, since nonferrous metal prices fluctuate more than steel, aluminum, and other ferrous metals, they are good indicators of business activity. When copper prices rise, for example, it is usually because of increased demand stemming from higher overall production.

Steel Production, Store Sales, and Other Statistics

Steel production figures are released weekly by the American Iron and Steel Institute and, of course, give you early indication of what quarterly earnings of the steel companies will be.

Weekly department store sales not only tell how Macy's, Sears, and the other big stores are doing, but also give a clue as to how well the textiles and appliance makers are doing.

Then there are figures for *life insurance sales, crude and refined oil production,* and countless other industries.

One not-so-noticeable statistic involves *wholesale price levels.* Food chains and soap manufacturers normally *increase* their profits in years when wholesale prices are low.

Needless to say, an owner of stocks or a potential investor should follow the *earnings* and *dividends* of companies. Later on, we'll explain how to use these figures in determining what price a stock should be selling for in the market.

FEDERAL RESERVE POLICY

No discussion of business forecasting would be complete without mention of the Federal Reserve Board. The importance of this governmental body cannot be overemphasized.

The Federal Reserve regulates the amount of money that flows through our economic system. Because money is the root of all business activity, the Fed has great power. Briefly, the Fed has the following tools:

1. It sets the *discount rate,* which is the rate of interest that the banks have to pay when they borrow money from the Federal Reserve. If the Fed raises the discount rate from 9% to 9½%, banks have to pay more for some of the money they loan out. To compensate for this ½ of 1% increase, the banks will have to raise their interest charge by approximately this amount. Theoretically, the higher interest charge should deter a certain amount of borrowing; thus the Fed can restrain lending by raising the discount rate. In contrast, lowering the rate has the effect of lowering interest rates throughout the country,

which invites more borrowing. Borrowing does not always increase, however, because when people get cautious about borrowing, even abnormally low rates may not generate enthusiasm. "You can lead a horse to water, but you can't make him drink." Most economists agree that the discount rate is more powerful in restraining business than in stimulating it.

2. The Fed also sets the *reserve requirements* of banks. This has a direct effect on how much money the banks have available to lend and this naturally has an important effect on the economy. The lower the reserve requirements, the more money the banks have "free" for lending; the higher the requirements, the less money available for lending. In addition, the Fed can affect banks' reserve positions through purchases and sales of government securities in the open market.*

3. The Fed has direct control over the use of credit in the stock market through the establishment of *margin requirements*. Margin is the amount of cash one has to put up when purchasing listed securities (you must put up all cash when buying most unlisted stocks). When margin requirements are 50%, a buyer must put up at least $5,000 in cash for the purchase of $10,000 in securities; the remaining $5,000 may be borrowed from the broker at an interest rate set by your broker. By raising margins, the Fed requires higher down payments and thus restricts speculation. Incidentally, changes in margins are *not retroactive*. If you made a $10,000 purchase with a down payment of $5,000 and the Fed raises margins to 70%, you will not be affected. You can keep that $5,000 loan for as long as you like. As a matter of fact, you can replace a security held in a margin account with an equivalent dollar purchase (and stay under the "old rules") as long as the switch is accomplished the same day. Any new purchases, however, will come under the new regulations.

---

*A detailed discussion of this complicated mechanism is unnecessary for our purposes. All you need to know is that the Fed decreases member bank reserve balances (restricts credit) when it sells government securities in the market, and vice versa.

4. The Fed can use *credit restrictions* (i.e., force car or appliance buyers to put up a given down payment). These have been employed only in rare circumstances such as war, but the early 1980 credit restraints instituted by the Fed had immediate impact on the economy.

The Federal Reserve Board has been criticized time and again for its policies. Tight money policies (higher discount rates, reserve requirements, and margin requirements) usually bear the brunt of attack by both labor and business because the tightness tends to hamper business. That's why it is especially important to understand the Fed's aims, which are generally to keep the economy on a steady rate of growth with only moderate inflation. The Fed certainly doesn't want booms which lead to busts—and it doesn't want rampant inflation. It estimates the country's achievable growth rate and tries to keep it on an even keel. I like to contrast the Fed's attitude with an experience I'm sure all of you have had as a driver or passenger of an automobile traveling along a boulevard that has stop signals set for a certain rate of speed. Perhaps you've seen drivers who insist on going 60 miles an hour for two blocks, only to have to screech to a halt at the next signal, while you make all the signals without stopping by driving 30 miles per hour. What happens to the 60 mph driver? He wastes gas by rapid acceleration, wears down his tires and brakes by quick stops, and ends up with constant aggravation. This is just what the Fed guards against. It wants the economy to go 30 mph and get to the destination with greatest ease.

The trouble is that the Federal Reserve Board cannot regulate the economy as you would the gas pedal of your car. Restraint may well choke business and create lower activity than originally planned (this was the complaint of many during 1956–57). But a temporary dip in business is always better than a sharp depression that might last for a long, long time.

In recent years various moves have been made to reduce the independence of the Federal Reserve Board through legislation. I consider this a mistake—one that would have serious consequences for the U.S. economy. This is not to imply that the Fed has always "behaved" as its role dictates; certainly its willingness to stimulate the economy in 1972, which "just happened" to be an election year, when the economy did not need such stimulation seemed strange (and inexcusable) to me. Its actions in 1978–1980 also left something to be desired—the Fed was more stimulative than those of us who feared inflation would have liked. In the early 1980's the Fed's restrictive policies led to high interest rates and a downturn in the economy. However, the result of such action proved to be the dismantling of painfully high rates of inflation built up through the prior decade.

By and large, the Fed's role is an admirable one in the best long-range interests of the country. If it were to lose its independence and become a political-type organization, its role as an economic "traffic controller" would be diminished. Monetary regulation is anything but an exact science, and even the best efforts of the Fed have not always produced the desired results. Until human nature changes radically, however, every economy requires monetary regulation—and its chances for success are enhanced with an objective, independent body such as the Federal Reserve Board.

9

What's the Market Doing?

When people ask, "How's the market?," most want to know what the basic trend is. Many experts contend that there's no such thing as a "general stock market." Instead, they say there are separate markets for individual stocks and that an investor should be more concerned with what's going on in individual issues rather than the overall list. While I, too, prefer this approach, one has to be conscious of a trend and that's what we're going to touch on here.

Most investors judge "the market" by what is happening to the Dow Jones Industrial Average (DJIA)—an index of thirty stocks* listed on the NYSE. Actually, there are numerous disadvantages to the DJIA. For one thing, it constitutes *only* thirty stocks—hardly representative of the whole market. Second, the thirty stocks are recognized blue chip issues; there are no secondary stocks (since there are more secondary companies on the exchange than blue chips, the DJIA does not reflect the majority). Third, the stocks in the average are not all equally weighted. In 1928 Dow Jones revised its average in such a way that any stock that splits has—after the split—less influence on the index than those that leave their price high. Because of this, in any given day a large fluctuation in just one or two high-priced stocks like Procter & Gamble or IBM can distort the average considerably. Thus, while the DJIA may

---

*The thirty include: Allied-Signal, Aluminum Co., Amer. Express, Amer. T&T, Bethlehem Steel, Boeing, Chevron, Coca-Cola, duPont, Eastman Kodak, Exxon, General Electric, General Motors, Goodyear, IBM, Inter. Paper, McDonald's, Merck, Minnesota M&M, Navistar, Philip Morris, Primerica, Procter & Gamble, Sears Roebuck, Texaco, Union Carbide, United Technologies, USX, Westinghouse El., Woolworth.

reflect the overall market trend *over the long run,* it is too often a very unreliable indicator of daily or weekly market action.

There are other averages one can follow. The most widely quoted are the Standard & Poor's 500 Stock Index and the New York Stock Exchange Index. Because of their breadth, these do not have certain of the DJIA's disadvantages. Actually, the S&P 500 has shortcomings, too, in that it is heavily weighted by a few dozen large capitalization (i.e., many shares outstanding) companies.

Broader indexes of the market than the DJIA and S&P are now available. The most broadly based is the Wilshire 5,000 Equity Index (compiled by the Wilshire Associates of Santa Monica, California). The "5,000" reflects the total market value of all stocks listed on the New York and American Stock Exchanges plus those "actively traded over-the-counter." The Value Line Composite Average, an equally weighted geometric average of stock prices expressed in an index form with June 30, 1961, set at 100, is another index, this one consisting of all of the approximately 1,700 stocks regularly reviewed in the Value Line Survey, 80% of which are listed on the NYSE. The problem with this index is that it's "equally weighted." It doesn't account for company size and therefore weights the performance of the tiniest company equally with that of the largest.

FACTORS TO CONSIDER IN JUDGING THE MARKET

There are countless factors to consider in judging what the market is doing. Here are some of the most important:

1. *Do* follow some of the averages listed above, but remember that the most important consideration is the percentage change over one day or a long period of time. The newspaper headlines can be deceiving: "Stocks Drop Ten Points" or "Market Declines Total $3

---

*Actually, it hasn't been a reliable indicator over the past ten years; from 1976 through 1986, the DJIA was up "only" 75% versus the S&P 500 performance of + 140%. The poor results of Bethlehem and USX, Eastman Kodak, General Motors, Owens-Illinois, Sears, Union Carbide, and others acted to depress the DJIA.

Billion." Remember that a 24-point drop in the Dow Jones Industrial Average, which is currently around 2400, is 1%. And that the total value of listed securities is over $2.5 trillion.

2. Look for the ratio of *advances* to *declines* in the market on any particular day. If more stocks are advancing than declining, perhaps the market is really strong despite the fact that the averages showed a decline for the day.

3. Also useful in determining the breadth of the market on any given day is the number of individual stocks that made *new highs* versus the number that touched *new lows* for the year. Obviously a market with a preponderance of stocks reaching new highs cannot be termed weak, even if the averages denote a decline.

4. What is the *volume of trading?* Like the preceding figure, this one appears every day in your local papers. The volume of trading is obviously the number of shares that were bought and sold—an important indicator because *volume usually moves with a trend.* That is, if the market is advancing on *low* volume and declining on *heavy* volume, most probably *the basic trend* is *down.*

5. How many shares have been sold short? The so-called short interest, which shows how many shares of each stock are held "short," comes out once a month (the data are gathered on the 15th and published a few days later). The larger the number of shares sold short, the more pessimistic people are. Oddly enough, it is *not* a bad sign when the short interest is up. Why? Because the time to buy is usually when most investors *are* pessimistic, which is of course when stock prices are low. And remember that a short seller must eventually buy back, so the more shares sold short, the more potential buyers there are "lying in the weeds."

6. *How do yields on stock compare with yields on bonds?* This "spread between the yields" is important because bonds and stocks are in competition for investor monies. For many years stocks provided a higher current income return (yield) than bonds; this seemed natural, because there is more ordinary risk in stocks

than in bonds. An investor would find the return on stocks anywhere from ½ of 1% to 2½% higher than the yield on bonds. As the 1958–1959 market boom progressed (stocks rose in value and bonds plunged), this situation changed to one in which a "minus spread between the yields" became standard. Since then, bonds have provided a higher return than stocks (in 1986 the return was as much as 4–7% higher for bonds than for stocks). The fear of inflation is primarily responsible for this "minus spread" since, as we have seen, bonds seldom provide the desired hedge against inflation, whereas many common stocks do. This realization is what has shifted investor emphasis away from current income paid out to the underlying earnings of corporations; in 1986, for example, most investors point to "*earnings* yields" (rather than dividend yields) in their assessment of markets and stocks. Still, from a historical standpoint, a large minus yield spread is a sign for caution and investors should watch these figures (shown weekly in *Barron's,* among others).

7. *What is "the public" doing?* One of the old adages of Wall Street is "The public is always wrong." Who is "the public"? Usually the smaller investor, who buys in smaller amounts—in odd lots—activity gauged by watching the summary of odd lot transactions, which shows how many shares in less than 100-share lots are bought, how many are sold, and how many are sold short. Also from a historical standpoint, it is time for suspicion when odd lot buys greatly overshadow the odd lot sells. Conversely, think about buying when the odd lot figures show heavy selling on balance.

8. *How much speculation is there in the market?* This can be judged by the types of securities that are most actively traded. One guide is the Standard & Poor's 20 Low-Priced Stock Index or similar indices found in *Barron's* and the SRC (Security Research Company) Red Book publication. Another is the list of the most actively traded stocks on the exchange either daily or weekly. A predominance of low-priced, low-quality stocks indicates that the market has "poor leadership," and that speculation, rather than long-term investing, prevails.

Another reliable indicator of speculation is the relationship of trading on the American Stock Exchange to that on the Big Board. Let's face it, the ASE is hardly the haven for quality issues—at least compared to the NYSE. Whenever the ASE is experiencing volume much above 50% of the trading on the NYSE for an extended period, it constitutes a strong sign for caution.

9. *How many "secondary offerings" and "new issues" are coming to market?* Secondary offerings (large blocks of stock being offered at a given price at one time) and new issues (initial public offerings, "IPO's," or shares of *privately* held companies being offered to public investors for the first time) pose a number of negatives. First, heavy IPO activity drains investors' dollars away from securities traded on the exchanges or over-the-counter. As with other commodities, a very sharp increase in supply of securities without a corresponding increase in demand will lead to lower prices. Second, a preponderance of IPO's usually signifies that a speculative attitude prevails—an attitude that historically has prevailed at market peaks.

10. *How high is the market in relation to earning power?* We will see later how to judge an *individual stock*'s merit on the basis of its earning power. The *market in general* should be judged the same way. Most statistical services show you how high the market is in relation to current earnings and in relation to projected profits—by figuring its "price-earnings ratio." This ratio is discussed fully in Chapter 22, but for now just remember that the lower the ratio, the better, and a higher ratio is a sign of warning. Over the past twenty-five years we have seen the market sell between the broad range of around 6 and 20 times earnings, with one year (1961) when the market sold well above 20 times earnings. Remember, however, that it is more important to determine how the market is selling in relation to *future earnings* (those of six to eighteen months ahead) than to past or even present profits.

10
The Bulls Versus the Bears

As you gathered from the last chapter, it is important for investors to analyze what is happening in the stock market. Accomplishing this simply prepares you to *forecast* better what lies ahead.

Cycles of various kinds are inevitable in the stock market, and you should be prepared to spot these cycles *before they arrive*.

The stock market is a place where many thousands of people "vote" every day. In the market, of course, there are only two ways to cast your ballot: you can vote that the market—or more specifically, a stock—will go up, in which case you buy; or you can vote your belief that it will go down—and you sell. As in political elections, a *trend* usually develops in favor of one side or another. If the trend is on the buy side, then the market goes up and we have what is called a "bull market." If, on the other hand, people are mainly pessimistic and are predominantly on the sell side, stocks go down and we have a "bear market."

Over the years, the stock market has experienced many bull and bear cycles. Fortunately, the bull trends have dominated, as the chart on page 72 indicates. Also, a study of U.S. stock markets shows that bull markets normally last twice as long as the declining bear trends.

You certainly want to develop a sense for these trends. Like a good fighter, you want to roll with the punches and be more fully invested in a bull phase than in either trendless or bear conditions.

PEAKS AND TROUGHS IN S&P 500

Peak		Trough		% Change Peak to Trough	Length of Peak to Trough (months)	% Change Trough to Next Peak	Length of Trough to Next Peak (months)
Date	S&P 500	Date	S&P 500				
Jun 1948	16.74	Jun 1949	14.16	(15.4)%	12	87.6%	42
Dec 1952	26.57	Aug 1953	23.32	(12.2)	8	111.8	35
Jul 1956	49.39	Dec 1957	39.99	(19.0)	17	51.3	19
Jul 1959	60.51	Oct 1960	53.39	(11.7)	15	34.0	14
Dec 1961	71.55	Jun 1962	54.75	(23.5)	6	69.6	43
Jan 1966	92.88	Sep 1966	76.56	(17.6)	8	41.5	26
Nov 1968	108.37	Jun 1970	72.72	(32.9)	19	62.3	30
Dec 1972	118.05	Sep 1974	63.54	(46.2)	21	69.1	27
Dec 1976	107.46	Mar 1978	86.90	(19.1)	15	61.7	32
Nov 1980	140.52	Aug 1982	102.42	(27.1)	21	—	—
Average				(22.5)	14.2	65.4	29.8

SPOTTING (AND DISTINGUISHING) BULL MARKETS

A good way to be ahead of the crowd in forecasting trends is to understand the characteristics of the *final* stages of a bull market. First, business is usually very good near the top of a market. This may sound paradoxical, but remember that wise investors are looking ahead and they know that booming business cannot last forever; it is normally followed by recession. Second, a robust economy encourages the majority* of investors to be enthusiastic and plumb full of confidence. It's quite normal to hear talk of the "new and golden era." Many stock market "experts" are exuding confidence, too, predicting higher and higher markets ahead. In addition, the following factors generally exist:

1. The market has attracted wide public participation. The total number of stockholders in the country takes a sudden spurt. The odd lot figures mentioned in Chapter 4 show far more buyers than sellers.
2. Stock splits are commonplace; this is because stock prices have risen so high that there are many more high-priced issues (obvious split candidates).
3. These warning signals appear: bonds are yielding way more than stocks; the market is probably selling very high in relation to current and, most important, prospective earnings, and there is a rash of offerings and new issues for the public to absorb. (Watch out when the "hot" new issues suddenly turn cold and "sticky.")
4. Additional signs for caution:
   a. Rallies, which used to carry a long way, don't carry as far.
   b. Bond prices start to fall sharply, thereby offering much higher returns to investors (a lot of money is attracted away from inflated stocks into deflated bonds).
   c. The key stocks in the market begin to fade and sell off (the leadership of the market is weakened).

*Note that I said "the majority," not necessarily the wisest.

d. The volume of trading on the advances slows down considerably (the tide of enthusiasm is ebbing).
e. The market does not react, as it used to, to good news (announcements that once created excitement and caused stocks to rise suddenly have no effect).

When you begin to spot these factors, it is time to switch from a heavily invested position in common stocks to a conservative approach. But don't expect your actions to prove correct overnight—the market won't plunge the day after you have lightened your holdings. There is little chance of your selling at the top, so expect to see the stocks you have sold go higher in price. In other words, don't be greedy and try to extract the last ounce of profit from a waning market. If the market continues to roll on, don't be deceived and buy back hastily.

It is equally important to be able to spot the end of a bear market so you know when to take a very aggressive position in the stock market. On a historical basis, bear markets last anywhere from one to four or five years, although overall downward trends have been much shorter in duration over the last twenty years (usually lasting little more than one year). In stark contrast to bull markets, bear trends produce a morgue-like mood; people are depressed and interest in the stock market is apathetic. Oddly enough, a sharp decline in the blue chip issues is a sign that the end of the bear market is approaching (since investors hold on to these till the end). As the decline nears an end, an investor is able to find real bargains in the market; dividends are high and stocks sell very reasonably in relation to earning power and book value. The market becomes resistant to bad news (announcements that used to cause stocks to sell off suddenly have little or no effect).

Once the market reverses, the volume increases, but gradually. You start witnessing more advances than declines, more new highs than new lows, and so on. In short, the storm has passed and it is time to look for the clearest of skies.

Let me emphasize here that, despite the analysis just presented, the stock market is seldom a feast-or-famine affair. There are stocks to buy in very bad markets, just as there are stocks to sell in a boom. The analysis is intended to make you aware of extreme danger signals and of exceedingly attractive opportunities that may (will!) present themselves sometime during your stock market life. Everything is relative, and successful investing results from having as much knowledge, information, and insight as possible. In essence, this is but one piece in the puzzle of success. The other pieces of the puzzle will fall into place as we go along.

PART IV
Some Facts of Life for Stockholders

11

Getting More Out of the Financial Page

Chapters 9 and 10 have pointed out that there's plenty to be gained from reading the financial pages. But there's still more! Now we'll take a look at the page that shows the daily performance of individual stocks.

DAILY PRICE MOVEMENTS

Common Stocks

Here are a few typical quotations from your daily paper.

Sls	Stock	High	Low	Close	N'Ch
266	GenMotors 5.00	80	79½	80	+ ½
1520	Rohm & Haas 3bas	730½	724	726	− 2

First of all, an explanation of the columns. Column 1, "Sls," means sales that took place in that stock on the particular day. These sales are in 100's; that is, you merely add two zeros to the figure under "Sls" to find out how many shares traded that day (in the case of General Motors above, 26,600 shares traded). The name of the stock follows—almost always abbreviated. Then comes the company's annual dividend rate, shown as 5.00

for GM, meaning GM pays $5.00 per share annually in dividends. The "high" column signifies the highest price the stock reached during the day, and "low" signifies the lowest. "Close" indicates the very last sale that took place on the exchange that day. And "N'Ch" means "net change," which is the change in market price of the stock between the previous day's close and this day's last sale price. In the GM example, the stock closed at 80 compared to yesterday's 79½ for a net gain of ½ point. Incidentally, stock prices are traded in fractions, with ⅛ of 1 point (12½ cents) being the smallest fraction for most issues (on lower-priced stocks a dollar price is sometimes broken down to ¹⁄₁₆'s, and "stock rights" are often bought and sold in fractions as small as ¹⁄₆₄'s).

What can we learn from the GM example, over and above the simple facts just presented? First of all, watch the volume figures ("Sls") because, like the market in general, individual stocks often show their *trend* by volume; that is, if GM consistently goes *up* on a large amount of "Sls" and shows consistently lower volume when it goes down in price, you might assume that the GM pattern is currently *up*. In stock market jargon such a pattern indicates a "strong technical pattern" for GM stock. Second, notice that the stock closed at its high for the day—so enthusiasm was building at the close, hinting that the stock might open at higher prices on tomorrow's market.

There are a few stocks on the exchange that do not sell in 100-share round lots. Certain high-priced issues like Rohm and Haas (shown above) used to be called "10-share traders," which means that 10 shares constituted a round lot (1 to 9 shares constituted an odd lot). I say "used to be," as most of these very high priced stocks have been split and their shares now trade in normal 100-share round lots. Rohm and Haas, for example, has been split and is a normal 100-share trading stock now. The only 10-share traders today are preferred stocks. In this case the explanation usually includes the letters "as," which means "actual sales." In such circumstances, you do *not* add two zeros to the volume figures at the left; in our Rohm and Haas example, 1,520 shares were the total traded during that day.

You might also have noticed the letter "b" after the "3" in

Rohm and Haas. It means the company paid out *stock* dividends in addition to the $3 annual *cash* payout. There are numerous other letters used to point out other information to the reader. Consult the small print either at the beginning or at the end of the price list to find out what the symbols mean.

Preferred Stocks

Sls	Stock	High	Low	Close	N'Ch
10	NiagMhk pf 4.10as				
		32	32	32	−3
110	do pf 5.25as	41	41	41	+ ½
20	do pf 4.85as	37½	37½	37½	

Our preceding discussion explains most of this. Just a few additions: The company's name is Niagara Mohawk; the "pf" stands for "preferred stock," and "do" means "ditto"—the same company as above.

Here we have three Niagara Mohawk preferred stocks. You may wonder why there is a big fluctuation of 3 points in the $4.10 preferred, especially since preferreds don't ordinarily fluctuate as much as commons. The answer: This preferred had not sold for quite some time—perhaps a month or longer—and the "−3" means the stock closed 3 points lower than *the last time it sold* (not the previous day, because it didn't trade then). You will often find large pluses or minuses on preferred issues and a time lag is usually the reason.

These prices on the three Niagara Mohawk preferred stocks serve as an ideal illustration of what has happened to preferred stocks for many years as well as explain how bonds and preferred stocks go up and down in price *with a change in money (interest) rates.*

Let's follow the history of these preferred issues. In 1954 Niagara Mohawk needed money and decided to sell some preferred stock to investors. The company sold 210,000 shares at $100 per share. But what dividend would it pay on these shares? The decision was made by asking, "What are comparable preferred stocks paying?" Assessing other such stocks, the company determined that it could sell these shares if it offered a rate of return just over 4%—4.10% to be exact. Thus a $4.10 dividend rate was set on the $100 stock to yield 4.10% yearly to its owners. The issue was sold on this basis. Incidentally, a call price of 103¼ was set, enabling the company to redeem all or part of the issue *at its discretion* at this price. *With such a call price, investors knew they couldn't expect the stock to rise very far in price, no matter how long it was held.*

As years went on, money rates changed in the United States. Whereas in 1954 investors were attracted by yields of 4.10%, by 1957 people were demanding higher returns, as indicated by the $79 market price of this preferred. Yes, the Niagara Mohawk $4.10 preferred had gradually declined to as low as $79.

Now Niagara Mohawk needed more money and decided to "float" a new preferred issue. It had only to look at its $4.10 preferred at 79 to know that a yield of around 5¼% ($4.10 divided by 79 gives you this yield of 5.25%) was "the going rate." So the company marketed 200,000 shares of a new $100 preferred with a $5.25 annual dividend rate, to yield this 5¼%. This time the company gave the buyers a little more upside potential by setting the call price at 107½.

Time marched on and once again money rates changed. Investors were getting lower returns on their money than in 1957 and were willing to pay more than $100 for the $5.25 Niagara Mohawk preferred. By 1958, the $5.25 preferred had risen to 108 in the market price (pretty much a maximum price for the stock because of its 107½ call price) and the $4.10 preferred had come back to around 85. And once again Niagara Mohawk was looking for capital and decided to issue another preferred (the company had, over this history, sold considerable amounts of bonds and common stock, too). By looking at the $4.10 and $5.25 issues, the company could see that a rate of around 4.85% was now attractive to investors,* so it set a $4.85 annual dividend rate on another $100 par issue. Call price this time was 106.

Although Niagara Mohawk's position as a company did not

---

*The $5.25 preferred selling at 108 was yielding 4.86% ($5.25 ÷ $108 = 4.86%) and the $4.10 preferred was at a price that gave a 4.83% annual return ($4.10 ÷ $85 = 4.83%).

change much over the next twelve years, by 1980 money rates had changed dramatically and Niagara type preferreds were selling to yield around 12¾%. Hence, the three Niagara preferreds were trading in the $30–$40 range. Then by 1987, the $4.10 preferred was selling at 44, the $4.85 at 56, and the $5.25 around 57, to yield 8½ to 9%, reflecting the past few years' decline in interest rates. It is obvious how horribly the original investors in these preferreds have fared. To watch an original investment at $100 per share decline to levels in the $40–$60 range is a discouraging but vivid lesson in the lack of protection a preferred shareholder has against rising interest rates. Bondholders likewise suffered a miserable experience over this twenty year period, but bonds at least contain maturity dates at which time the original investment is returned to the investor, thereby limiting losses compared to those suffered by preferred holders.

Convertible Preferred Stocks

Although the majority of preferred stocks and bonds fluctuate with money rates and do not provide a normal hedge against inflation, some issues have a "kicker" in the form of a *conversion feature.* When a preferred or bond has this feature, it gives you the right to convert it into *common stock at a given price* under certain conditions at *your* option. For example, let's assume that back in 1960 you were considering the purchase of the Pacific Coast Company's $25 par value convertible preferred, which paid an annual dividend of $1.25 per share. Were this a straight preferred, you could never expect more than the $1.25 dividend each year and you couldn't expect the stock to sell much over its call price, which in this case was $25 per share. This preferred, however, was *convertible* share for share into Pacific Coast Company *common* anytime until 1965. Thus if the *common* were to rise to $50 per share, your $25 preferred would be worth $50, because you could take the preferred and exchange it into one share of common (worth $50) whenever you wanted, up to 1965. The conversion feature obviously gives you a chance to grow with the common.

It so happens that the 1960 market price of Pacific Coast common was only $15—not $50—and thus the conversion feature was not of any *present* value. You certainly wouldn't turn in a $25 preferred for one share of common worth $15, so you had to hope the common would eventually move up in price past the price of the preferred. Because the common was at $15 and the conversion feature was of no present value, the preferred sold pretty much like any *non*convertible preferred (on the basis of its yield alone) and thus traded around $20.

In contrast, let's see what happens to a convertible preferred when the common advances in price and makes the preferred valuable. Georgia-Pacific, a large, vertically integrated, forest products company, has a preferred issue outstanding, each share of which is convertible into one share of common stock. Because of this conversion feature, the preferred can be expected to sell at least at the price of the common. Here's how both the common and the preferred showed in the newspaper in July 1986:

Sls	Stock	High	Low	Close	N'Ch
1141	GaPac .80	32⅛	31⅝	32⅛	+ ½
23	do pf 2.24	40	39½	39½	. . .

As you can see, the preferred sold for more than 7 points *more* than the common. This is because the former pays a healthy $2.24 per year to its owners in cash dividends, while the latter distributes only 80 cents. Investors were willing to pay a premium of over 7 points for the privilege of receiving the larger cash return—and for the possible increments from the conversion feature.

Convertible Bonds

Conversion features have the same meaning for bonds as for preferred stocks—they give them added potential. Here are two examples of convertible bonds.

1. *When the conversion feature is of no present value.*

EXAMPLE: Douglas Aircraft 4% convertible debentures,* 1977 maturity date; each $100 debenture convertible into 1.08 shares of common stock until 1977. This debenture was originally issued when Douglas *common stock* was selling around $85 per share. (All of this, of course, took place before Douglas's merger with McDonnell Aircraft.) The debenture might have looked attractive at that time; after all, if Douglas common rose to 100, the bond would have been worth at least 108 (1.08 shares of common selling at $100) and might have sold well above 108 because of its interest rate and the prospect that the common would rise further.

Unfortunately, Douglas common went the other way—it declined to $35 per share in mid-1961. Was the conversion feature of this Douglas bond of any immediate value anymore? The answer is: Yes, it has value, but obviously well below its $100 original issue price. After all, to convert a $100 bond into 1.08 shares of common now selling at $35 would give only $37.80 worth of common (1.08 × $35 = $37.80).

Where was our $100 bond selling in 1961? Around $80! The bond never skidded down to $37.80 because investors were attracted to it at $80 mainly as a straight (*non*convertible) bond. At $80, the $4 interest rate gave an annual return of 5% ($4 ÷ $80 = .05, or 5%), *and* the bondholder knew that Douglas would have to pay back the original $100 at maturity (1977). Thus the person who bought the bond at $80 in 1961 expected to realize a $20 gain by 1977—and this $20 plus the 5% yield attracted him. For the conversion feature to be of any value, Douglas common had to climb back to about $75 ($80 bond price ÷ 1.08 = $74)—a long way from its then market price of $35. As it turned out, Douglas did stage a dramatic recovery. By the end of 1965 it was back to the $75–$80 level, which naturally brought recovery to the bond price, too.

*"Debentures" are bonds that have the general credit of the corporation behind them. No specific real estate, property, or securities are pledged directly to debentures. Naturally these bonds rank above preferred stock in every way, but they are inferior to secured bonds.

The Importance of "Yield to Maturity"

Ignoring the convertible feature for a moment, it is important for you to figure both the current return of the bond *and* its change in value to maturity (as a percentage rate of return). The combination of these two gives what is known as *yield to maturity*. In the case of this Douglas debenture, the $20 increment (the bond was to be worth $100 at maturity compared to its then-present price of $80) amounts to a gain of almost 1½% a year over the fifteen years remaining to its 1977 maturity. This 1½% plus the 5% current return produces a yield to maturity of almost 6½%. *Only through the use of yield to maturity can you compare the relative values of bonds; only through this can you realistically measure potential returns.*

Using the Douglas example, if instead of the bond selling below $100 (selling at a "discount" as we say), the bond sold *over* $100 (at a "premium"), you would have to subtract the premium to arrive at the yield to maturity. For example, a 5% bond due in one year that sells at 101 will have a yield to maturity of 4% (5% current return minus the 1 point, 1% loss in capital = 4%). This is very important to understand—especially because marketers of bonds (including bond mutual funds) often advertise high current yield when in fact yield to maturity may virtually guarantee a loss of capital (e.g., where premium bonds such as my final example are owned). Do not be fooled by this—be sure to ask the question "what is the yield to maturity?" before buying.

2. *When the conversion feature is presently of value.*

EXAMPLE: R. H. Macy 5% convertible debenture, 1977 maturity date; each $100 debenture convertible into 12½ shares of common stock at $8.00 per share until maturity date. When this bond was first issued, Macy common stock was selling at a little under $7.50 per share. Thus the debenture gave the investor a 5% return, plus a long-term call on the common at $8.00.

Macy common rose from the approximate $7.50 figure to $37.50—up exactly five times since the 1957 issue date of the debentures. Obviously, the conversion feature of the bond was of considerable value. Since each $100 bond could be exchanged into 12½ shares of common, the debenture sold for 12½ times the price of the common. In this case, the common stock price of $37.50 made the debenture worth over $468 (12½ × $37.50 = $468.75).

A FEW RULES ABOUT CONVERTIBLE PREFERRED STOCKS AND BONDS

Here are a few generalizations that will be helpful to prospective owners of "convertibles":

1. Do *not* buy a convertible issue unless you think the outlook for the company's common stock is especially good.
2. Try to figure what your maximum downside risk is before buying. There are two considerations here:
   a. Ask: What is the investment value of the bond or preferred as a "straight" security—that is, what is its value without the conversion feature? Unless income yield demands by investors change, this investment value should constitute your downside risk. Then, even if the company's common stock market price declines substantially, the convertible should not be affected beyond this "yield value."
   b. Obviously, the investment value will fluctuate with the trend of interest rates—and you may want to estimate what your maximum market risk is by assuming higher interest rates will prevail in the future. If your bond (or preferred) yields 7% but you fear 10% rates someday, you can calculate an approximate market price under these conditions.
3. When you buy a convertible bond or preferred whose conversion feature is already of value, the bond or preferred *will generally fluctuate directly with the price of the common.* In the case of the Macy convertible, if the

common declines from 37½ to 30, the debenture will fall from 468 to 275 (12½ × $30 = $375).

4. In many cases when you find a convertible issue selling way above 100, you are better off buying the common stock directly. This is especially true if the common stock provides a higher rate of return than the bond at these advanced prices. For example, if a 4% bond is selling at 200 (giving a yearly return of 2%) and the common stock of the same company is yielding anything *above* 2%, you might as well buy the common directly.

5. Whereas your borrowing power on a corporate *bond* through your broker is limited to the existing margin requirements at that time (1987: 50% borrowing allowed on listed convertible bonds and listed nonconvertible bonds), and whereas a broker cannot grant margin on all *un*listed securities, *banks can lend large amounts* (generally between 50% and 75%) on such unlisted securities under certain circumstances. For example, assume you are considering the purchase of an 8% convertible bond of the XYZ Company. Let's say that each $100 bond gives you the right to convert the bond into 2 shares of common stock. XYZ stock is selling for $47. On a straight conversion basis, the bond is worth 2 (the number of shares you get for each bond) × $47 (the price of each share on the market), or $94. The bond is certainly going to be worth more than this pure conversion value, however. For one thing, the interest rate on the bond (8%) is probably higher than the yield on its common stock, but even if it isn't, the bond no doubt carries less risk than the common, and with the conversion feature giving you a long-term call on the common, this minimized risk warrants your paying a premium.

Thus the bond may be selling for 105, 110, or even more. Let's say you buy it for 108, which means that the common has to rise to 54 for you to be even (2 × 54 = 108). Let's also assume that the stock goes a lot higher than 54—to 70! The bond will be worth 2 × 70, or 140, which is a 32-point profit on your $108 purchase, or an increase of almost 30%. But suppose you hadn't put up

the full $108 purchase price. Suppose you had bor-
rowed 70% of the $108 from the bank and invested only
30%, or $32 of your money. The 32-point profit on the
bond is exactly the amount of your cash investment—
and thus you actually doubled your money. Because of
your borrowing, you turned a 30% gain into a 100%
gain, minus the interest paid on your loan. By the same
token, a 64-point rise in the bond would realize you a
200% profit, a 96-point increase would mean a 300%
advance, and so on.

Naturally the reverse is true if the bond declines—
you will suffer a larger percentage loss on your investment dollars because of the borrowing. Needless to say,
borrowing of any kind involves risk and you should be
very cautious about it. Still, you can see the dramatic
possibilities in borrowing on the right convertibles.

6. Convertible issues that provide more income than the
common stock can be expected to sell at a premium over
their conversion value (for instance, the Georgia-Pacific
preferred on p. 84).

7. Most convertibles are "protected against dilution" in
that the conversion feature changes along with the
issuance of stock dividend splits, splits of the common
stock. If XYZ convertible preferred, for example, is
now convertible share for share into common and the
common is split 3-for-1, the conversion privilege will
change after the split. Each preferred will become
convertible into 3 shares of common, instead of 1. If
you are considering the purchase of a convertible, make
sure it is protected against dilution.

Also, *always find out if and when a conversion privilege
expires or changes.* Not all convertibles give the owners
the right to convert into common for the full life of the
issue; and in many cases, the original provisions of the
convertible provide for a change in the conversion
feature as time goes on.

8. Well-chosen convertibles are an excellent investment
medium. They can give you a high and stable return, a
"senior" position above the common in the event things
don't go well for the company, and a chance to grow
with the common stock over the years.

12

More About That Financial Page

STOCK SPLITS

Perhaps at some time you've opened to the financial section of your paper to see headlines like "Minnesota Mining Splits 3-for-1." Stock splits make news. And they capture the imagination of investors and speculators alike. *Yet stock splits are merely the breaking up of a large pie into smaller pieces.* When a stock is split 3-for-1, the company gives you two new shares for each one you already own, giving you a total of three shares (including your original) for each one you started with. This would be sensational if the market price of the stock remained the same after the new shares were issued to you. Unfortunately, this is *not* the case! Once the new shares are issued, the stock will sell for about one-third its pre-split price. In a way it's like a pack of gum. The pack of five pieces sells for 40 cents; open the pack and you have five separate pieces—each worth 8 cents. After you've opened the pack and *split* the gum into five separate pieces, you have no more and no less than you had when you started.

Then why, you might ask, do people get excited and rush to buy a stock if they think a split is coming or after one has been announced? After all, aren't three shares of Minnesota Mining worth $60 each the same as one share at $180? Absolutely!

There are, however, many investors who won't buy a stock

selling as high as $180 per share. "How much money can I make," they ask, "by owning only 10 shares?" Yet they'll not think twice about buying 30 shares of the same stock selling for $60. That's just human nature. And if more people are attracted to buying a stock at $60 than at $180, what does it mean? That the stock will *go up* in price after it is split and sells for $60. And this is the main reason investors are attracted to newly split issues.

There's another, and perhaps more basic, reason for being attracted to a company that has announced a split. *A well-managed company will not split its stock unless it is optimistic about its future and can foresee the prospect of raising its dividend or showing higher earnings in the immediate future.* You can be sure when Minnesota Mining splits its stock that management is reasonably certain business will be excellent in the current year. And chances are that the annual dividend rate will soon be raised.

Management usually states that it wants to improve its stock's "marketability" by splitting it. It hopes that fluctuations will be less (even on a percentage basis) if a person wants to buy or sell the $60 stock than they would be at the $180 rate. This improved marketability is encouraging to investors, and this, too, makes the split attractive.

All of this brings us to three warnings. First, be skeptical of $10–$20 stocks that announce splits. A split in these instances smells of promotion because there is no real reason to bring a stock down in price from these low levels. Second, never buy a stock *only* because it's being split; be sure you want to own that company and look for good values rather than splits alone.

And third, remember that investors in higher-priced stocks expect splits at some time in the future (so, again, buy stocks for the *values* they represent—not for less important reasons).

Here's how splits show in your daily stock prices.

After stockholders approve the split proposed by the company's board of directors, a stock is traded on the exchange in two ways—"regular" (the stock at its old price) and "when-issued" (the new split price). It may show as follows:

Sls	Stock	Div.	High	Low	Close	N'Ch
12	MinnMng&Mfg	1.60	183	179	180	+1½
45	do wi		61	59¾	60	+ ½

Trading will continue this way until the new stock is actually mailed out. The first day after the official mailing the stock will show with the word "New" after it, meaning that from here on it will only be traded at the lower split price. The exchange allows the two-way trading as shown above as a convenience to buyers and sellers. Say, for example, you want to buy $6,000 worth of MMM stock. If there is no "wi" (when-issued) trading, you have to buy 33 shares of the $180 stock; in this case, you may have to pay some premium for the odd lot and you end up with 99 shares after the split and will then have to transact a one-share buy order to round out your shares to 100. Both these disadvantages are overcome by buying 100 shares of the $60 stock. You don't have to fuss with odd lots and you end up with the exact number of shares you want, without making another purchase. The term "when-issued" means you cannot take physical delivery of the certificate until the new stock is mailed out, but still it's your stock, and if you turn around the next day and decide to sell it, you can do it (on the "wi" basis).

MERGERS AND "ARBITRAGE"

More and more often these days, two companies will announce they are merging, which is the corporate way of getting married. For example, in March 1958 Texaco and Seaboard Oil announced that the board of directors of both companies had agreed to a plan whereby the two companies would merge. They agreed that each share of Seaboard would be exchanged into an equal share of Texaco (and that Texaco would be the surviving company). They announced that the stockholders of both companies would vote on the merger proposal and that the results of their voting would be ascertained at a special meeting on May 23. Here is the way the stocks of Texaco and Seaboard traded on the stock exchange between the time of the merger announcement and the day the merger became official:

| | Market Price on | | | |
	Mar. 13	Apr. 10	May 5	May 23
Seaboard Oil	58	60⅝	66¾	66
Texaco	61⅛	62⅜	67⅜	66
Difference in market price between the two	3⅛	1¾	⅝	—

Even though the two companies' directors had agreed to the terms of the merger, there was a difference of 3⅛ points between the two stocks on March 13. Why shouldn't they sell at the exact *same* price? Simply because the merger was not yet *official;* many things could happen between March 13 and May 23 (the directors might change their minds for many reasons or the stockholders might fail to approve the plan or the government's antitrust forces might object to the merger). Thus the market reflected this element of uncertainty, with Seaboard selling 3⅛ points lower than Texaco.

As the approval date grew closer, however, the spread in price between the two narrowed: by April there was only a 1¾-point differential; in early May there was only a ⅝-point spread; and finally they sold at the same price after the approval. This is an illustration of a typical merger and respective market prices, but in most cases, the spread will be far wider than 3⅛ points (just 5% away from Texaco's $61 market price). You will often see a 10–15% disparity even if the approval date is as soon as a few months away, and an even wider discount when additional elements of uncertainty are involved.

These spreads provide a *guaranteed* way to make a profit *if you believe the merger* is going to be approved. If you buy the Seaboard Oil in March at 58 and at the same time sell the same amount of Texaco stock *short* at 61, you will give yourself a 3-point gain (you eventually cover your short sale of Texaco by delivering your Seaboard stock—remember, the Seaboard actually becomes Texaco stock after the approval). The transaction would look something like this:

Sell 100 shares of Texaco short and receive	
approximately	$6,100
Buy 100 shares of Seaboard and pay approximately	5,800
Your profit	$300

You have effected what is known as *arbitrage*, which is the buying and selling of similar securities for profit. Of course you have no guarantee of profit, because the merger could be broken off and you'd own 100 shares of Seaboard Oil that you could no longer use to cover your Texaco short sale. Chances are that Seaboard would fall in price if the merger talks were terminated, and you would stand to take a loss on your purchase. At the same time, Texaco would probably rise in price because short sellers would be rushing to cover—and thus you would lose on your short, too.

There are some types of arbitrage, however, that do not carry such risks and that do guarantee a profit, albeit a small one. One way to accomplish this involves buying a convertible bond or preferred stock and selling the common stock of the same company if it sells higher than the convertible issue. For example, let's assume that ABC Company stock sells at 101 today and the company's convertible bond (which is exchangeable share for share into common) sells at 100. You have a guaranteed profit if you buy the bond at 100 and immediately sell the common at 101, and then exchange the bond into the stock and deliver this stock to cover your short sale. In this case, you make a 1-point profit with no risk whatsoever. The only drawback is that you have to put up significant capital to accomplish the buying and selling; thus, the return on your money is likely to be small—perhaps a profit of only ½ of 1% on your capital. But if you can achieve a guaranteed profit of ½ of 1% on your money 200 times a year, your annual return is a handsome 100%. Unfortunately, unlike exchange members or large institutional investors, the average investor usually can't do this for several reasons. To begin with, it generally takes sophisticated communication and computing power to spot and take advantage of favorable spreads that suddenly appear. These opportunities don't last very long, and the individual lacks both the information and the implementation ability to compete in this arena. Second, exchange members incur small costs in their arbitrage transactions, whereas individuals have to pay commissions which often exceed the spreads. Third, brokers generally won't allow individual short sellers to keep any of the interest earned on the invested proceeds of their short sales (institutional investors, and arbitrage competitors, are often allowed to retain as much as 85% of this interest).

There is one thing to keep in mind here. Whenever a company has a convertible issue outstanding, it *may* be subject to an arbitrage which produces constant short selling in its common stock. This selling may place temporary pressure on the stock and hamper its upward movement somewhat. If and when the convertible issue is called for redemption by the company, this short selling will cease and the stock will have an easier road.* Many fine stocks, however, do have convertible issues outstanding, so don't let that fact alone be a deterrent to buying them. As we'll see later, buy good value and the rest will take care of itself.

Finally, all of the above must be differentiated from "*risk* arbitrage," in which securities are purchased with*out* the ability to hedge. In the flurry of merger and buy-out activity of companies in the 1980's, many individuals and organizations have engaged in pure speculation on the outcome of such mergers or buy-outs.** Using the Seaboard-Texaco example of pages 92–94, a risk arbitrageur might have simply bought the Seaboard (and not hedged with a shorting of Texaco)—betting either on the merger going through or on the possibility that another buyer for Seaboard would appear and offer a more attractive price than Texaco did.

---

*Of course, the sudden conversion of bonds or preferred stock into a large amount of common means the company will have more common shares outstanding, which tends to dilute earnings *per share*. By itself, this should hamper the stock, though the retirement of debt or preferred stock will reduce interest or dividend expense for the company, increasing net worth or earnings; furthermore, accounting rules today encourage management to report a figure called fully diluted earnings per share, which represents what e.p.s. would be if all convertible issues were exercised. Absence of the short selling—as described above—is, therefore, usually a stronger factor than the dilution of earnings, which is why the stock can be expected to do better after the conversion.

**Sadly, too many instances of this were based on "insider information" and related illegal tactics; fortunately, many of the cheaters here have been identified and are being prosecuted.

13
About Those Dividends

IMPORTANT DATES TO KNOW

Ah, those lovely dividend checks! How important they are to so many millions of Americans. Unfortunately, some essential facts about dividends are understood by only a small percentage of stockholders.

I'm referring mainly to the term "ex-dividend date" and its importance in determining just who is entitled to dividends.

There are four dates to consider when a company is paying a dividend to its owners:

> Declaration date
> Payment date
> Record date
> Ex-dividend date

The declaration and payment dates are simple: the former is merely the day the board of directors meets to consider paying a dividend; the latter is the date they set to *mail out the dividend checks.*

Think how many stocks change hands daily and you can imagine the problem of deciding who is entitled to which dividend. The directors have to draw a line somewhere, so they set a record date, which is the date you must have your name *on the corporation's books* to be paid that particular dividend.

The trouble is that the corporation (or the transfer agent

bank that generally handles dividend payments for the company) is not informed the very day a stock changes hands. As a matter of fact, a seller has *five business days* (excluding weekends and holidays) to deliver his stock certificate to his broker; a buyer doesn't have to pay for his purchase for the same five-day period. In other words, the company doesn't know for five days who sold and who bought its stock. Thus, if Friday is the established record date for a certain dividend, you have to buy it *five days* before—on the preceding Friday—to have your name on the company's books and be entitled to the payment. If you buy the stock *four days* before the record date (in this case, on Monday), your name will *not* be on the books and you will miss the dividend. You can see, therefore, that there is a big difference between owning a stock four days before and five days before its record date. For this reason, the stock exchanges (and the OTC market) inform investors that they must buy a stock five days before record date to be entitled to a dividend, and if they buy in four days before, they are out of luck—they are not entitled to it. To simplify the situation for investors (to save them from having to count back the days), the dividend declarations signify which day is *four (business) days before record date*—and they call this *"ex-dividend date"* ("ex-dividend" means "without dividend"). *Anyone buying the stock on or after the ex-dividend date is not entitled to that payment.* In other words, you have to buy *before* the ex-dividend date to get that dividend.

Obviously, the reverse is true if you already own the stock. If you sell before ex-dividend, you miss the upcoming payment; if you sell on or after ex-dividend, the dividend check is yours (even though you will receive the check a number of weeks after you have sold the stock).

Let's trace a theoretical $1.25 quarterly dividend by General Motors:

Declaration Date	Ex-Dividend Date	Record Date	Payment Date
April 10	April 19	April 23	May 30

If you already own GM, you need to hold it *through* April 18 to be entitled to this May 30 payment. If you sell it on April

19 or after, the dividend is still yours. As a new buyer of GM, you must buy the stock *before* April 19. The new owners on April 19 will not get the dividend. So someone who buys on April 20 is getting $1.25 less value than he would have received had he bought on April 19. *For this reason, a stock should be expected to decline by the amount of the dividend on the ex-dividend date.* As a matter of fact, all open-limit buy orders are automatically reduced on the specialist's book by the amount of the dividend each time a stock goes ex-dividend (the $1.25 dividend is equal to 1¼ points, so all such orders on GM stock are lowered in limit price by 1¼ points).

The stock exchanges designate that a stock has gone ex-dividend by placing the letters "xd" after the dividend figure in the daily quotations. General Motors, which in 1986 distributed a total of $5.00 including extras, would show "GenMtrs 5.00xd." If the stock closed at 80 the day *before* ex-dividend and closed at the same price *on* ex-dividend date, the stock actually rose *in value* by the 1¼ point dividend, so the paper will show the net change as +1¼. In other words, the stock was expected to drop by that 1¼, and because it didn't it was actually up 1¼. If GM stock closed at 81—a 1-point gain over the previous day's close—the net change would be +2¼.

One general rule comes to mind here in answer to the obvious question: Should I wait to buy a stock on its "xd" date when it's lower in price, or buy it the day before and get the dividend? *Given a static market,* I would always advise you to buy before "xd" (so you will be entitled to the dividend), because chances are the stock will recover the amount of the dividend not too long after "xd."* In the same vein, if you're going to sell a stock and it's the day before "xd," wait till the "xd" date or after because odds are that the stock will recover whatever amount it declined due to the "xd" and you will still be entitled to the dividend check when it comes a month or so later.

---

*Investors in extremely high tax brackets might be the exception here. They might prefer to buy the stock at the lower "xd" price rather than buy it before "xd" and have to pay a heavy tax on the dividend. This assumes, however, that the investor's tax rate on dividend income is higher than the capital gains tax rate (not true for investors after December 31, 1987, under the new tax law).

STOCK DIVIDENDS

So far I have been discussing dividends paid out in the form of cash to stockholders. This is not the only type of payment made by corporations, however. Many firms either supplement cash distributions or substitute for cash with payments of additional stock; these stock payments are called *stock dividends*.

As a supplement, stock dividends can be interesting. Suppose, for example, that Company A—whose stock sells for $100 per share and pays an annual *cash* dividend of $3 per share—declares an additional 10% stock dividend. This 10% distribution means that existing stockholders will get 1 share free from the company for every 10 shares they own. This sounds like a bonanza and would be except that (like stock splits and cash dividends) once the stock goes "ex," it will drop in price by the amount of the dividend. As with cash dividends, there is an "ex-dividend" date on stock dividends and all open-buy limit orders on the specialist's book are reduced by the amount of the dividend. In the case of Company A, its stock will drop by about 10% on the "ex" date—from $100 per share to about $91.* With this in mind, you might ask what is so valuable about a stock dividend. What's the difference whether you own 10 shares of a stock at $100 per share or 11 shares (1 extra share from the 10% stock dividend) of the same stock worth $91 apiece? Actually you are correct in your reasoning that there is no difference. Remember, however, that Company A is also paying a $3 per share *cash* dividend, and *if no change is made in this payout, the stock dividend has the effect of increasing the stockholder's cash dividend income*. In our example, an owner of 10 shares of A stock was receiving $3 per share yearly in cash, for a total of $30 income. After the 10% distribution, ownership increased to 11 shares—and these 11 shares with the same cash payout of $3 now provide income of $33 a year. Therefore the real advantage of the 10% stock dividend was that it increased the stockholder's cash dividends. If instead of retaining the $3 cash rate after the distribution, the cash rate was reduced by

*100 ÷ 1.10 (the 10% stock dividend) = $90.9, to be exact.

10%, the stockholder would receive no material benefit at all. *In the vast majority of cases, companies do retain their present cash rate after a small stock dividend, and the increased income resulting is the main reason for viewing small stock dividends optimistically.* Incidentally, *large* stock dividends (50%, 100%, 200%, etc.) *are termed stock splits* and therefore fall under the discussion in Chapter 12.

After this conclusion you have probably gathered that *there is no benefit from stock dividends that are a substitute for cash.* If, in the example of A, the company is *not* paying out any cash dividends at all, what good is the 10% stock payout? In effect, the company is simply giving you more stock certificates, but with these extra certificates your holdings are worth no more and no less than they were before the stock distribution. Many investors argue that the stock dividend without a cash rate gives the stockholder a tax advantage; that is, the stockholder is not forced into reporting cash income, on which he will have to pay income tax; if he wants cash income, he only has to sell off whatever stock dividends he gets and these sales will be taxable at capital gains tax rates (Chapter 29). The trouble is that—*if and when the stock dividend is sold—the investor has reduced his actual ownership in the company.*

Another argument for stock dividends without corresponding cash payouts is that after the stock goes "ex" and is reduced in price by the amount of the distribution, it will go back up in price to where it was before. In theory, this should *not* be the case, because the company's earnings per share, book value per share, and comparable fundamentals are also reduced by the amount of the stock dividend. In practice, stocks often do recoup the stock dividend amount not too long after "ex." When this happens, we should assume that the subsequent rise in price is not due to the stock dividend. Instead, it is due to the more important factors you will soon learn about, i.e., attractive industry and company, increasing net income, and the like.

14
Stock Rights

When a company raises money through the sale of publicly held securities, it can resort to numerous channels. It can sell bonds, in which case it is *borrowing* money for a specified period of time. It can sell preferred stock, which gives it permanent capital (unlike bonds, there is no maturity date set for any money to be repaid). Or the company may allow investors to share ownership through the sale of its common stock.*

Assuming that it decides to market more common stock, there are basically two ways this can be done:

1. Through sale *to the public* of an agreed number of shares.
2. Through the offering of stock to *existing stockholders*.

The first method may be the simplest, cheapest, and speediest way to raise the money. The company considers the present market price of its stock, sets the number of shares it needs to sell to get the needed money, and then "hires" a group of brokers (called "underwriters") to sell those shares to the public at around the existing market price. One criticism of this plan is that it does *not* guarantee existing stockholders that they will be able to buy any of this additional stock if they choose. In other words, a stockholder's current ownership position is not protected. For example, if you currently own 10% of the XYZ Company and the company sells new stock—of which you buy none—you no longer own 10%. Assume the company has

*Chapter 18 on *leverage* explains the pros and cons of issuing different securities.

100,000 shares outstanding, of which you own 10,000 or 10%; if an additional 100,000 shares are sold and you buy none, your ownership has been decreased to 5% of the 200,000 new total shares of the company.

For this reason, many companies prefer to offer new stock to *existing stockholders first* and always provide an incentive for the stockholders by giving them the right to buy the stock *at a reduced price*. But what happens if you, the stockholder, have no more money to invest or simply choose not to buy any more of the company's stock? Remember, you have been given the option to buy the stock at a discount and this option to buy at a cheaper price than the prevailing market should be valuable to someone. It is! And the company allows you and other stockholders to sell this option if you want.

The option to buy stock at a price below the market is called a stock "right." Let's trace through an example of these rights, how they work, and how you compute their value.

Assume the ABC Company has 1 million shares of common stock outstanding and its stock is selling for $50 per share. The company has expansion plans and needs new money in the amount of about $4 million. It decides that it will offer new stock to existing owners at a discount of $10 per share from the present $50 price—or at $40 per share. At $40 per share, the company will have to sell 100,000 shares to raise the $4 million. Since 100,000 shares constitutes one-tenth of the 1 million shares outstanding, you can see that the company plans to sell 1 new share (at $40) for each 10 outstanding. In giving written evidence of this right to buy, the company *issues 1 "right" for each share outstanding and then explains that it will take 10 of these rights to buy one share at $40.*

Thus, if you own 100 shares of ABC Company stock, you will receive 100 rights from the company. Your 100 rights entitle you to buy 10 shares at $40 and if this is what you want, you merely mail in your rights and $400 to the company and wait for your new share certificate.

If, however, you decide *not* to buy more stock you can sell your option to buy at $40 per share to somebody else. Because many people choose to sell their rights, the stock exchanges (or the over-the-counter market) set up trading in these rights just as they do in stocks. For the few weeks that the option is open to buy at $40, "do rts" will appear under the name of the stock ("do" means "ditto" and "rts" means "rights"). For example, the financial page might show the following for ABC Company:

Sls	Stock	Div	High	Low	Close	N'Ch
52	ABC Co	2.00	50	49	50	
150	do rts		1	⅞	1	

Notice that the rights have a value of $1 when the stock is $50. This is because it will take 10 rights to get the $10 discount (to buy one share at $40) and thus each right is worth $1. The formula for figuring how much rights will be worth is:

$$\frac{\text{Stock's current market price} - \text{Subscription price to stockholders}}{\text{No. of rights needed to buy 1 share at subscription price}}$$

In the case of ABC, the formula would work like this:

$$\frac{\$50 - \$40}{10} = \frac{\$10}{10} = \$1 \text{ (the value of each right)}^*$$

Naturally, as the current market price of ABC stock goes up, the right to buy the stock at $40 has more value (and vice versa). If ABC common rises from $50 to $55, the rights will rise from $1.00 to $1.50:

*This is the formula for determining the value of rights *after* the stock has gone "ex-rights." As with regular dividends, you have to own a stock before it goes "ex" to be entitled to rights. Also, you should expect a stock to decline on "ex-rights" day by the amount the right is worth, since the buyer on "ex-rights" day gets less in value than the person who bought the stock the day before.

Because there is the value of 1 right in each share before it goes "ex-rights," a different formula is used in computing how much each right is worth *before* the ex-rights date. This formula is:

$$\frac{\text{Stock's current market price} - \text{Subscription price to stockholders}}{\text{No. of rights needed to buy 1 share at subscription price} + 1}$$

In our ABC example, the value of each right would be:

$$\frac{\$50 - \$40}{10 + 1} = \frac{\$10}{11} = .91 \text{ or 91 cents}$$

$$\frac{\$55 - \$40}{10} = \frac{\$15}{10} = \$1.50$$

Notice here the speculative possibilities in buying rights. With the common rising $5, a 10% increment on a $50 stock, the rights went up 50 cents each—a 50% increase on a $1.00 original price. By the same token, you can take a large percentage loss if you buy rights and the stock declines very sharply during the rights period.

Now to some generalizations about rights that should be helpful to you in the future:

1. Under normal conditions, a stock price will be somewhat depressed during a rights offering. This is because numerous stockholders will decide to sell their option, and since the stock and the rights will fluctuate together during the offering period, any heavy sales of rights will force the rights lower in price, which in turn will also force the stock lower.

2. If you own stock in a company that is issuing rights, your decision to buy more stock at the option price or to sell the rights should depend strictly on how you feel about the stock as an investment. People may argue: How can I turn down the chance to buy the stock at $40 when it's selling at $50? The answer is: If you decide to sell the rights instead of subscribing at $40, you will realize the $10 from the sale of your rights, so it's six-of-one, half-a-dozen of the other as to which you should do.

3. Remember, you lose your proportional interest in a company by selling the rights. If you own 10% of a company and subscribe to the new stock, you will still own 10%; if you sell your rights and do not add to your holdings, you will own less than 10%. This is not of great consequence to the average stockholder who owns only a small fractional interest in a company.

4. Any company issuing rights is adding to the number of common shares outstanding; thus it will have to in-

crease profits to keep the net income *per share* at least equal to that of the previous year. In many cases, the new money received from the offering goes for new production facilities, introduction of new products, or other elements that should increase the company's long-range potential. Profits from these additions, however, will usually not show up for a year or more, and thus stockholders often see earnings *per share* temporarily reduced. There are times, however, when common stock financing may actually produce an immediate *increase* in earnings. If, for example, a company has been borrowing money at 14% or 15%—which amounts to a hefty net charge to income—*and* if its price-earnings multiple (see pp. 181–183) is above approximately 11, the company's earnings per share may rise as the proceeds from the stock sale are used to reduce its borrowings.*

5. Rights have a normal life of only a few weeks. Therefore, as a stockholder in a company such as ABC, be sure you either exercise the rights (buy the stock at the discount price) or sell them before their expiration date. If you don't, you have thrown money away.

6. Rights do hold attractive speculative possibilities, but you have to consider point 5 when you buy them with the idea of making money on them. Since the rights are worth zero at their expiration, you either have to sell them before that date or be in a position to subscribe (by putting up $40 per share, in the case of ABC) before that date.

7. Since stocks are normally slightly lower in price during their rights offering period, this period can create attractive buying opportunities. A stock usually recovers in price shortly after the expiration date of the rights.

*Given a top corporate tax rate of 34%.

15
Warrants

"Make 1,000% on your money through warrants."
"A chance to make a fortune through warrants."

Perhaps you've seen advertisements like this in the financial pages of your newspaper or in finance magazines. These ads are not pure hokum—people have made fortunes by buying warrants and have done far better than 1,000% on their money through their purchases. As you can well imagine, these are exceptional cases, but let's examine this explosive area and see what makes it tick.

In the previous chapter I explained how stockholders are sometimes given "rights" to buy more stock at a reduced price for a specified period of time. Warrants are just like rights. They, too, give their owners the privilege to buy stock at a set price. The differences are that warrants may be perpetual or have a life of *at least a few years* (remember, rights last only a few weeks), and the option price of a *warrant* is usually set *above the stock's market price at the time it is issued* (rights give you the option to buy stock at a discount).

Warrants are born differently than rights. Whereas the latter are created to raise money immediately for the issuing company, warrants are brought into the world as a "financing gimmick" and a method of possibly raising money for the company in the future. Warrants usually start out as a way of "sweetening" a company's proposed new issue of either preferred stock or bonds.

Let's say that ABC Company needs money, decides to float a bond issue, and is told by its investment banker that it will have to pay a 12% interest rate to potential bondholders. ABC management is concerned about this 12% obligation, especially over the twenty year life of the bond. If ABC were to throw in a "kicker," however, it might get away with offering a 9% or 10% bond, or even one at 7½%.

The "kicker" in this case might be a warrant. Each $1,000 8% ABC bond might carry with it one warrant that entitles the holder to buy 100 shares of ABC common stock any time over the next ten years for $12 per share. The present market price of ABC common is $10 per share, but you can see that this warrant could become extremely valuable to its owner over the years if ABC does well and its stock rises above $12 per share. If this happens, the warrant owner can turn in his warrant and $1,200 (for 100 shares at $12 per share) to ABC and receive the 100 shares that have been set aside for him. If ABC common is now at $20 per share, these 100 shares are actually worth $2,000 in the open market, and he can turn right around and sell the same 100 shares that cost him $1,200 for $2,000 and make himself an $800 profit. And remember he still has his $1,000 8% ABC bond.

Thus, by using warrants, the ABC Company accomplished two objectives: (1) it sold its bond issue successfully and with a lower interest cost; (2) it received an additional $1,200 for each $1,000 bond, possibly solving a future financing problem for the company.

HOW TO EVALUATE WARRANTS

When the 8% ABC bond was sold, the holders were advised that they could detach the warrants from the bond if they desired. They had the choice of keeping the bond and the warrant or selling either one separately. Then, instead of there being just one market for the bond *with* warrants, there commenced a market for the bonds themselves and the warrants by themselves.

In figuring how much the warrants should be worth, you should ask: What is the worth of a piece of paper that entitles me to buy ABC common at $12 per share anytime in the next ten years, when the stock is now selling at $10?

You might think that this piece of paper—this warrant—isn't really worth anything. Why should you pay anything for this warrant to buy the stock at $12 per share when you can buy the stock itself right now for $2 less, for $10 per share? Right you are to question this—but consider the following. If you buy the stock right now you have to put up the $10 per share. But if you only have to pay, say, $2 for the warrant, you can get the option on five times as much ABC stock through the purchase of the warrants as opposed to buying the common stock outright.

Assume you have only $1,000 to invest in ABC. You can buy 100 shares of the common at $10 per share. Or, *if* you buy the warrants at $2, you can buy 500 warrants, which give you the option to buy 500 shares of ABC at $12 per share over the next ten years. Assume that a few years from now ABC is selling at $20 per share. Had you bought the 100 shares outright at $10, your $1,000 investment would be worth $2,000. You would have doubled your money!

How did your 500 warrants come out? Assuming you sold your warrants instead of exercising the option—because you didn't want to put up any more money—here's how you would have fared:

Each warrant would be worth a minimum of $8 ($20 current market price of ABC − $12 option price) and thus your 500 warrants would be worth at least $4,000—you would have quadrupled your $1,000 original investment.

If ABC common had gone to $40 per share over this period, the comparison is even more startling. You would have quadrupled your money by buying the common outright ($10 stock advancing to $40). This is fine, but let's see how much the warrants would be worth now:

Market price of the common stock	$40
Less option price of the warrant	12
Minimum worth of the warrant	$28

The warrant you paid $2 for is now worth at least $28—your investment has appreciated at least 14 times.

You can see the possibilities that exist in warrants. You get a tremendous play for the money invested. For this reason, you will usually find warrants selling much higher than this ABC example. Instead of paying $2 for the ABC warrant, you might find the market $4–$7, depending on how optimistic people are about the future of ABC Company.

From a near-term standpoint, once the warrants have established a base, you will often find the common stock and the warrant fluctuating by the same amount. In other words, once the ABC warrants are traded separately and the market is established at, say, $4, you will probably find the warrant going up 1 point to $5 if the common rises 1 point to $11. Of course a 1-point rise in a $4 warrant is a 25% advance, while the 1-point increment in the $10 common is only 10%. By the same token, declines in the common would bring about much more severe declines in the warrants on a percentage basis.

Remember, too, that warrants never pay dividends—you must depend solely on the warrants' going up in price to make your money. As shown, they can provide terrific gains for you, but they are highly speculative. If you find a stock you like very much and it has warrants outstanding, you should consider this medium for investing in the company. But do not buy warrants unless you are really enchanted by the stock's growth promise.

16

Puts and Calls (Options) and Related Vehicles (Index Options and Futures; and Futures Options)

The two preceding chapters were devoted to forms of *options* to purchase stocks, namely:

1. *Rights,* which provide stockholders with the *temporary* option to buy more stock at prices lower than the existing market price.
2. *Warrants,* which are originally issued as a financing "sweetener" and serve as an option to buy stock at a set price for a longer period of time.

Both rights and warrants are issued by a company primarily for its own selfish purpose—to raise capital; the fact that these options are bought and sold after their issuance and that profits and losses result from their existence is incidental to their purpose. *As we have seen, rights and warrants are popular profit-making vehicles because they provide their owners with leverage—with the opportunity to control a maximum amount of ownership for a minimum amount of invested capital.*

Another type of option—and one that provides even greater leverage than rights and warrants—exists in the form of *puts* and *calls.* In a book such as this, which is intended to give you A to Z coverage and instruction in the stock market, some discussion of puts and calls is essential.

Options differ from rights and warrants in that they are *not* issued by operating companies. These options are not corporate securities and have no place or effect on a company's capitalization, balance sheet, or income statement. Instead, puts and calls come into being through a group of brokers and dealers who arrange for the buying and selling of these option contracts and who collect a fee for their work.

Now let's look at these unusual instruments and see what makes them tick. First of all, we'll answer the question: What is a call?

A *call* is a contract that gives its owner *the option to buy a specified number of shares of a stock* (usually 100 shares) *at a set price for a stated period of time.* When you buy a call, you are buying a privilege to purchase the stock anytime during the agreed period at an agreed price. Naturally you don't have to exercise the option, you don't have to buy the stock; but if the stock rises appreciably anytime within the contract period, you can direct the maker (of the contract) to sell you the stock at the agreed-to (lower) price and make a nice profit.

A put is the opposite of a call. A *put* is a contract that gives its owner the *option to sell a specified number of shares at a set price for a stated period of time.* In this case, you are purchasing the privilege to *sell* the stock anytime during the agreed period at the agreed price. You will profit if the stock declines substantially during the contract period, because you can buy the stock on the open market at the low price and direct the maker to purchase it from you at the agreed-to higher price. Or, of course, you can close your position by selling the put itself.

You buy a call if you think a stock is going up in price, and you buy a put if you think it is going down.

The life span of any put or call option contract is determined by the expiration date. Each option contract will have only one expiration date, which normally occurs on the third Saturday of a specified month. After the close of the business day preceding that third Saturday, the option contract is essentially dead. The holder of a call option has either to purchase the stock at the specified price or to close out the option position by selling the call itself before the expiration date. Similarly, the holder of a put option has to exercise the put by selling the stock at the set price or to close out the position by selling the put prior to expiration. If none of these actions are implemented, the option expires and is worthless.

Options on a given stock generally have three expiration dates, set in different months. The months may be spaced out quarterly, monthly, or irregularly, depending on where the issues trade. When one set of contracts expires, a new contract with an advanced expiration date will be created to keep the option contracts rotating around the calendar.

The set (exercise) price for an option contract is often referred to as the *strike price*. Any number of strike prices can be set for a particular stock; typically, a stock will carry four exercise prices spaced at $5.00 intervals. For example, if ABC stock is trading at $65.00, there might be option contracts with exercise prices at $60.00, $65.00, $70.00, and $75.00. Incidentally, if a stock's market price equals its exercise price, it is said to be trading "at-the-money." If ABC trades at $65.00, an ABC $65.00 call would be at-the-money. If ABC's stock price is below the exercise price, the call would be "out-of-the-money." With ABC trading at $62.00, for example, the ABC 65 call would be out-of-the-money by $3.00. In contrast, if ABC trades at $67.00, the ABC 65 call would be "in-the-money" (by $2.00). Conversely, put options are "in-the-money" if the stock price is less than the exercise price and "out-of-the-money" if the stock exceeds the strike price.

The price of an option, like the price of an insurance policy, is usually called the *premium*. Needless to say, the amount of this premium you pay is crucial—and it is both complicated and hard to generalize how much you should pay for these options. Pricing depends basically on 5 factors: a) the relationship between a stock's market price and the exercise price of the option; b) the amount of time until the expiration date; c) the volatility of the underlying stock; d) the dividends payable on the stock before the expiration date; and e) the level of interest rates. The first factor mentioned—stock price compared to exercise price—measures the intrinsic value of the option; of course, there is no intrinsic value to an option unless it is trading in-the-money.

If XYZ stock trades at $45.00, a call option would have an intrinsic value of $5.00 if the exercise price stands at $40.00; a put option would have an intrinsic value of $5.00 if the exercise price is $50.00. Suppose, however, the XYZ 40 call premium was $7.00 when the intrinsic value remained at $5.00. This $2.00 difference is referred to as the "time value" of the option. The difference is attributable to the fact that XYZ stock may move up in price within the time remaining before expiration and therefore the call option has more value than the intrinsic value alone. Let's briefly go through each of the basic factors in option pricing to see how this works.

When an option has no intrinsic value (i.e., it's out-of-the-money), an investor will be concerned with how far the stock price needs to move to reach the exercise price. The closer the stock price to the exercise price, the greater the potential for the option to become in-the-money. Thus, for a call option with an exercise price of $30.00, you would naturally pay more premium when the stock stands at $29.00 than at $25.00.

It is logical to expect to pay a larger premium for both a longer time period until expiration and a higher volatility stock. The more time you have and the more potential (upward) movement a stock possesses, the more opportunity exists for a successful option venture.

While no dividends are paid to the holders of option contracts, dividends do have to be considered. As discussed previously, stock exchange "specialists" and OTC market makers adjust orders on their books downward by the amount of the dividend for stocks on their ex-dividend dates. No such adjustment is made, however, for exercise prices of options. It is important, therefore, to be aware of any ex-dividend dates scheduled to occur before option expiration dates and to allow for this in any calculation of "deserved premium." Naturally, you should pay a lower premium for a call option where dividends will be paid and you should pay a higher premium for a comparable put.

Interest rates can also affect option premiums, although this is usually less of a concern. Since the initial outlay for buying an option is much less than for purchasing a stock—and the difference can be invested in Treasury bills or other interest-bearing securities—higher interest rates tend to cause higher option premiums.

A sixth factor influencing options' pricing is the general level of interest in the options market itself. As with all investing, supply and demand determine price. Bull markets create higher premiums on calls just as bear markets create higher premiums on puts. The more speculative the attitude of the investors, the greater the costs involved in playing this (speculative) options game. Of course, premiums paid should vary according to *conviction*. The more convinced you are of a stock's potential, the more you should be willing to pay to leverage your investment. After all, puts and calls are bought (instead of buying and selling the equivalent number of shares in the marketplace) for the reason mentioned earlier—you are able to control a lot of stock for a small amount of money. Assume, for example, that you wish to purchase ABC stock, which is presently selling for $50 a share. If you buy 100 shares, you will have to put up $5,000, or at least $2,500 if you are operating under 50% margin requirements. If ABC rises 12 points to $62, the resulting $1,200 gain amounts to a 24% profit on a $5,000 cash outlay, and almost a 50% gain if you margined your purchase and put up only $2,500. Assume that, instead of buying the stock itself, you purchase a six-month call on 100 shares of ABC stock at $50 per share for a cost to you of $600. The $1,200 appreciation in this case is reduced to $600 (since the $600 outlay is gone—it has been paid to the put and call dealer), but this gain amounts to a 100% increase on your cash outlay of $600.

The same thing goes for the purchase of puts. Suppose you believe XYZ stock is overpriced at $60 per share, where it is now selling. You decide you want to speculate that the stock will go down in price from these levels. To do this, you can sell XYZ short, and if you engage in a 100-share transaction, this will mean an outlay of $6,000 in cash, or $3,000 on 50% margin. To control the same number of shares through a put might cost you only $600, however, so you can imagine the prospect for greater return on invested capital from buying the put. For the sake of example, let's assume that your judgment proves correct and that XYZ does decline from $60 to $45 and that an approximate profit of $1,500 results. Here's how you will come out under the three possibilities mentioned:

1. Short sale of 100 shares at $60 with full cash outlay of $6,000: a $1,500 profit amounts to a 25% increase on invested capital ($1,500 ÷ $6,000 = .25 or 25%).

2. Short sale of 100 shares at $60 with 50% margin cash outlay of $3,000: a $1,500 profit amounts to a 50% enhancement ($1,500 ÷ $3,000 = .50 or 50%).
3. Purchase of a six-month put on 100 shares at $60 for a $600 cash outlay: the $1,500 profit is reduced to $900, since the $600 cash outlay is gone (it has been paid out to the put-and-call dealer); the net profit of $900 amounts to a 150% increase on invested capital ($900 ÷ $600 = 1.50 or 150%).

You can see how puts and calls offer money-making possibilities. In addition, puts and calls have the advantage of *limited risk in dollars* for their owners. *If you buy either the call on ABC or the put on XYZ, you know from the start that the very most that can be lost is the original $600 premium,* regardless of what happens to the respective stocks. You can't make this statement about buying or selling short on a regular basis. Of course, if you lose the full $600 on the put or call, you have lost 100% of your invested capital, so you can see that there are two sides to the coin. There are other disadvantages to put and call options, and I'll cover these a little later. In the meantime, let's explore other motives for putting money into these contracts.

One such motive involves using puts and calls as a hedge while buying or selling stocks in the normal manner. Assume that you are interested in ABC stock at $50 per share. You think it will go higher in the next six months, but you want to protect yourself and limit your loss in case you are wrong. In this case, you might buy 100 shares of ABC on the market, and at the same time purchase a six-month put on ABC at $50 per share for, say, $600. Now you can relax a little, knowing that no matter how low ABC goes in price, you can always exercise your put and sell your stock to the put dealer at $50. Therefore the most you can lose is the cost of your put, or $600 (plus commissions, taxes, etc.). Naturally, if ABC goes above $50, you will let your option lapse and sell the stock itself in the open market. Since whatever profit you make on the transaction will have to be reduced by the $600 cost of the put, you can see that both your upside and downside potential have been tempered by this hedging. Certainly a hedge such as this is unsuitable for the vast majority of stocks. It only makes sense if you are buying the type of stock that might fluctuate widely either up or down. The trouble is that with such volatile stocks, the cost of the put might be higher than the $600 example. Incidentally, the reverse of this illustration can be accomplished by the investor who is selling short and wants to hedge with the use of a call option.

Another reason for buying puts and calls might be to protect a profit on a stock owned or on one sold short. Suppose you bought a stock some time ago and now have a sizable gain on it—to the point where you are worried about it declining sharply. Uncertain about the future, you can purchase a put on the stock. Then, if the stock continues to rise, you can eventually sell at a larger profit and disregard the option. If, instead, the stock plummets, you can fall back on your put and sell the stock to the maker at the agreed price. By the same token, you can protect a profit on a short sale by the use of a call option.

A third motive for using options is to turn a short-term gain into a long-term gain—a differentiation which existed for many years but which ended with the 1986 tax reform. Since laws change, the example of its prior use is worth explaining. For most of the past, six months was the dividing time between a short-term and the highly advantageous long-term capital gain. If a person had a short-term profit on a stock and was *very* uncertain about the stock's immediate future and was tempted to sell the stock, he could avoid the excessive taxation of a short-term gain through the use of options. In this case the problem could be solved by buying a put on the stock—one that expired after the six-month period following the original purchase of the stock. If the issue held its gain beyond the six-month date, there was no need to exercise the put; he could sell the stock in the open market. But if the stock fell sharply over this period, he could exercise his put and sell the stock at the option price to the maker. By doing this, he preserved his profit (less the cost of option contract) on the favorable long-term tax basis.

Option contracts are obviously created by someone— sometimes by people directly invested in the underlying securities and sometimes by those without related investments. You can participate in either. For example, you can sell or "write" options and get part of the premium instead of paying it (you only get part, as the broker or options dealer creating the instrument gets part, too). If, for example, you own some XYZ stock and want to write (as opposed to buy) an option, you negotiate with an options dealer; in exchange for part of the premium you agree to deliver your XYZ stock—which of course may be called away at any time. Since you already own the XYZ, you have written a "covered" (as opposed to "naked") option. Suppose XYZ is selling at $50.00 and an XYZ 50 call option, expiring 3 months out, has a premium of $5.00. You could write a covered call and collect a portion of the $500 premium. Certainly the extra income (your portion of the $500) looks nice, but what are you sacrificing? If XYZ stock moves above $50.00 in the next 3 months, you may be forced to deliver your 100 shares if the buyer exercises his option. If and when XYZ appreciates more than your share of the premium, you start to lose potential profit. Hence as a writer, the most you can make is your premium income and the worst that can happen is lost opportunity which is unlimited.

The mechanism for handling puts and calls has changed drastically over the past fifteen years with the formation of options markets (the major one is located in Chicago), which are central marketplaces where options can be easily bought and sold. Thus a market now exists for these option contracts, providing investors with greater flexibility (and lower costs) than was previously possible. So many changes are taking place in this area that I advise anyone contemplating the option vehicle to obtain a copy of rules and regulations from either their normal brokerage affiliation or from a specialized option broker.

A great deal has been written about the burgeoning new options markets. I direct your attention to some interesting facts uncovered by a thorough study of puts and calls made by the SEC in the years 1959 and 1979 (the most recent study performed). Here are some of the pertinent findings, including my interpretations:

Option buyers in the earlier study paid an average of 14% of the value of the stock optioned for most six-month calls. Excluding the very low priced and very high priced stocks, six-month calls were priced at an average of 12% of their existing market price at the time. As mentioned, the new options markets have lowered costs for put-and-call buyers and sellers. Both the costs and the relative prices for various contracts, as explained below, are very much different from the 1959 study conclusions.

The premium paid to buy six-month options was about double the amount paid for *thirty-day* contracts (this means that the average fee for thirty-day options was 6–7% of the stock's market price).

The premium paid to buy six-month options was about 1½ times the amount paid for *ninety-day* contracts (the average fee for ninety-day options was 8–10% of the particular stock's market value).

Calls are slightly more expensive to purchase than comparable puts.

Premiums charged on puts and calls depend not only on the market price of the stock involved but also on the volatility of the stock. The stock that has a record of erratic price behavior in the market will cost more on an option than the relatively stable performer.

The SEC completed a special survey of six-month calls bought in June 1959. Despite the fact that the stock market in general (as measured by the Standard & Poor's 425 Stock Index) increased slightly over the six months from June 1959 to January 1960, the experience of call buyers was most disappointing. *Overall the public lost about 43% of its investment on these calls. Over half (54%) of the call money invested turned out to be completely worthless. Another 28% of the money wound up with losses amounting to an average of 60% of invested capital. Only 18% of the call money ended up with a profit—although this select group did reap a return of about 150% on investment.* Although this study is obviously dated, its conclusions are probably not much different from 1980's experiences.

Before going into the disadvantages of puts and calls and some conclusions, I should point out two unusual contracts, namely "straddles" and "spreads." Both straddles and spreads are "double options" in that both a put and a call are written simultaneously on the stock involved. In the case of a straddle, one buys or writes both a put and a call—at the same exercise price and expiration date. An investor can buy a spread, created by being both buyer and writer of the same type of option (puts or calls) but at different exercise prices and/or expiration dates. These double options give their owners flexibility; they provide the opportunity to make money on both up- and downswings in the market. Obviously, anyone who makes a profit on both sides of a stock is extremely lucky. Straddles and spreads are expensive to buy and a person has to count on wide price fluctuations in the stock to make them at all profitable.

Quotations on stock options in the financial section of your newspaper will appear as follows:

Option & NYSE Close XYZ	Strike Price	Calls-Last			Puts-Last		
		Sep	Dec	Mar	Sep	Dec	Mar
61⅞	60	3	5⅜	7	¾	2	2¾
61⅞	65	⅝	2½	4⅝	3⅞	4¾	5½
61⅞	70	⅛	1⅛	2⅝	7½	8	9⅜

As you can see, this format is almost self-explanatory. The first column lists the stock's name and the most recent price; the second column lists the various strike prices on available contracts; quotations on call options with expirations in different months are in the next three columns and a similar display for put contracts fills the following three columns.

STOCK INDEX OPTIONS, STOCK INDEX FUTURES, AND FUTURES OPTIONS

Stock Index Options

Prior to 1983, available options contracts dealt only with individual securities. If you wanted to buy or sell XYZ Corp., you could use calls, puts, or straddles to attempt to achieve your goals. Brokers (and others) sensed that single options on single stocks weren't enough and that some investors might prefer to deal in the same way with a whole basket of securities. In 1983, the first such "basket" option began trading—first through a contract matching the underlying securities of the NYSE Index and later through many additional indexes, including the S&P 500 and the S&P 100 Stock Index (contracts on the S&P 100 are the most popular). These stock index options work much the same way as individual stock options (except for the mechanics involved in transactions). Losses are limited to the price you pay for the option and no more, but of course this amounts to 100% of your investment and is therefore little comfort except when comparing against very leveraged investments (some of which follow). Thus, if you want to "play" the general market or that of any index which represents some segments of the market, you can do so. Choose the index, find the contract which represents it (call, put, or straddle), pay the price, and hope for good results.

Trading in stock index options has become very widespread. Many investors simply invest in them as they would buy options on a chosen stock; and many use them to hedge their portfolios against broad market movements. To hedge, an investor with a diversified portfolio who is worried about a possible market setback but who prefers not to sell the individual securities held might well buy S&P put options, recognizing that these puts will rise in value as the market declines and provide protection for him. Conversely, an investor who is worried that he isn't invested enough may choose to hedge his bets by buying an index call option rather than buy a raft of individual stocks. In both cases the option ploy allows you to control more assets than your contract price amounts to, with the limitation that you can only (!?!) lose the amount of money ventured.

Assume it is now March with the S&P 100 at 282.79 and you want to bet that the market will rise between now and, for example, June. You decide to use options rather than buy individual securities, and you find option prices on the S&P 100 to be as shown below (as they would be listed in the financial pages):

INDEX OPTIONS

S&P 100

Strike Price	Calls-Last			Puts-Last		
	Mar	Apr	Jun	Mar	Apr	Jun
280	6¼	8⅜	10	⅞	3	4¾
285	2⅞	5⅜	7⅛	2⅜	5	6⅞
290	1	3¼	5	6	8	9¾

The Index: high 284.77; low 280.71; close 282.79, −0.68

You can buy a call on the index either at 280 for $1,000 ($100 per point times the 10 points listed for the June call at 280), at 285 for $712.50 (7⅛ points × $100), or at 290 for $500 (5 points × $100).

You decide to purchase the June call contract at 290 for $500, meaning that to reach your breakeven point, assuming nothing else changes but the underlying S&P 100 index itself, requires a 12.21 point move in the index—figured as follows:

Strike price chosen	290.00
Minus: Current price of the index	282.79
Increase in Index required to reach the strike price	7.21 points
Add: Your call contract cost	5.00 points
Move in index needed to break even	12.21 points

Therefore, the S&P 100 must rise to 295.00 to reach your breakeven point as shown:

Index level necessary to break even:
Required move in index	12.21
Add: Current index level	282.79
	295.00

You can see that:

1. Your $500 investment "controls" $28,279 worth of stocks (the 282.79 S&P 100 index × $100 per point).
2. Your $500, the equivalent of 5 points, amounts to a little under 2% of this $28,279 ($500 divided by $28,279 = .018).
3. The 290.00 contract price you chose is 7.24 points above the current 282.79 index level, which is another 2+% required move in the index.
4. The total of #2 and #3 above equals 12.21 points. The index will have to move 12.21 points, or from 282.79 to 295.00, for you to break even. This means that the market must increase over 4% before you stand a chance to profit.

If your judgment is correct and the index rises sometime between now and your June expiration to, say 297.63, you have achieved the following (either through exercising the option itself or selling the contract to someone else):

Ultimate price of index	297.63	($29,763)
Minus: Strike price of contract	290.00	(29,000)
Profit *before* your cost	7.63	($763)
Minus: Your cost	5.00	(500)
Net profit	2.63	($263)

The 2.63 point profit ($263.00) on the 5.00 point ($500) investment = 0.526 or a 52.6% return on investment.

Of course, if the index never exceeds 290, your option contract is worthless—you have lost 100% of your $500. If the contract rises above 290 but below your 295 breakeven point, you will still want to exercise in order to reduce your losses to less than 100%. It is possible, too, for the contract you purchased to move either to a premium or discount from the spread which existed when you bought it. The 2% premium you paid could move up or down on an interim basis. The closer you get to expiration date (in this case, June), however, the less change you can expect in such premiums or discounts.

It is probably worth mentioning again that, although you can only lose the money you invest in stock index options (small consolation!) options constitute a leveraged way of betting for or against price appreciation prospects. In this example, you controlled about $29,000 worth of stocks for three months for just $500, or just 1.7% of the total; your breakeven was over 4%. As with all leveraged situations, small moves in the investment values produce large percentage moves in your return potentials. If the S&P 100 index rises less than 2%, you lost 100% of your investment, just as an approximate 6% move makes you about 100%.

Now—on to a discussion on the even-more-leveraged stock index *futures.*

Stock Index Futures

Stock index futures differ considerably from index options. Futures contracts, be they on wheat, sugar, Treasury bills, or a stock index, allow you to buy or sell at a fixed price on a fixed date. Contrary to options, however, futures have *no limitation on potential losses* because you are obliged to exercise at expiration—though nothing prevents you from selling the contract at any time before expiration and taking your gains or losses up to that date. Think of futures as a highly leveraged way of *owning* (in our example) the index of your choice. Unlike options, futures require daily cash settlements (similar to margin calls on stock or bond positions purchased with borrowed funds), in which the cash value of the difference between today's futures contract value and yesterday's is exchanged; so you do not have to wait until expiration to realize your results—both gains and losses.

In the case of the S&P 500 futures, the size of any contract is $500 times the current price level of a contract. If a contract is currently trading at a 290.00 level, your investment is $500 times this 290.00, or $145,000. With futures contracts, unlike stock index options or futures options (discussed in the next section), you have to put up only a small percentage of the total contract price. Minimum margin requirements for futures contracts are set by the exchanges but brokers often require additional amounts. The initial margin is usually 5-10% of the total value of the contract (or $7,250–$14,500 with the S&P at a level of 290.00). This margin may be raised one day. Authorities are concerned that the leverage is too liberal and that it may lead to excessive volatility of both futures and the stock market itself. Maintenance margins are usually 75–80% of this amount and margin calls are initiated if equity in the account falls below this level. The contract's price is quoted in increments of .05 (i.e., 290.05, 290.10, 290.15). Two point moves in the index always represent a $1,000 absolute gain or loss (the percentage change obviously depends on the level of the index at any time).

As you can readily see, these contracts are inherently volatile. If you buy a futures contract with the S&P at 290.00 with margin requirements at 5%, a two point move in the index (less than a 1% move for the S&P at 290.00) produces a 14% gain or loss on your invested capital ($1,000 result divided by your initial capital investment of, say, $7,250)—assuming there is also a one-for-one move in the futures contracts. It takes only a 15 point (5.2%) decline in the S&P 500 at the 290 level to completely wipe out your $7,250 investment.

For example, say you bought a September futures contract on Sept. 4, 1986, when the S&P 500 was at 253.83 and the March 1987 contract was trading at 252.90 (a discount of less than one percent for the contract versus the underlying S&P index). Your total position would have been $126,450 (252.90 × $500) but your invested capital at a 5% margin would have been $6,320. On Sept. 12, only 6 trading days later, the S&P stood at 230.67 (a 23 point or 9.1% decline) and March contracts were trading at 230.80 (a premium of .06%). You would have lost 175% of your original invested capital of $6,320 (252.90 − 230.80 × $500 = $11,050). This is not just a "paper" loss since the broker could require that you actually add these dollars to your account, regardless of whether you decide to hold or sell your position. To avoid daily trips and checks to your broker, most futures dealers require that you deposit a larger sum—perhaps $20,000 per contract—that would be invested in Treasury bills on which you earn interest but which can be readily credited to the broker should the future go against you.

Premiums and discounts were mentioned on page 122. You should realize that they will vary. In the Sept. 1986 example above, the discount of .37% changed to a premium of .06% as the market dropped (investors obviously expected a recovery from the recent sharp decline). As investor sentiment changes, however, discounts don't have to turn into premiums, and vice versa. If the discount on the futures contract in our example had remained at its original level of around .37%, losses would have amounted to $11,530, or 182% of original invested capital, as shown:

S&P contract level at time of purchase. . .   252.90
S&P contract level 4 trading days later. . .   229.84
(given a constant discount of .37% to the index)   ———
Total level decline. . .   23.06
× $500/pt.
= LOSS. . . $11,530

The futures section of the financial pages is more complicated than that on options. Using an S&P 500 futures contract, information will appear as follows:

FUTURES

S&P 500 Stock Index (CME) $500 times index

	Open	High	Low	Settle	Chg	High	Low	Open Int.
Mar	292.60	293.85	287.50	287.95	−4.70	295.30	227.00	78576
Jun	294.40	295.50	288.65	289.40	−4.95	298.40	249.50	26217
Sep	295.85	296.80	290.20	291.00	−5.00	299.00	274.50	2207

The Index: high 293.30; low 288.14; close 288.52 −4.41

The last three columns of the futures section demand explanation. The third-to-last and second-to-last columns represent the highs and lows on these contracts since the contract was opened. The last column simply represents the number of contracts outstanding.

Futures Options

As if this isn't complicated enough, another vehicle exists which allows you to buy options on futures—called futures options. Options on index futures are options on a specified *futures contract* for the underlying index rather than on the underlying index itself (as with stock *index* options). When exercised, an amount equal to the difference between the exercise price and the current price of the futures contract is exchanged. The cost for each futures options contract (for the S&P 500) is $500 times the current trading level of the instrument. With futures options you can purchase both puts and calls on the underlying futures contract and your potential for losses is limited to only (!) 100%.

For example, assume it is March and that you are very bullish on the market and buy a futures call option on the S&P 500 with a June strike price of 300.00 when the futures contract is trading at 286.28. Say the futures call option is trading at a level of 3.35 (see chart below); your total position would be $1675 ($500 × 3.35) per contract. By paying this amount you control $143,140 worth of stock market assets ($500 × an index value of 286.28). Your $1675 position only represents 1.17% of these assets. Options on the S&P 500 futures contract are so-called European options: you can only exercise these options on the expiration date. Stock index options, on the other hand, are "American" options: you can exercise these at any time up to and including the day of expiration.

Back to our example, let's assume your market judgment proved correct and the S&P 500 futures contract has advanced to 303.72 on the expiration date—at which time you exercise your option. Your proceeds will be $1860 (303.72 − 300.00 × $500) for every contract owned or a gain of 11% on your invested capital ($1860 − $1675 divided by $1675). In contrast, if the futures contract at expiration is below, or equal to, 300.00 your futures option contract will be worthless; it doesn't matter how much below 300.00 it is, since you don't have to exercise your option (you have lost all of your invested capital, the worst thing that can happen). If the index has advanced above 300 but is below your breakeven point, you will still want to exercise your futures options in order to reduce your losses.

The financial pages carry a section called FUTURES OPTIONS. The format for these instruments is very similar to the format for stock index options:

FUTURES OPTIONS

S & P 500 Stock Index (CME) $500 times premium

Strike Price	Calls-Settle			Puts-Settle		
	Dec-C	Mar-C	Jun-C	Dec-P	Mar-P	Jun-P
290	6.50	10.60	20.40	10.50	10.00	9.50
295	4.70	8.40	10.60	13.65	13.15	12.75
300	3.35	6.75	8.65	17.25	16.05	15.75

Est. vol. 3,256; 1,940 calls; 1,568 puts
Open interest; 15,356 calls; 12,011 puts

The format of this section of the financial pages does not include a quotation of the stock index futures contract. You will have to look elsewhere in your newspaper for this.

Program Trading

Publicity about so-called "buy or sell programs" relates to the effects of futures contracts. The fact is that the expiration dates of large index futures programs create sudden and wide fluctuations in the stocks underlying such indexes. Large trading firms, brokerage houses, and arbitrageurs initiate (sometimes massive) buy or sell orders for a basket of stocks likely to perform like a given index. At the same time they take opposite positions in futures contracts on the index being near-duplicated. They do this if and when they believe that the difference between the index level and the contract price of the future (called the spread) appears out-of-line with a theoretical spread that should prevail given the interest and transaction costs represented by this difference in prices. Program traders expect to profit from this "aberration" by buying futures/selling stocks when the futures contract is "underpriced" and stocks are "overpriced" and vice versa when the situation is reversed. As they buy or sell the prices of stocks and futures move back into theoretical "equilibrium" and this activity becomes unprofitable until the next time futures and stocks become "mispriced." These activities can cause wide variances in the stock market and therefore create more nervousness than would be the case without them.

SOME CRUCIAL WARNINGS

Time now for a magnifying-glass look at puts and calls and some conclusions about them:

1. You receive no return on invested capital from dividends when you place money in puts and calls.
2. Puts and calls now have marketability; in some cases, trading volume of option contracts exceeds that of the underlying securities. Options are, however, available on only a limited number of securities—thus you may not be able to use the vehicle for the stock of your choice.
3. You are limited by the time element of options. Good investments often take time—generally considerably more time than thirty days, ninety days, or even six months or a year. Your idea may be completely right, but you may be thwarted by the restriction of a short period of time in controlling stock through options.
4. The high cost of puts and calls amounts to a significant burden. You start out with a high break-even point when you purchase option contracts. For example, a six-month call on ABC at $50 per share for $600 means that the stock has to advance to at least $57 ($600 option cost plus about $100 in commissions) for you to break even.
5. A new and interesting field has evolved for those who are willing to "write" options on stocks they own or contemplate owning. Option writers are the source of puts and calls, and they receive a part of the premiums

(described earlier) that are charged to the put and call buyers and sellers. Some high rates of return have been earned by those who have written options. And some investors have insisted that option writing equates to "riskless" returns. Such is not really the case; just because you own XYZ stock and write an option for a fee against this holding does not mean that your return is guaranteed or that you incur no risk. Market moves in the stock you have written an option against may be so volatile that you cannot protect yourself as you would like; and the ability to manage your investments might be hampered by certain stock movements. Lastly, more and more investors (including certain institutional portfolios) are becoming involved in writing options, which signifies to me that the margins will be lowered substantially over time.

CONCLUSIONS

My conclusion is that *puts and calls should be used on only isolated occasions*. If you happen to come across a stock that greatly excites you, one for which you can visualize a very large advance in the market, then a call might be useful in your planning. Or if you are dealing in securities for truly speculative purposes, then options certainly give you an outlet.

If you do invest in options, I have one bit of advice: *Do not buy them with a time fixation in your mind.* Too many people purchase options with the fixed idea (either conscious or subconscious) that they will do nothing with them until the expiration date. Too often they see their price objectives on a stock reached before the option's expiration, only to procrastinate on exercising or selling the option till the very end. Invariably the stock will retreat in the interim and these option holders find that their profit has faded away. So set some kind of price objective when you purchase the option and do not let the expiration date of the option interfere with your investment judgment.

I caution you against active participation in the put-and-call market. It is my contention that the percentages will "eat you up" in time. The statistics (you are working against a high break-even point and a time element) are against you from the start, so you will have to choose unusually good stocks to make consistent profits in puts and calls over the years.

Stock index options, futures, and futures options allow you to make general market bets with considerable potential leverage existing in all three. Index options at least provide some downside protection even though this "limitation" is 100% of the capital you invest. Futures serve a function, but they constitute new and more volatile elements for investors using them (you can lose more than 100% of your investment). Futures options have similar downside limitation as index options, but since they represent bets on very volatile futures contracts, they are bound to be very volatile themselves. All three vehicles present new and complicated factors for stock investors to reckon with in the future. The inherent leverage existing in these instruments obviously presents dramatic opportunities for the very astute (or very lucky). The risks are equally obvious and, as mentioned, they portend greater nervousness for all involved—something the stock market (and investors) frankly can do without.

PART V
Security Analysis
Made Easy

17
Tools to Build Your Success in the Market

One of the basic rules of investing is "Get the facts before you invest," or "Investigate before you invest." Fortunately in stock market investing the facts are available to you in research bulletins from brokerage firms, annual reports from individual companies, statistical services, and other publications. It's up to you to use these facts correctly, and if you do, your successes will be greater.

Some of these facts involve fundamentals, such as understanding a little something about a company's financial position and earning power. The basic aim of this book is to show you how to make money—big money—in the stock market. To understand what is to come, I ask you to start by building the foundation for your success. After all, no builder starts with the roof.

THE BALANCE SHEET

It's obvious that part of the risk you take investing in a stock stems from the financial condition of the company involved. That's why it's important to know something about a company's financial status before you invest in its stock. This kind of knowledge is available to you from a quick glance at its *balance sheet, which provides a detailed snapshot of a company's financial condition at one particular date.*

Perhaps the simplest way to familiarize you with this first tool is to compare it with the balance sheet of a typical American family.

The left-hand column is concerned with "assets," a fancy term for "these are the things we *own*." First of all, we have "*current* assets," which are those that are *easily converted into cash.*

JONES FAMILY BALANCE SHEET
AS OF DECEMBER 31, 1986

Current Assets			Current Liabilities	
Cash		$ 5,000	Accounts payable	$ 1,000
Savings bonds		1,000	Balance due on car	2,000
Common stocks		20,000	Notes payable	2,000
Total current assets		26,000	Total current liabilities	5,000
Other investments		10,000	Mortgage on home	25,000
Fixed Assets				
Automobile				
Cost	$ 9,000		TOTAL LIABILITIES	$30,000
Less reserve for depreciation	3,000		NET WORTH	67,000
		6,000		
Home		50,000		
Home furnishings				
Cost	10,000			
Less reserve for depreciation	5,000			
		5,000		
Total fixed assets		$61,000		
			TOTAL LIABILITIES	
TOTAL ASSETS		$97,000	AND NET WORTH	$97,000

Next comes "other investments," which could be anything, but in this case probably represent a small business thought to be worth $10,000.

Next comes "fixed assets," which are tangible items that are not as easily converted into cash as the current assets. Listed under fixed assets are an automobile, home, and home furnishings. Notice that the auto and the furnishings have a "reserve for depreciation," which has reduced their carrying value on the balance sheet. Why? Because these items depreciate, or are worth less, as time wears them out. The minute you drive a new car out of the showroom it becomes a "used" car and is worth less on resale than you paid for it. The same thing goes for furniture and other home furnishings. You might make the buy of the century on a new sofa, but get it home and try to resell it and you'll know that it has already "depreciated."

Because of depreciation, you would only be deceiving yourself if you valued your car and furniture at their original retail price. To know what your assets are truly worth, you should subtract this depreciation from their original price. In our family balance sheet you can see that the $9,000 original cost of the auto has been reduced by $3,000 of depreciation, for a more realistic net value of $6,000.

But, you might ask, how much depreciation should one account for? The correct way to figure this is to *estimate the life of the asset itself*. In the case of the car, assume it has a useful life of five years, or sixty months. After that time, you figure it'll be ready for the junk heap. If you take the original cost of $9,000 and divide it by this sixty-month "life," you'll come up with $150 a month depreciation to subtract from the $9,000 cost. At this rate, the car will be worth $8,850 after the first month,* $8,700 after the second, and so on until, at the end of sixty months, it will show on the balance sheet as having no value. Actually, the car will have some small value at the end of this period, so you can see that depreciation is seldom exact, but it is

---

*This is an example of "straight line" depreciation in which an even amount is deducted each month. Many companies use more realistic depreciation methods where higher depreciation is taken in the early stages of an asset's life. Such "accelerated" depreciation should be used by individuals, too, because for most assets, the resale value drops very sharply right after purchase.

realistic and does give you a good idea of the worth of what you own as time goes on.

Notice that I did *not* set up a reserve for depreciation for the Jones home. Real estate values have traditionally risen over time, roughly in line with inflation rates. There's a good chance that the Jones's home has appreciated, not *de*preciated, in value over the years. In this case, you should set up a reserve for appreciation by the amount you estimate your home is worth.

Adding all these things the Jones family owns gives us "total assets" of $97,000. Is this what the Joneses are really worth? No! They *owe* something to somebody, and naturally we have to deduct this from what they *own* to find out what they're really worth. Now we come to the right-hand side of this balance sheet, the column "liabilities" (amounts *owed*). The first item shown is "current liabilities," which states the debts the Jones family has to pay *within one year* (here are charge account bills and any other obligations that must be met within the year).

Next we have to show any other debts due over a longer period of time than one year. When the Jones family bought the $50,000 home shown under assets, they borrowed $35,000 from their bank, which was to be paid off over a period of twenty years (and which has been paid down to $25,000 in our example). We have to show this *long-term debt* separately from the current liabilities. Now we've listed all the debts and have totaled them under "total liabilities": $30,000.

At last we can tell the real worth of the Jones family:

Total value of what they *own* ("Total Assets")	$97,000
Less total amounts they *owe* ("Total Liabilities")	30,000
Total amount they are worth ("Net Worth")	$67,000

The balance sheet has served its purpose—it realistically states the Jones family's current financial position and its net asset value if they cashed in all their chips on the date this statement was compiled. Remember, however, that the home has to be valued "at market" rather than at cost in order to arrive at a realistic net worth.

THE CORPORATION'S BALANCE SHEET

A company sets up its balance sheet just as a family does. Below is a typical corporate balance sheet (of the Ichabod Crane Company).

ICHABOD CRANE COMPANY BALANCE SHEET AS OF DECEMBER 31, 1986

Current Assets			Current Liabilities		
Cash		$ 2,000,000	Accounts payable		$ 1,000,000
Marketable securities		1,000,000	Notes payable		1,000,000
Accounts receivable		2,000,000	Accrued wages, taxes,		
Inventories		3,000,000	expenses		2,000,000
Total current assets		8,000,000	Total current liabilities		4,000,000
Other investments		2,000,000	Long-term debt		4,000,000
			Total Liabilities		8,000,000
Fixed Assets					
Property plant			Net worth		
and equipment			Common stock		
Cost	$10,000,000		(1,000,000		
Less reserve for			shares)	$1,000,000	
depreciation	5,000,000				
Total fixed assets		5,000,000	Capital		
Prepaid expenses		200,000	surplus	1,000,000	
Deferred charges		500,000	Earned		
Patents and goodwill		300,000	surplus	6,000,000	
			Total net worth		$ 8,000,000
			TOTAL LIABILITIES		
TOTAL ASSETS		$16,000,000	AND NET WORTH		$16,000,000

The "current assets" contain the very liquid items the company owns, but there are two items here not usually found in the family's balance sheet. A company in business has large sums owed to it by those who have bought its goods, and these are shown as "accounts receivable." Then, a company has a supply of its own products on its shelves waiting for sale (in this case, cranes), and these "inventories" are also a part of the current assets. In analyzing the current assets, we would normally prefer to see more cash items (cash, marketable securities, accounts receivable) than inventories because the latter are less certain of being converted into cash.

There's no telling what you will find in a corporate balance sheet under "other investments." Most often you have to read the small print shown as "notes to the financial statement" to determine what these other investments include. Some interesting facts can be learned from digging into these footnotes. For example, the Matson Navigation Company owned 500,000 shares of Honolulu Oil for years and always showed this holding under "other investments"—valued at Matson's original cost, which happened to be *50 cents per share*. In case you weren't aware of the real market value for Honolulu Oil (then listed on the New York Stock Exchange), the footnote explained that this value as of the balance sheet date was *not 50 cents a share but closer to $50 per share*. Thus instead of Matson's 500,000 shares being worth $250,000, as shown, the holding was worth about $25 million. Quite a difference! Many balance sheets are like this (management is being conservative by not writing up these hidden values) and the investor should be conscious of this "carry-all" category, which can lead to profits for those who are alert. Incidentally, some large profits were made on Matson stock—the company partially liquidated in 1959 and stockholders realized how valuable Honolulu Oil stock was (its actual liquidation price was $100.85 per share).

Next under the asset column of the corporation come "fixed assets." Rather than show these fixed assets separately, most companies lump them into one category "property, plant, and equipment." Like the Jones family's automobile and home furnishings, Ichabod is realistic and depreciates this carry-all asset—thus the "reserve for depreciation." Deducting this reserve from the original cost of the property, plant, and equipment may (but may not) give a more realistic appraisal of the fixed assets.

The last asset items on Ichabod's balance sheet are termed "intangible assets." They include prepaid expenses, deferred charges, patents, and goodwill. Another example might be a prepaid pension expense. If a corporation has previously funded more than enough to cover expected retirement benefit payments, this would be an intangible asset. Many stocks have risen substantially in the recent past when investors uncovered such "hidden" assets. Whereas the "prepaid expenses" item is generally legitimate, the "deferred charges" can be a "hideout" for expenses that really should be charged currently. This is an area open to considerable interpretation. For example, let's assume that the $500,000 on the Ichabod Crane balance sheet is explained in the footnotes (all balance sheets have explanatory footnotes to certain assets and liabilities) as "deferred research and development expenses." In such a case, the company will no doubt explain that it has poured excessive efforts into one or more programs from which it does not expect sales for some time in the future. In essence, management is claiming that it should not be penalized currently for something that appears certain to provide revenues (and profits) in the future.

Legitimate though this reasoning is, the crucial question is whether the products being developed will be as successful as projected. If they are, then the deferrals can ultimately be written off against the revenues and a profit may still be forthcoming from them. If the products are ultimately *unsuccessful,* however, the company has nothing to write deferrals off against—*and the deferrals have to be charged off.* Thus some unpleasant surprises may be forthcoming.

Frankly, I am extremely skeptical of large deferrals. Management can always rationalize their existence, but I prefer owning companies that charge off everything currently.

Incidentally, one attractive part of most large high-quality companies such as IBM and MMM is that normally they engage in very conservative accounting. Not only does this practice eliminate sudden writeoff surprises but the higher charge-offs mean lower reported profits, which in turn mean lower taxes paid; thus the company has the use of money that a deferring company must pay in taxes.

Investors who ignored the deferred balance sheet items of Cordura, Memorex, and countless other companies lost huge sums of money.

A word about "patents and goodwill." Even though a company's patents have large value and its name and reputation (goodwill) are also extremely valuable, it is conservative accounting practice to carry patents and goodwill on the balance sheet at the nominal figure of $1. This is because there is no way of evaluating what they are worth. Beware when you find patents and goodwill carried for huge amounts on the balance sheet—management may well be deceiving you!*

When we total all Crane assets, they add up to $16,000,000. But, like our Jones family, Ichabod has some bills to pay, too.

First of all, we find "current liabilities"—those that have to be paid within one year. Here we have "accounts payable" (current bills), "notes payable" (possibly to the bank), "accrued wages, taxes, and expenses" (all of which are to be paid out in cash shortly), and so on.

Just as the Jones family took out a mortgage on their home to be paid over twenty years, Ichabod needed some money for a long period of time, too. This borrowed money is termed "long-term debt" when it has *more* than one year to run.

Now we total the current liabilities and the long-term debt and come up with "total liabilities" of $8,000,000. Finally we can gauge approximately what Ichabod is worth if it goes out of business tomorrow:

Total assets	$16,000,000
Less total liabilities	8,000,000
Total net worth	$ 8,000,000

The total net worth of $8,000,000 is divided between "common stock," "capital surplus," and "earned surplus" on the balance sheet. It's not necessary to our discussion to distinguish between these terms. All three represent values to the common stockholder, and the main thing to consider is the total of the three.

We're through now with the fundamentals of the balance sheet. The next step is to put these fundamentals to work and learn how to judge whether a company is financially strong or not.

---

*An exception may be when one company has recently purchased another, in which case it may have paid for patents, goodwill, and so on, and these will be written off (amortized) over the years.

18

Some Simple Surgery on the Balance Sheet

Balance Sheet Analysis

Analyzing a balance sheet can become highly complicated. Ordinarily, however, only a few simple tests are necessary to determine whether the company of your dreams is financially sound.

You want answers to the following questions:

1. Can the company pay its bills?
2. What is it worth in the event it goes out of business or is bought by or merged with another company?
3. Has the company gotten itself too deeply in debt?

It may come as a surprise to you, but a very cursory glance at the balance sheet will answer these questions for you. Here's how.

1. *Can the company pay its bills?*

You pay your bills out of your checking, savings, or money market account, or the money you have stored in the sugar bowl. You depend on your cash items. You do not depend on your auto, home, home furnishings, or similar assets to do this. In other words, you depend on your current assets (readily convertible into cash)—not your fixed assets—to pay your current liabilities (which have to be paid within one year).

Thus it's easy to see whether you can pay your bills by comparing your current assets with your current liabilities.

The same thing applies to a company. You can determine

its ability to pay bills by comparing its current assets with its current liabilities. To compare companies of all sizes, you simply divide current liabilities into current assets and arrive at what analysts call the *current ratio*. For example, Ichabod's balance sheet showed:

Current assets of	$8,000,000
Current liabilities of	4,000,000

By dividing current liabilities of $4,000,000 into current assets of $8,000,000, you obviously arrive at a current ratio of 2 to 1. In other words, there are twice as many current assets as current liabilities. The more assets, the better; thus the higher the current ratio, the better.

What Is a "Normal" Current Ratio?

A company generally needs an infusion of cash from somewhere if its current assets are less than its current liabilities. By the same token, a company with a current ratio of 1 to 1 (current assets the same as current liabilities) can't keep living from hand to mouth forever. *As a general rule, a current ratio of 2 to 1 or better is preferable for a company. But the ratio will vary from industry to industry.* For example, your gas and electric company will no doubt have a current ratio of only a little over 1 to 1. It doesn't need a ratio higher than this because its revenues are steady and are paid in cash monthly; plus it does not have the problem of carrying inventories on its shelves. In contrast, companies that have to build up inventories for seasonal sales will need a higher current ratio.

Two words of caution here! First, always look to see what portion of a company's current assets consists of immediate cash items. A company can have a high current ratio and have almost no cash in the till. A large portion of inventories is not as reliable because you can't be sure when and at what price these inventories will be sold and converted into cash.*

*To measure real liquidity, compare cash and marketable securities alone (omit accounts receivable and inventories) to current liabilities and get the company's "quick ratio." A quick ratio of 1 to 1 is exceptionally good.

Second, don't buy a stock only because of a high current ratio. We'll see later just what to consider in buying and selling stocks, but remember that one of the most disappointing stocks in the 1950–1960 decade—Texas Gulf Sulphur—had one of the highest current ratios—about 11 to 1. Still, you should consider the current ratio for background because it's reassuring to know the company of your choice has the ability to pay its bills.

2. *What is the company worth in the event it goes out of business or is bought by or merged with another company?*

Recall how we determined the balance sheet net worth of an individual or a corporation. It is important to adjust these figures for any under or over-statements of value (such as the Honolulu Oil–Matson situation discussed previously) to arrive at a true net worth.* Then divide this by the number of common shares outstanding and you get net worth, or "book value" as it is usually called, per share. This will usually be done for you by management in its annual report, but just in case it isn't, here's how Ichabod Crane book value would be figured:

Total net worth of $8 million ÷ 1 million shares = $8 per share.

In other words, this company would be worth $8 per share were it to liquidate tomorrow (assuming no adjustments were in order for the stated balance sheet items). While stated book value tells you something, you should also consider the company's "going concern value"—i.e., how much its business may be worth to other owners. This is bound to be an inexact number to the outsider, but some attempt should be made to approximate this.

How important is it to know a company's liquidating value? Striking examples in the past few years have illustrated the potential for sudden, large gains in stock prices once understated balance sheet items were recognized. Companies coveting these assets, liquidators, the so-called "corporate raiders", and even existing, internal management have sought large

---

*Preferred stock usually appears under "net worth," but it should be deducted, since we are interested in what the *common* stockholders would get in liquidation.

positions in companies in the belief that they could realize greater values for its various parts than reflected in its value in the market. Mergers and acquisition activity—sometimes referred to as "takeover mania"—has swept through corporate America. Large profits have been made in stocks such as Getty Oil (acquired by Texaco), General Foods (acquired by Philip Morris), and Levi Strauss (taken private by management).

However, I suggest that you de-emphasize book value unless:

1. There is a chance that the company will liquidate its business (this is a rare occurrence for very large companies).
2. There is a chance that it will merge with another company in the future (in such a merger book value would be given some weight in arriving at a price).
3. There is some likelihood of tender offer (attempt at control of the corporation) by outside investors.

If you believe one of these three possibilities may occur, you can make fine returns from those investments that go one of the routes. So long as it is cheaper to buy whole companies through the marketplace (at premiums to quoted market prices) than it is to build new plants or establish businesses, the "buying assets" philosophy can bring excellent returns for investors.

If, however, you see little chance for the three prospects listed, ignore book value in your appraisal of the stock. Incidentally, let me point out that the term "par value" has no significance whatsoever in the appraisal of a stock, even though it appears on a balance sheet. Since it bears no relationship to book value, earnings, or market price, simply ignore it.

3. *Has the company gotten itself too deeply in debt?*

Have you ever considered how much money to put up in cash to buy a home or another piece of property? If you can put up all cash—and thus avoid a mortgage—you will have no monthly payments to make (except for taxes and insurance). Your worries will be small. You can even lose your job and still know you'll have the roof over your head.

Assume that instead of paying all cash for this house, you

are forced to take a large mortgage from the bank. You borrow $50,000 or $75,000 and have to make payments of $600 or $1,000 per month. Now what happens if you lose your job and the income isn't rolling in? You're in trouble.

The same principle applies to companies that have to borrow to conduct their business. The more they borrow, the higher the "monthly payments" they have to make and the greater the risk they take. This is because the interest becomes a *fixed* charge that must be paid through thick and thin.

You may remember the song "What a Difference a Day Makes." Following is a song you should get to know—let's call it "What a Difference a *Debt* Makes."

Assume you're looking to buy the business of the Hotentot Pot Company. Last year Hotentot earned $20,000 before taxes, or $17,000 after taxes.* You and the present Hotentot owners agree on a selling price of $100,000 for the business and now it's yours.

You shell out $100,000 *in cash*. This year the business once again earns $17,000 after taxes, and thus you are realizing a 17% return on your cash investment.

Then you think: Why should I tie up my cash in Hotentot? I can use some of that cash to buy some more businesses. And the interest rate from the bank is only 6%. So you arrange with your banker to borrow $70,000 of the $100,000 purchase price—and to pay the bank 6% on the $70,000, or $4,200 per year in interest. Now you only have $30,000 cash invested in Hotentot.

The next year Hotentot once again earns $20,000 before taxes. Of course, now you have an expense of $4,200 for interest and you have to deduct this from the $20,000. Here's how you'll come out:

Net income before interest and taxes	$20,000
Less interest expense	4,200
Net before taxes	$15,800
Less income taxes (15%)	2,370
Net income	$13,430

*The corporate income tax is only 15% on income under $25,000.

Your net income shows at $13,430 instead of $17,000, but now you have only a $30,000 investment in the business. Here is what has happened to the return on your money:

Before: $17,000 net income ÷ $100,000 investment = 17%
Now: $13,430 net income ÷ $30,000 investment = 44.8%

Such genius! Merely by borrowing the bulk of the purchase price, you have increased your rate of return from 17% to 44.8%.

Next year Hotentot has a booming year—net income before interest and taxes advances to $40,000. Let's see what this means to profits under both conditions (full $100,000 in cash and borrowing $70,000):

	All Cash Purchase	Borrowing $70,000
Net income before interest and taxes	$ 40,000	$40,000
Less interest expense	None	4,200
Net income before taxes	$ 40,000	$35,800
Less income taxes (15%)	6,000	5,370
Net income	$ 34,000	$30,430
Cash investment made	$100,000	$30,000
Return on original cash investment	34%	101%

Fantastic! You have tripled the return on your money by going into debt (by "leveraging" your investment as they say in investment circles). Of course, you know that there are two sides to this coin. So now we have to ask: What happens if Hotentot's business slides off? Assume the net before interest and taxes declines to $4,000:

	All Cash Purchase	Borrowing $70,000
Net income before interest and taxes	$ 4,000	$ 4,000
Less interest expense	None	4,200
Net income before taxes	$ 4,000	$(200) Loss
Less income taxes (15%)	600	——
Net income	$ 3,400	$(200) Loss
Cash investment made	$100,000	$30,000
Return on original cash investment	3.4%	Minus return

The fixed interest charge of $4,200 looms large when business falls off and, because of this expense, you have a loss instead of a profit. The risk of borrowing has reared its ugly head.

This discussion should be helpful to you in deciding how much borrowing you should do if you buy a business, invest in real estate, buy stocks on margin, or undertake some other venture. Actually, with 1987 interest rates running even higher than the mythical 6% used in our examples, leverage (borrowing) is even riskier. But back to stocks!

One of the things to investigate before buying a stock is the amount of borrowed money a company is using. Since heavy borrowing entails risk and corresponding rewards, you ought to check what kind of leverage exists before buying.

There is no way to set a dollar limit on how much companies can soundly borrow because you will be looking at companies of all sizes. The debt figure means something only if we relate it to the amount of each company's total capital. A $5 million debt to a $100 million company is nothing, but to a $10 million company it constitutes half the capital. Here's how to determine how heavily leveraged a company is:

1. Total all the invested capital in the business by combining these figures:
   a. All the *long-term debt* shown on the balance sheet (this may include bank loans, notes, bonds, debentures).
   b. All the *preferred stock* (if any exists), also as it is shown on the balance sheet.

c. All the *common stock money that is invested in the company.* Rather than use the common stock and surplus figures as they show on the balance sheet (we have just seen how this net worth, or book value, may have little significance in appraising a stock's real value in the marketplace), it may be more realistic to use *the market value of all the common stock outstanding.* In other words, *multiply the number of common shares outstanding by the stock's current market price.*

2. See what percentage of total invested capital (a + b + c) is represented by the securities that have fixed charges on the company—i.e., by long-term debt (a) and preferred stock (b).

On Ichabod Crane's balance sheet you would figure leverage as follows:

1. Total all invested capital by combining:
   a. Long-term debt, which in this case is ... $ 4,000,000
   b. Preferred stock, which in this case is .... None
   c. Common stock
   Instead of using the $8,000,000 book value figure shown on the balance sheet, multiply the company's 1,000,000 outstanding common shares times the present market price on the stock (assume it to be $16 per share), for a total of $16,000,000
   Total Capital $20,000,000
2. See what percentage of total capital ($20,000,000) is represented by long-term debt and preferred stock ($4,000,000):
   $4,000,000 ÷ $20,000,000 = .20 or 20%

Thus, Ichabod has 20% of its capital in debt. Naturally, the higher this figure, the more risk the investor takes. Like the current ratio, the "proper" amount of borrowed capital will vary according to the industry and the individual company. Once again, your gas and electric company can afford considerable borrowing because of its stability—it may have as much as two-thirds of its capital in debt and preferred stocks.

But this kind of leverage might be suicide for industrial companies. In fact, any time the leverage is over 25% you have to be very conscious of the possible risks.

In a growing and profitable industry some amount of debt shows management aggressiveness. As in our example, some borrowing can greatly enhance the return on your money. As a matter of fact, management may well leave itself open to criticism if it fails to take advantage of "cheap" borrowed money. After all, a company that consistently earns 10–20% on its invested capital may have acted foolishly in not expanding when borrowed money cost only 5% or 6%—or even higher. Perhaps management was overly conservative; on the other hand, the business may simply not have possessed opportunities that warranted further capital investment.

I must mention that some companies are in the fortunate position of having ample cash to handle their business and take care of expansion as well. They simply may have no need for debt or preferred stocks. They have what is called a *clean capitalization—free of debt and preferred charges.* The stockholders of these companies can relax some, knowing that there are no fixed interest charges to cause extraordinary swings in their profits. Companies such as Apple Computer, A. T. Cross, John Harland, and Kelly Services have had clean capitalizations, with no debt, and yet have been able to show sufficient (in some cases, quite spectacular) growth to provide their owners with both a feeling of security and very attractive capital appreciation over the years.

The prospective investor should consider a company's leverage in order to know what risks investment in that company entails. It's another "background" fact to know about a stock before making the plunge.

Other Balance Sheet Ratios

Other clues to a company's health—and to future prospects—are also available through balance sheet analysis. I do not want to turn this chapter into an accounting course, but a lot can be learned from considering:

a. The sales/inventory ratio—i.e., are inventories building up in relation to sales (if inventories are rising too fast, it may indicate "stale merchandise")?

b. Sales/accounts receivables—i.e., are the company's collections lagging?

c. Depreciation (see p. 135)—if it is declining, management may not be realistic in assessing replacement needs of the corporation in years ahead.

Finally, a study of notes to the financial statements is a must. Explanations of deferred charges (pp. 138–39), unfunded pension liabilities, pending legal matters, stock options, company investments, inventory evaluation, and so forth can all give a clue to the future. Therefore my advice to you is similar to good legal advice: Read the small print!

CONCLUSION

The *current ratio*—easily figured and usually computed by management in its report to stockholders—shows you a company's current financial position and tells you whether the money is there to pay the bills.

Leverage tells you whether the company is too heavily laden with debt and gives you a hint of certain risks that may exist.

Book value is useful in specialized instances.

These are by no means the only yardsticks for balance sheet analysis, but when you understand the relative importance of these, you will have the background necessary to back up your decisions. I emphasize that they give *only background* because, as we shall see very shortly, most decisions will stem from other considerations.

19
More Profit-Building Tools

You now know how to judge the solidity of a company by whether it can pay its bills, by determining whether it is too much in debt, and by knowing how much it would be worth if it were to go out of business tomorrow or possibly be bought by another company (or outside investor).

Overlooked here is one all-important consideration: *How much money is the company earning?*

As emphasized later, it is present and potential earning power that normally makes a stock a buy or a sell candidate. Hence, you must understand the accounting statement that tells the world about a company's earnings—the so-called *income statement* (also called the *statement of profit and loss* and/or the *statement of earnings*). The income statement tells *how much money has been earned over a given period of time.*

Despite the importance of the income statement, its analysis is relatively simple. There are, however, a few pointers to prepare you to judge which stocks to buy and when to buy them.

HOW EFFICIENT IS THE COMPANY?

You've no doubt had contact with inefficient people. You wouldn't invest a plug nickel in them, I'm sure. Nor would you be eager to invest in inefficient companies.

RUM DUMB RUM CORPORATION

INCOME STATEMENT
FOR THE YEAR ENDED DECEMBER 31, 1986

Net sales		$100,000,000
Less:		
Cost of goods sold	$70,000,000	
Selling, general & administrative expenses	10,000,000	
Depreciation	5,000,000	85,000,000
Profit from operations		$ 15,000,000
Less interest charges		1,000,000
Net profit before taxes		$ 14,000,000
Add nonrecurring income		4,000,000
Total profit before taxes		$ 18,000,000
Less income taxes		8,000,000
Net Profit		$10,000,000

But how can you determine whether a company is efficient when you are so detached from it and have no personal contacts? One answer: by looking at its *margin of profit.*

The margin of profit tells you how much gross profit the company is getting from each dollar of sales and is arrived at by relating the "profit from operations" on the income statement to "net sales." In the case of Rum Dumb, the margin of profit would be:

Profit from operations ÷ Net Sales = Margin of Profit
$15,000,000 ÷ $100,000,000 = 15%

In other words, on every $1 sale, Rum Dumb makes 15%, or 15 cents (before interest, taxes, etc.).

Obviously a company that makes 15 cents on every $1 of sales must be far more efficient than one that makes only 10 cents on the same $1. Thus, *in the same industry,* you can compare the efficiency of any number of companies by comparing their margins of profit. Notice I have stressed comparison *in the same industry*. This is because every industry has its own profit structure and mode of doing business.

The food chain industry, for example, is a high-volume business and the margin of profit on each $1 of sales is very low. You can't compare the margin of profit of Safeway—the world's largest food chain—with that of IBM. The latter's equipment and services provide a significantly larger profit in each $1 of sales than there is in the stable, high-turnover food business.

Assuming that you are comparing companies in the same line of business, however, you can conclude that *the higher the margin of profit, the more effective management is in getting profit for the stockholders*. It is the *trend* of margins that is most important. Rising margins are very healthy, but they may also signal caution. An industry or company used to a narrow range of margins—which may suddenly surge—may be benefiting from an abnormality. Oil and oil service companies experienced exactly this in the late 1970's. Margins went out of sight—way above the norm and high enough to attract enough new competition and supply as to cause a complete reversal in the 1980's. Hence, you should differentiate healthy, sustainable margins from unsustainable ones.

BUYING "INEFFICIENCY"

Certainly it is normally better to buy the *most* efficient companies. Still, there are times when it is *very profitable to buy companies that have been plagued with inefficiency*. Of course, this only holds if there is some definite change in philosophy, circumstances, or personnel that makes a sudden endeavor to improve efficiency and the margin of profit.

Take the case of Safeway Stores! The years 1949–1955 were spent building up sales. But it is not volume of sales that pays off for stockholders, it is profits—and here is where Safeway had fallen down. Here's the company's record over this seven-year span:

Year	Sales (Billion)	Margin of Profit (%)	Earnings per Share
1949	$1.1	2.7	$1.68
1950	1.2	3.2	1.61
1951	1.4	2.1	.75
1952	1.6	2.3	.67
1953	1.7	3.0	1.36
1954	1.8	2.8	1.16
1955	1.9	2.8	1.08

Despite the increase in sales, Safeway's profits per share had declined (the company had added to its common stock outstanding and this dilution forced earnings *per share* down over this period). As a result, Safeway common stock was a dull performer. Something was obviously wrong because the company was operating at a margin of profit *about half of what the average company in the industry was doing.*

New management took over in 1955 and it was their announced intention to improve the efficiency—the margin of profit—of Safeway. This change of philosophy offered some real money-making opportunities to stock buyers. All you had to say was: "I believe that new management at Safeway will be able to reach industry averages of efficiency" (no more) and you could have bought the stock with assurance. After all, if Safeway doubled its margin of profit, its earnings would at least double and the stock would be a good investment.

Here's what happened at Safeway in the ensuing four years:

Year	Sales (Billion)	Margin of Profit (%)	Earnings per Share	Market Price of Safeway Stock
1955	$1.9	2.8	$1.08	19⅜–14
1956	2.0	4.1	2.04	23⅞–16⅞
1957	2.1	4.3	2.43	27½–20⅛
1958	2.2	4.4	2.60	41¾–24½
1959	2.3	4.5	2.82	42½–34⅝

You can see the importance of efficiency here. Earnings went from $1.08 per share to $2.82 and the stock rose from a low of 14 to a high of 42½. There are countless examples of constructive management changes that have achieved similar results. Over the five years from 1975 to 1980, Amcord, Boise Cascade, General Dynamics, General Instruments, Litton Industries, and Rohm and Haas were just a half dozen of hundreds of companies in which successes were made by "investing in inefficiency." From 1980 to 1986, many more emerged—including GAF and Celanese. Remember, however, that improving margins is not an easy task, so do not assume that it will be accomplished overnight.

IS ANY PART OF NET PROFIT "UNUSUAL"?

Naturally you want to know whether a company's reported profits will continue at the same levels in the future. You certainly want to know if one year's profits have been "bloated" by some nonrecurring gain. Say, for example, a company sells a plant or some real estate in one year. It will have a gain to report, and since it may be many years before it sells off another large asset such as this (perhaps it never will), you should not be deceived by this gain.

Therefore I caution you to look at a company's income statement to see if there are any large "nonrecurring profits." Rum Dumb had just such an addition to its profits—in the amount of $4 million. You should deduct this $4 million (approximately $3 million after capital gains tax) from Rum Dumb's net profit to arrive at the company's "true" earnings for the year.

Usually management will do this for you: it will separate the nonrecurring income from the normal income and tell you what the company actually earned on an operating basis. *If it does not do this, it is to be criticized.* To my way of thinking, it's a sign of weakness if management doesn't advertise the truth, rather than attempt to hide it. Look for this, too, in assessing management.

Likewise, a company may have some nonrecurring *expenses* or *writeoffs* that *reduce* normal profits. Writeoffs will usually show separately on the income statement, but nonrecurring expenses (such as the opening of new facilities or moving to a new plant) will usually be lumped together with normal expenses rather than be shown separately. In either case, you can count on management to explain these nonrecurring items and tell you how much they reduced profits. Naturally you'll want to allow for these items when you appraise the company's efficiency.

Another item you will want to consider is a company's reporting on pension matters. With the Financial Accounting Standards Board's (FASB) adoption of new rules for pension accounting in 1986, many company reports will be distorted in the future by over- and underfunding which occurred in the past and by variations in the investment results of their defined-benefit plans (companies with defined contribution plans don't have to deal with this, as the new standards don't apply to them). Reported net income will be affected both positively and negatively by these non-operating considerations.

These new methods will also affect the balance sheet. Financial Accounting Standard (FAS) #87 requires that companies compare pension fund assets and liabilities (accumulated benefits) on a plan-by-plan basis. If a plan has a net liability, that amount must be shown as a liability in the company's balance sheet. Plans with net asset balances, however, are ignored.

WHAT IS THE NET INCOME PER SHARE?

When you buy a stock on the market, you pay for it on a *per share basis*. Whether you buy 10, 20, or 100 shares, the important thing is what price you pay for each share. Thus it makes sense to know how much money the company is earning on a per share basis.

Almost all companies report their earnings in both total dollars and on a per share basis. Just in case you're wondering how the latter is figured, it is done as follows:

Net income (after taxes and after preferred dividends, if any) ÷ number of common shares outstanding.

In the case of Rum Dumb—which had 1 million shares outstanding—net income per share would be:

Net income of $10 million ÷ 1 million shares = $10 per share

Rum Dum management would no doubt deduct the nonrecurring income for you and show you that net income from operations is $7 million after taxes, or $7 per share.

As we'll see later, the relationship of a company's net income per share to its market price per share tells us a great deal about whether or not its stock should be bought.

WHAT IS THE "CASH FLOW" PER SHARE?

In Chapter 17 we discussed "reserve for depreciation," the accumulation of the periodic adjustments companies (or individuals) make in writing down their assets to realistic figures. There are various methods of computing depreciation: some companies use accelerated depreciation and write down their assets just as rapidly as possible, whereas others use the straight line method. A company that uses the former method is going to have *higher current depreciation expense and correspondingly lower reported earnings* than the company that uses the latter. Take Companies A and B, both of which just completed new plants costing $50 million. Company A decides to depreciate this plant very fast, and in the first year charges off depreciation expense of $5 million; Company B uses a slower method and incurs a depreciation expense of only $3 million for the same year. Because of this accounting decision, Company A is deducting $2 million more than B from its sales, and solely for this reason, A will have to report lower net income than B. But A is not really any less profitable than B, and therefore it should be obvious that an investor has to be conscious of depreciation expense in an income statement.

In order to compare companies like A and B more fairly, analysts use what is known as *cash flow—the total of net income after taxes plus depreciation.* As in the case of net income, it is important to compute this figure on a *per share basis.* In the case of Rum Dumb, cash flow per share would be:

Net profit (after deducting $3 million
    after-tax nonrecurring income) $7,000,000
Add depreciation   5,000,000

  Total cash flow $12,000,000
  Per share ($12 million ÷ 1 million shares) = $12

In the same industry, it is often very important to compare companies on the basis of *cash flow per share*. In extreme cases like that of A and B, cash flow per share can be the most realistic measure of comparison.

Cash flow has become more and more important to investors in all industries. Analysts have concentrated heavily on "free cash flow"—that which is available to management for anything from paying higher dividends to shareholders to buying back the company's stock, buying other companies, etc. Indeed, reported earnings may be far less significant than cash flow—hence you should understand its importance and utilize it in any common stock analysis.

CONCLUSION

You can easily learn what you need to know from a company's income statement. You now know how to judge a company's efficiency and how—in rare cases—you can profit from both too much of this and from spotting inefficiency (accompanied by a change in management or a change in philosophy). You also know how to uncover some hidden items and how to arrive at the all-important net income and cash flow per share. All of these are valuable tools for your future investing.

PART VI
How to Buy the Right Stocks at the Right Prices

20
What to Buy—Part One

Studies have shown that workers are happier when they have soothing background music while they work. Not only are they happier, they also get more work done, and this increased productivity leads to higher wages for themselves and higher profits for their employers.

In a way, the last few chapters have provided you with the "background music" for investing in the stock market. Your "productivity" should improve by knowing the few important facts I've emphasized.

But background music isn't enough. If workers haven't been properly instructed in how to assemble the product they're working on, the music will do them little good. In fact, it might just put them to sleep.

The same thing goes for investing. We've turned on the background music—now let's see how to assemble the product so you know *what to buy* in the market.

Knowing what to buy entails a fairly simple and very logical procedure. Actually, it's similar to buying a house, where your top priority is likely to be *location*. Regardless of its beauty, you're not going to buy it if it's located next to the city dump. The most logical approach to house hunting is to determine *where* you want to live and then find the property you want for the right price in this approximate location.

Buying stocks involves the same approach. The first thing to do is to find the best location for your money—that is, the *best industry*.

MY INDUSTRY APPROACH THEORY

Most of the mistakes made by stock investors stem from not giving proper weight to the industry in which a company is engaged. People get excited about companies for a variety of reasons, but in so many cases they could save themselves a lot of time, bother, and money by putting a magnifying glass on the industry involved. After all, even the very best company in a poor industry will generally be only a mediocre investment. And a mediocre company in a poor industry will usually be a very poor investment.

My industry approach theory emphasizes one basic rule: *Before you invest, be satisfied that the industry is attractive.*

The industry approach theory is not a new one. All security analysts are trained to use it. My theory involves asking a few important questions about the industry you are considering. Here they are:

1. *Is the industry growing?*

This is so obvious I'm almost ashamed to list it. The person considering an investment in International Buggywhip in the early 1900s—just when the automobile was going into mass production—should have known enough to ask this, too. His answer would certainly have been: No, this industry is not growing—it has reached maturity and will eventually be replaced by the advent of the automobile. Yet there were many who lost "Buggywhip money" at that time because they failed to ask themselves whether the industry was in its early stages of growth or had reached maturity. The same question exists today about steel (aluminum, plastics, and glass all aim at markets that now belong to steel), glass (plastics are penetrating more and more markets), rayon (newer synthetic fibers have made sharp inroads into rayon usage), and so on. Always ask this first important question about the industry you are investigating.

2. *How important are labor costs?*

It is said that there is nothing certain in life but death and taxes. Add "and higher labor costs" to this and you have a broader truism. The disadvantages of heavy labor involvement are obvious, starting with the broad generalization that the more people you have to manage, the more problems you have to overcome. In addition, heavy labor content industries often have to face stiff competition from countries with sharply lower wage standards and while many service-type industries with high labor content (like hotels, restaurants, financial and business services, etc.) may face little or no foreign competition, they still face strong obstacles. The fact is that companies with high labor charges have to depend on either (a) corresponding increased productivity from their workers, or (b) increased selling prices of their products, or they will see their profits squeezed in the future. Naturally there is no guarantee that they will be able to accomplish either of these remedies over the years. Therefore it is important to recognize the importance of labor costs in the industry you are considering.

3. *What is the pricing structure of the industry?*

Certain industries compete solely on the basis of the selling price of their products and are always waging "price wars" among themselves. Other industries are not subject to these wars because they have disciplined themselves (I am talking about firm price-policy groups that do *not* resort to collusion or price fixing), realizing that price wars are injurious to everyone involved.

Asphalt, plumbing fixtures, plywood, and most building materials are typical industries that often engage in price wars. The record shows that most companies in these industries have lacked the consistent year-by-year increases in profits to be found in certain other industries.

In contrast, consider Bristol-Myers at the time it brought Bufferin to the market. Here was a product that was intended to penetrate the aspirin market, so you might think that Bufferin was introduced at a price either under aspirin or at the same level. If it had sold *under* aspirin's price, then the aspirin producers might have been forced to cut their prices and down would go profits for all the companies involved.

Instead, Bufferin was marketed to sell *much higher* than aspirin and, of course, was a success. It did penetrate the aspirin market and it became a profitable item for Bristol-Myers. What happened to the aspirin producers? They subsequently *raised* the price of their branded aspirin and were, prior to the introduction of Tylenol, making as much money—or more—on this product than they did before the advent of Bufferin.

Proprietary drugmakers (proprietary drugs are those that can be purchased without prescription) have found that price is *not* the key to the success of their products. If the public thinks Bufferin or Pepto-Bismol or XYZ formula will accomplish the job in mind, the public will pay the price. For example, right now test your own "knowledge" of prices of nonprescription drugs that you might buy to relieve yourself of some discomfort. Think of products like cold pills, laxatives, pain relievers, cough medicines. Then see if you can pinpoint the selling prices of these products. Chances are that you won't be too accurate. Of even greater importance, however, ask yourself whether an extra dime or 20 cents or even 50 cents added to these product prices would cause you to switch to something else. If the products are any good at all, you'll be inclined to continue purchasing them, *despite price differences*. Of course, this type of loyalty is of great benefit to the manufacturers.

Another example of "firm pricing" exists in the dry cereal business. It is *not* price that apparently motivates cereal buyers most; consumers do not consider Rice Krispies as identical to Life cereal or Cheerios or whatever is most appealing at the moment. The breakfast food producers, sensitive to this, do not concentrate on lower pricing as a business-enhancing ploy.

The earnings records of companies heavily involved in such products bear this out, with the ability to show consistently rising profits over the years.

One of the fine examples of what makes a good investment and what makes a poor one emanates from a former "member of the club" of firm-price-structure industries. Norwich Pharmacal, though never the most dynamic proprietary drug merchandiser, had compiled a record of consistent growth over many years—and I used it (and its key product, Pepto-Bismol) as an example in lectures for many years. In contrast to the Pepto-Bismol, I would point to a carton of salt—which, of course, is a nondifferentiated product that lacks the characteristics emphasized above.

Lo and behold, one day in 1969 Norwich announced its

intention to merge with Morton International—the makers of—guess what?—Morton's salt (among other products).

I wrote Norwich management, told them I felt they were making a mistake, sold all the Norwich stock I had outstanding, and placed the money in "pure" companies that would not have to struggle with saltlike products. This was certainly the right decision as the Morton-Norwich company experienced poor operating results for the next seven years—and its stock fell from the $50 level to a low of $11! It wasn't until 1982, after management changes and an ultimate merger with Thiokol, that the stock surpassed its 1969 price.

'Nuff said?

Other industries that have at least a fairly "disciplined" price structure are: cosmetics, soft drinks, tobacco, and selective "service" areas.

4. *How easily can new competition enter the scene?*

A famous American industrialist made an extremely sage and interesting statement some years ago: *It is easier to make ten million dollars than to make a hundred thousand.* The comment was shocking to many people, but actually it made a great deal of sense. Why? Simply because there are relatively few people in the world who have the capital, the know-how, and/or the fortitude to engage in multi-million-dollar deals, whereas the world is full of individuals who are trying to make $100,000. How very true this is. And how valuable this lesson can be to investors—so valuable that I insist you keep it in mind at all times when considering an industry for investment.

Naturally you don't want to invest in an industry in which new competition can easily set up business and cut into your market. Be wary of what I call "garage" industries—ones in which persons can easily set up similar operations to yours, without substantial capital requirements. Invest instead in industries that require some real know-how, heavy capital, or control of important resources. In short, invest in industries where new competition is going to be scarce.

Some years ago there was a wild flurry for boat building stocks in the market. As sure as night follows day, I was convinced that this flurry would end in disaster for most investors. The reason: Small boats can be made locally for competitive prices by small operators and it was obvious that most glamour boat companies would soon fall by the wayside—which, in fact, they did.

5. *Is the industry cyclical? (Is it extremely sensitive to the business cycle?)*

I mentioned earlier that the Federal Reserve Board and other authorities endeavor to keep business on an even keel—with a gradual upward slope. Despite this, fluctuations are inevitable. Business is bound to have its ups and downs over the years.

Certain industries are very sensitive to changes in business conditions. When business in general is good, they may thrive. When business turns bad, they show rather drastic declines. I will discuss later how money can be made from buying and selling so-called cyclical stocks (those that are very sensitive to the general economy). I don't recommend that the average investor invest in many cyclicals because success from them requires great flexibility, which most investors lack. *Buying cyclical stocks entails making frequent decisions,* which are both difficult to time and hard to handle emotionally. When you buy cyclicals, you are competing with owners who for the most part are conditioned to frequent selling and who know how to anticipate cycles in order to maximize their returns. They are tough competition. Because of this, and because you, too, know that cycles cause volatility, you are less apt to be relaxed with your investment (and don't think that this is unimportant—after all, investing should bring you peace of mind along with a good rate of return).

This is not to imply that you can take a Rip Van Winkle approach to noncyclical growth-type stocks. However, the proper growth companies do allow you more time as a holder (i.e., less frequent buys and sells are necessary). Besides, their growth should bring steadily increasing dividends and less-nervous fellow shareholders.

Evidence of an industry's cyclicality exists in its past record. You should determine whether it has been subject to violent ups and downs. If it has, ask one question: Have enough changes occurred in the industry to eliminate these fluctuations?

If not, then you should beware! Or at least recognize what to expect and condition yourself to prosper from the volatility.

6. *What is the overall outlook for the industry?*

The answer to this question involves a summation of what we have just discussed plus many other factors influencing the future. Let your imagination help you decide what the future has in store. I recommend a "vacuum approach" to reach your conclusions. Put yourself in an emotional vacuum! Be completely objective about the pluses and minuses and decide what the overall outlook is for the industry you are considering. Later on—in Chapter 27—I will do some of this vacuum thinking for you.

CONCLUSION

By now you should be able to make a more practical decision about investing in an industry. If your conclusion is negative, then look elsewhere for your success—consider owning stock in a company in a more favorable industry environment. I can't stress the importance of this industry approach enough.

21
What to Buy—Part Two

MY COMPANY APPROACH

After you've decided that a certain industry is attractive for investment, the next step is to rate the company you are considering. I have compiled a few questions you should ask of every company you consider for investment.

1. *How good is management?*

Obviously management is all-important. A company is no better than the people who make its major decisions and form its backbone. There are endless examples of the difference good and bad management can make in an organization.

Perhaps the classic example is Montgomery Ward and Sears, Roebuck. In 1947 sales of Montgomery Ward were $1.1 billion and those of Sears amounted to $1.9 billion. Both companies had been battling for the consumers' business and both had achieved considerable success. Following World War II, however, the two companies differed enormously in their attitudes about the future:

Montgomery Ward was pessimistic about the future of the United States. Management felt a depression was right around the corner and that it was necessary to conserve cash and reduce operations so that overhead and expenses would be at a minimum.

Sears envisioned the opposite. It saw startling prospects.

The buying of almost all items had been curtailed during the war, so there was a pent-up demand for good merchandise. Now was the time to modernize existing stores, build new ones, expand into suburban shopping centers.

The results are startling. Here's what happened to Sears and Montgomery Ward from 1947 to 1967:

	Sales 1947 1967 (Billions)		Per Share Earnings 1947 1967	
Sears, Roebuck	$1.9	$7.3	$0.75	2.51
Montgomery Ward	1.1	1.9	4.43	1.31

And here's how the stockholders of these two companies fared over the same period:

	MARKET PRICE OF STOCK Mean Price 1947 1967		Percent Increase over 20 Years	Dividends per Share 1947 1967		Percent Increase over 20 Years
Sears	5⅞	52½	793%	$0.29	$1.20	314%
MW	28½	26	−8.8%	1.50	1.00	−33%

What a contrast—due solely to a difference in management philosophy and know-how. There are countless other illustrations of companies engaged in identical fields whose sales performance, earnings, and dividends—and stock performance—are as different as day and night. In the vast majority of cases, the difference between success and failure is attributable to management and management alone.

Perhaps you're wondering how you can judge management from your living room chair. Well, there are many ways of doing this. First of all, your broker may be able to help you. His firm may have research people who call on various companies throughout the year and who can provide a first-hand "feel" about management through the research reports they publish. There are many caveats for you to consider in relying on such reports, however. Analysts commit errors too, and some have conflicts of interest which hamper their objectivity. Furthermore, if too many of these "researchers" share a common belief, unanimous popularity may be creating too many buyers and too few sellers—the classic definition of "too high a price." Second, read the annual report of a company you are analyzing, so you can get your own "feel" of management and its ideas and planning. There are many other management guideposts, among them: stress on research, ability to bring out new products, trend of profit margins, and trend of sales and profits.

A word of caution: Remember that management is inclined to be biased; it is bound to be optimistic about how the company is managed, how it can market products, and so on. Research reports, annual reports, and the like should all be read with this bias in mind.

2. *How good is the company's research?*

As you know, research is the backbone for the future. Top companies generally possess strong research teams and put a strong emphasis on R&D. Here are a few hints in analyzing a company's research:

A. Is the company spending a higher or lower *percentage of sales* on research and development than other companies in the same industry?
B. How many new products has the company developed successfully in the past few years?
C. What percentage of last year's sales came from products recently introduced?

Don't think research is important only to glamorous industries like electronics and chemicals. It's equally important in even the most conservative food company. What allowed Procter & Gamble to outperform its competitors for many years? Strong research and new product development, for one thing. Actually, heavy R&D spending in some industries is more a matter of survival than great growth potential. If product obsolescence is rapid and/or if competition is simply "overspending," the R&D you see may not portend at all the future it suggests.

Still, the future lies with those who prepare for it. The

efficient research companies will continue to outstrip their competitors, so give this element strong consideration when you are considering a company for investment.

3. *Is the company diversified?*

As you know, it's dangerous to put all your eggs in one basket. Likewise, it may be dangerous to own companies that have only one product. Someone comes up with a better mousetrap and you're out of business.

One interesting example of a company that was one-product for many years is Clorox. Here was a well-managed business making a product that had become a household word. Yet Clorox Chemical lived under a "one-product black cloud." If someone developed a capsule that when dropped into a gallon of water made a bleach like Clorox, the latter's extensive bottling facilities would become relatively obsolete. Here was a risk that Clorox stockholders faced every day of their lives— whether they knew it or not. Like most one-product companies, Clorox eventually merged with another company (in this case, Procter & Gamble) and stockholders finally could breathe easily with good diversification. (Later P&G was forced to divest itself of Clorox and the latter became an independent entity again— after which management moved into numerous areas to diversify.)

Most companies have sought diversification in recent years. But some have "overdiversified," entering a variety of industries on a helter-skelter basis—i.e., the so-called conglomerates. It's a difficult job indeed for management to become familiar with the ins and outs of many businesses and be able to make correct decisions for all. Some companies have been able to succeed in a multitude of businesses and have built admirable records. For the most part, however, the burden of proof rests with the optimist. There are many obstacles to overcome, and failure and mediocrity are far more common than dramatic success among conglomerates.

Diversification generally has been most successful when it has fit a pattern: diversification in related businesses. American Home Products is a good example. This fine company diversified from drugs into foods and related household products. This makes sense, because drugs and foods go to similar markets, take similar merchandising, distribution, and production. Success is not so difficult to achieve when diversification is in a related field.

4. *What new products does the company have?*

It's certainly unnecessary for me to tell you to watch for new products that might suddenly increase a company's sales and profits sharply. Yet I would be remiss if I didn't list this as a factor to consider.

Some new products are easy to observe. In the 1960s the smoker shift to Kent cigarettes provided an obvious boom for Lorillard. In the 1970s the same kind of enthusiasm for Marlboro hyped the earnings of Philip Morris. Polaroid's Land Camera had the market all to itself until Kodak entered it in 1978. Gatorade introduced a special niche into the beverage industry in the 1970s. The automatic pinspotters produced by AMF and Brunswick pretty much revolutionized bowling—and created profits for these two companies for half a decade. Automatic teller machines produced a five-year bonanza for Diebold in the late 1970s and early 1980s. Prescription drug companies are constantly seeking (and achieving) new product penetration that can lead to bonanza profit periods for them.

Other new products are not quite so obvious, but can be equally important. Ages ago (in the late 1950s) a company considered to be dull and suitable mainly for income (not growth of capital)—Otis Elevator—had a bonanza from the conversion of manual to automatic elevators. Hewlett-Packard's sophisticated calculators, introduced in the mid-1970s, may have been too complicated for most people—but they created huge profits for the company. All types of computer products provided investment opportunities in both the manufacturing companies and those supplying the components (semiconductors) throughout the past decade.

5. *What kind of patent protection or specific know-how "protects" the company from outside competition?*

This is as apparent as the preceding point, but has to be mentioned. DuPont had the synthetic fiber market to itself for many years, until other companies developed their own processes. Minnesota Mining's Scotch Tape patent protected it for many years. Kimberly-Clark's "pop-up" Kleenex patent allowed it to get a hold on the tissue market. Owens-Corning was one of the few companies in the country that had the know-how in production and fabrication of fiberglass. Xerox's advanced office copying literally destroyed companies that offered only wet-process machines. Once others developed the dry-process, however, Xerox's domination faded.

These few examples point out the importance of patent protection and know-how in analyzing a company's strength.

6. *How well does the company control its costs?*

As we saw in the discussion of profit margins, some companies operate far more efficiently than their competitors. It goes without saying that an investor will fare much better with an efficient company than with one that is a bit sloppy in controlling the costs of doing business. Some companies have better manufacturing plants, some have more efficient labor, some boast greater distribution capability of their products, and some know how to control their inventories better. These factors should be prime considerations in analyzing an individual company and I urge you to consider them. There is an additional important factor that can affect cost control: *How dependent is the company upon others for raw materials, etc.?*

Confucius might well have said: "Person who depends on neighbor for sugar three times a week will eventually drink unsweetened coffee." Just as a person will be more secure not depending on other people for everything, a business that is less dependent on others is better off.

Thus, in looking at prospective investments, give more consideration to self-sufficient companies than to those at the mercy of others for their existence. These self-sufficient ("fully integrated") companies have the following advantages:

A. They have control over their resources.
B. They are not as vulnerable to shortages. Example: Chrysler, after some very lean years, finally came up with a model car in 1959 that was slated to be successful. But then its glass supplier got involved in a drastic strike. Result: Chrysler had another bad year.

C. From the standpoint of reported profits, certain companies with their own resources can choose which resources to use at what time and thereby "fix" their reported profits. Example: Certain forest products companies, which own huge timber holdings. When plywood prices are low, they may be able to cut low-cost timber and thus may show better profits than those without this flexibility.

D. If inflation re-emerges, natural resource companies (such as those owning timber) should see their reserves worth more and more over a long period of time.

E. Companies that have to buy from others have to pay their suppliers a profit—a profit that would be their own if they did the work themselves.

Naturally there are notable exceptions to this reasoning. A company such as Bristol-Myers, for example, does not want to tie up its capital and management in the production of containers for its product. For one thing, it prefers the flexibility of being able to switch to whatever container it desires—which it might not do if it were tied to its own manufacturing output. In other words, management concentrates on producing the right products and putting the most efficient merchandising behind these. The small profit paid to someone else for the right container is insignificant in relation to the central goal.

7. *What is the company's past record and future outlook?*

In many cases, a company's past record will provide a clue to its future outlook. Therefore, just as when you analyze the overall outlook for a specific industry, you should start out by looking at a company's past record and ask: "What, if anything, makes this company's outlook any different today from what it has been over the past three or five or ten years?"

If the answer is, "Nothing is any different," then you may be able to project its future pattern. Conditions, however, are seldom static in this world. Thus, you have to consider all the previously mentioned factors to conclude whether the company's rate of growth will be faster or slower than its recent past.

CONCLUSION

You are now prepared to assess whether the *industry* you are considering is attractive and whether the *company* within this industry is for you. Does this guarantee you a successful investment? No. Because your timing in buying the stock may be wrong.

Our next step, therefore, is to determine when a stock should be bought and when it is overpriced and should be sold.

22
What Tools to Use

Earlier I discussed some yardsticks you should apply in analyzing the stock market in general. I hope you will use these yardsticks, but I feel it is equally important to learn when individual stocks are too high or too low. After all, there are times when individual stocks will rise sharply while the general stock market is declining—and just as many times when individual stocks will fall while the market in general is rising.

You're probably aware that there are a multitude of yardsticks and ratios that can be used in analyzing stocks. Actually I don't think it necessary that you bother yourself with most of these.

We've already discussed balance sheet analysis and decided that the various yardsticks given can be used to bolster your confidence in a company or to warn you of certain dangers. We concluded that the balance sheet can be the determining factor mainly when market price is below either stated book value or what might be termed "going concern value."

One problem for the book-value stock buyer is that most companies that sell at big discounts from liquidating value do so for a reason; oftentimes they are not particularly well situated competitively, or they are very cyclical or they are not particularly well-managed. So, in many cases, it is like buying property that is *not* in the very best location. Still, buying assets "cheap" is one very legitimate strategy—one that reaped big profits for investors in the early to mid 1980s—and it should not be overlooked.

Most common stock purchasing, however, is done on the basis of owning sound businesses that seem to have attractive future prospects. Here, there are three major yardsticks to consider, namely *yield, market price in relation to earnings,* and *cash flow.* Let's look at these separately.

YIELD

"Yield" is a word describing "annual rate of *income* return on your investment." This is figured by *dividing the yearly dividend rate of a stock by its present market price.* Thus a stock paying $4 per year in dividends and selling at $100 gives an annual rate of income (yield) of 4% ($4 ÷ $100 = .04 or 4%).

This is like figuring your return from money in a bank savings account or similar money market instrument. If you deposit $100 and keep it there a year and the bank pays you $6.25 interest, the yield is 6¼% on your money.*

Many investors place great weight on yield in deciding whether a stock should be bought or not. This is fine if current return is your investment objective. If you have to depend on dividends from your stocks for your everyday living or for necessary "luxuries," then yield should be your major consideration in buying stocks.

Oddly enough, most investors don't really need the dividends right now. Most people are looking to the future. They are more interested in building up capital and *future* income than in present yield.

If growth of capital is your objective, *give only limited consideration to yield.* If you have invested your money in a growing company, it may be better that they do *not* pay out high dividends now. Here's why:

1. If dividends are paid to you, you will have to pay income tax on them. Under the present tax structure, this could amount to as much as 30–40% (including state taxes) of the dividend income, payable to the government in your next income tax filing.

---

*Actually you will get slightly more than 6¼% if the interest is computed more than once a year.

2. You may spend the dividends and not "let them ride" and compound for you.
3. If you don't spend them, you may not be able to reinvest the dividends at the same high rate that the company could invest them for you. Most growth companies earn 10–20% (and some considerably higher) return on their invested capital. The question follows: Can you invest this dividend money (especially the amount left after your tax payment) and earn rates of return as high as the 10–20% *company* return on capital? If you place the after-tax income from dividends into some sort of savings acount which pays a lower return than the company earns, you are better off delaying receipt of those dividends.

If it's growth you want and you're looking to the future, deemphasize dividends and yield now. Most important, consider annual growth of your capital as the major part of your "annual return" equation. Take what is called a "total return" (income *and* capital appreciation) approach to your investing.

Yield, of course, can be very important in a declining stock market. It can provide a "floor" for your stock and limit your downside risk. Take a stock paying a $1 annual dividend and selling for $16 on the market, for a yield of over 6% ($1 ÷ $16 = .0625 or 6¼%). If that $1 dividend is safe, isn't there a minimum market price you can count on? If it declines to $10, the $1 dividend gives a 10% yield, which might be awfully high compared to savings instruments, bonds, or other common stocks (other than the very mature industry groups such as utilities and steel). Perhaps the lowest the stock might go is 12½ or so, because the yield there would be 8%—and this might be high, too. In other words, because of the (safe) $1 dividend, you can feel secure your stock will not decline below 12½. If there is no dividend on the stock, you may not be able to pinpoint downside protection. Who knows, maybe the stock will go to 10 or 8. Yield, therefore, can be an important consideration if you cannot afford much risk in your investments.

The above illustrations also indicate how yield *can* provide some *temporary* appreciation in stocks. The example of the stock that declines to 12½ (with a secure $1 dividend) is a case in point: the very high yield of 8% attracts considerable interest from investors, and before long this "bargain" stimulates buying and the stock recovers—perhaps back to the 16 level or higher. The rise from 12½ to 16 (a gain of almost 30%) may be due to yield and yield alone. The trouble is that this rise will probably constitute the major part of the stock's appreciation potential, *unless the company's earnings are growing*.

As you can see, I contend that *the best defense is a good offense*. Buy a stock that you think is a good value and that you feel confident will go up in price. If you're right and the stock goes from $16 to $20, $25, or $30, then your worries about it going down to $12 or even $16 should diminish.

It is difficult, of course, to have your cake and eat it. High-yielding stocks generally lack significant growth potential. As a matter of fact, they *generally indicate weakness*. The statement "it looks attractive because it's paying X% yield" is often a trap. Usually:

1. The outlook for the industry or the company is very poor and there are few good reasons to buy the stock.
2. Or the dividend is *not* adequately covered by the company's earnings—i.e., the present dividend rate is *not safe*.

Many years ago a friend called me and asked about Waldorf System common stock (then listed on the New York exchange). He was interested because Waldorf stock was selling at 16½ and paying a $1 annual dividend, for a yield of over 6%. I looked at this company and found that it was in the restaurant business, which at that time was not a particularly productive field. I noted Waldorf's earnings for the preceding five years, which were as follows:

1955	$1.01 per share
1956	.90
1957	.98
1958	.91
1959	1.08

The company had exhibited little growth over this period; unless there were some new developments on the Waldorf scene, or unless the company's book value suggested it should be owned for merger or liquidation of assets reasons, the stock held little attraction for growth. The stock's major attraction was its $1 dividend, which, as my friend pointed out, gave a yield of over 6%. But was the $1 dividend secure? Definitely not! First of all, Waldorf was paying out $1 in dividends out of a bare $1.08 in profits. Only a minor decline in Waldorf's business would place earnings *below* the $1 dividend and place it in jeopardy of being reduced.

Furthermore, a check of Waldorf's earnings for the first few months of 1960 indicated the profits were running below the 1959 levels. Now it was doubtful that there was *any* coverage of the $1 rate.

After appraising Waldorf's business and discovering that the dividend was not well protected, I advised my friend against investing in the stock. Only a few months later Waldorf was forced to reduce its quarterly dividend from 25 cents to 15 cents; the $1 rate had suddenly become only 60 cents, and that 6% yield had faded to 3.6%. It wasn't long before Waldorf stock reflected the new unattractive yield and fell to 11½.

Remember, then, that there is usually a good reason for a stock offering an exceptionally high yield—and it is normally a mistake to reach for the highest yields. I have a motto that sums it all up: If growth of capital is your goal, concentrate on *outcome,* not income.

WHAT YARDSTICK SHOULD YOU USE?

If you were to buy a business or a property, the price you would be willing to pay would normally reflect *the present and potential earning power* of the business or property.

Common stocks should be bought the same way. You should buy them based on their present earning power and most particularly based on what you believe they should earn in the future.

To do this, you should emphasize one ratio—the *price-earnings multiple*. This is not a new yardstick; in fact, it has been the backbone of security analysis for years. But the applications of this multiple have changed considerably over the years.

My application of this yardstick is somewhat different, and it will help you decide when a stock is a good value and when it is overpriced in the market.

The Price-Earnings Multiple

The price-earnings multiple is simply the relationship between a *stock's market price and its earnings per share.* It is arrived at by *dividing a company's earnings per share into the market price of its stock.* For example, suppose Company A earned $1 per share last year and Company A stock is selling for $10 per share. The price-earnings multiple is 10:

$$\$10 \text{ Market price} \div \$1 \text{ Earnings per share} = 10$$

Let's suppose that Company A had earned $2 per share instead of $1. What would the price-earnings multiple (let's call it P/E from now on) be?

$$\$10 \text{ Market price} \div \$2 \text{ Earnings per share} = 5$$

Naturally you'd rather buy Company A stock at $10 with $2 earnings (P/E of 5) than with $1 earnings (P/E of 10). Thus you can see that the *lower the P/E multiple, the more value you are getting.*

Another way of looking at this is to say that the P/E multiple tells you how many years you will have to wait to recoup your investment *if earnings remain the same in the future.* In Company A's case, if it continues to earn $1 per share each year, it will have earned your $10 market price back in ten years (remember, 10 was the P/E multiple, or as we say in our business, "the stock is selling at 10 times earnings"). If Company A earns $2 per share every year, you will only have to wait five years to have your $10 market price earned for you.

Naturally the quicker your investment is earned back, the better for you—which is another way of saying that the *lower* the P/E, the better.

If companies earned the same amount of money every year, it would be easy to decide which stocks were the best buys: you would simply compute the P/E and buy the stocks with the lowest ratios. The trouble is that companies do *not* earn the same amount of money year after year. There are always fluctuations, either up or down. Thus *you can't buy stocks on the basis of existing P/E alone.*

Instead, *the price you pay for a stock should depend on what you expect the company's profits to be in the future.* Let me show you the vast difference between four theoretical companies, all of which are now earning the same $1 per share—but which are going to grow in very different fashions over the next ten years. The first of these is a *supreme growth company,* with an expected 30% annual compounded growth rate over the next ten years; the second is a *normal growth company,* with a 10% annual growth rate; then comes *stable company* (no change in earnings expected at all), and the *stagnant company,* which is going downhill.

Here's how these four will change in this ten-year period:

Year	Supreme Growth (30%)	Normal Growth (10%)	Stable (no change)	Stagnant (declining)
Base Year	$ 1.00	$ 1.00	$ 1.00	$1.00
First	1.30	1.10	1.00	.95
Second	1.69	1.21	1.00	.91
Third	2.20	1.33	1.00	.87
Fourth	2.86	1.46	1.00	.83
Fifth	3.72	1.60	1.00	.80
Sixth	4.83	1.76	1.00	.76
Seventh	6.28	1.94	1.00	.73
Eighth	8.16	2.13	1.00	.70
Ninth	10.61	2.34	1.00	.67
Tenth	13.79	2.57	1.00	.64
TOTAL EARNINGS FOR THE TEN YEARS	$55.44	$17.44	$10.00	$7.86

What amazing differences between these four companies. *Supreme* earned a total of $55.44 over the ten years, which is more than 3 times what *normal* earned ($17.44), about 5½ times what *stable* earned ($10.00), and over 7 times what *stagnant* reported ($7.86).

In addition, take a look at the difference in earnings per share *in the tenth year. Supreme* is earning $13.79 per share in this year, which is over 5 times *normal*'s $2.57, almost 14 times *stable*'s $1.00, and over 21 times *stagnant*'s 64 cents.

It is obvious that you should be willing to pay a far higher market price for the *supreme growth company* than for the others; by the same token, you should pay more for the *normal growth company* than for the other two; and you shouldn't be interested in buying either of the latter two, *if growth is your objective.* Note that you could have paid $50 or even $100 per share for the *supreme growth* stock in the first year and only $10 for the *stable company* (5 or 10 times as much for *supreme* as for *stable*) and still had a far better investment from the growing company. So it is obvious that *you should be willing to pay a premium in the marketplace for growing companies.*

But just how much? How does one know whether one should pay 7, 10, 15, 20, 40, 80, or 100 times earnings for a growing company?

One answer lies in my *compounding growth theory.*

A COMPOUNDING GROWTH THEORY

Guesswork will always have a lot to do with the stock market, but it is amazing how stock prices *eventually* revolve around their basic values. Rates of return demanded by investors—competitive with returns from other investment vehicles—are important determinants of stock prices. But both the general market and the evaluation of individual securities also adjust (in time) to what kind of growth is in store. Low P/E multiples evolve when growth rates are falling, and high P/E's result from an acceleration of profits.

For example, at the time of *Primer*'s first edition, I

computed the growth in profits in the United States over the fifteen years that followed World War II—and then did the same for the companies constituting the Standard & Poor's 425 Stock Industrial Index. I found that the figures coincided at about 4% (growth) per year. Then I looked at the stock market itself over the previous decade and found that its average multiple of earnings was around 14½ times. Thus investors had been willing to pay around this multiple for an average of 4% growth.

Some years later I recomputed the growth in profits, this time using the 1951–1965 span. I found that earnings were going up approximately 6% per annum and that the market had adjusted to this acceleration and had averaged around 16 times earnings over the period.

Let's see whether there is a common thread running through all this. To make it simple, let's substitute an individual company for the whole market and see what five years of growth at various rates do when we start with a base year's profits of $1 per share—and then apply the kind of average multiples described above both to the base year's earnings and to those five years hence. Here is the way 4%, 6%, and 7% growth companies would look:

Annual Growth	Base Year	Fifth Year	Market Price Paid for	
			Base Year	Fifth Year
4%	$1.00	$1.22	$14.50	$11.88
6%	1.00	1.34	16.00	11.90
7%	1.00	1.40	17.50	12.50

The interesting statistic here is contained in the last column on the right, where all the figures cluster around $12. Thus, whereas the price of $14.50 was paid for $1.00 earnings for the 4% growth company in the base year, that $14.50 amounts to a price of $11.88 for the $1.22 earnings in the fifth year ($14.50 ÷ $1.22 = $11.88). The same thing goes for the 6% and 7% companies. *The purchase price amounts to approximately 12 times earnings at the end of the fifth year.*

Using these assumptions, let's see what market price an investor should pay for a company growing at a 10% compounded rate. Here's the way a 10% growth company's record will look over five years:

Earnings per Share

Now	$1.00
First year	1.10
Second year	1.21
Third year	1.33
Fourth year	1.46
Fifth year	1.60

Earnings per share will be $1.60 in five years. Using the assumption that 12 times earnings in the fifth year is a reasonable price, today's investor might be willing to pay a market price of $19.20 per share (12 × $1.60 = $19.20). Thus, whereas we paid $14.50 for the 4% growth company, we might pay around $19 for this 10% growth stock.

Now let's look at our *supreme growth company*—with a 30% rate:

Earnings per Share

Now	$1.00
First year	1.30
Second year	1.69
Third year	2.20
Fourth year	2.86
Fifth year	3.72

Multiply 12 times the $3.72 earnings (12 × $3.72 = $44.64) and we find that we should be willing to pay almost $45 for this stock compared with $19 for the 10% company and $14.50 for the 4% stock.

Setting this up mathematically, here is what we should be willing to pay for stocks according to their projected rate of growth over a five-year period:

Company's Expected Annual Rate of Growth (%) in Earnings per Share over Next Five Years	Multiple You Should Be Willing to Pay
5	15.4
10	19.2
15	24.0
20	29.7
25	36.6
30	44.5
35	53.7
40	64.3
45	76.7
50	91.0

There is one glaring problem with accepting the mathematics and conclusions on price-earnings multiples just shown: *Competitive interest rates from bonds and other investments are bound to change from the long twenty-year period used as the basis for the formula*. Whereas, for example, interest rates through most of the 1950s and the early 1960s were in a range of 3½ to 5%, we found ourselves in 1980 with the competition of 11–15% high-grade bond interest rates. By 1987, rates were back down to 7–9%. *On this basis alone, the multiples shown should be cut by about two-thirds*. Therefore, at any point in time, the investor has to make adjustments to our mathematical table depending on competitive rates from bonds and other available vehicles.

There are other factors to consider in this or any other evaluation table. One is the difficulty at projecting growth rates over any period. Because of this, other changes should be made to the pure mathematical formula.

First of all, I vigorously warn you not to assume companies will grow at rates like 20–50% a year indefinitely. After all, *the areas that promise such growth invite competition* and this competition will no doubt cause a reduction in the growth rate of almost all participants in the field.

Second, many companies currently growing at 20–50% rates are smaller companies that don't have to show very large increases in their business *at the beginning* to grow at high rates.

For example, a company with $20 million in sales need add only $10 million the next year to show a 50% increase, and perhaps just one or two new products will add this $10 million. As the company expands, however, it takes larger and larger increases in volume to continue this growth rate. Once this same company reaches $100 million in sales, it has to add a whopping $50 million the next year to keep up the 50% growth rate, and this may necessitate bringing out more new products than it is capable of doing.

Third, the industries that are showing the fastest growth rates are often in some phase of technological advancement and are dependent on new discoveries to realize their growth. The industries that are advancing at slower rates may be depending mainly on population increases or gradually changing habits of consumers—and these are more reliable than technological breakthroughs. The spending on health and beauty aids is an illustration of a dependable growth pattern, which is why you can project with more assurance the growth rate of American Home Products, Johnson and Johnson, and similar companies than those that are now *apparently* in this 20–50% growth class.

For these reasons, I insist the pure mathematical table on p. 186 be changed. (A new table is presented to you in Chapter 24.) The P/E multiples for companies projecting unusually rapid growth should be lowered. And the multiples should be altered on the basis of varying competitive interest rates from high-grade bonds. Each case has to be considered on its own merits, with particular attention given to varying *risks* being assumed, but you have to be pretty certain of your growth projections to pay more than 12 or 15 times earnings for a stock.

But there's another reason why you can't rely on a mathematical table alone. Investors, being human, may appraise two companies with identical growth patterns in entirely different ways. Take Company A and Company B, both earning $1 per share and both expecting to grow 10% a year. You may find Company A stock at one level, and Company B stock substantially higher or lower than that (Co. A) price. Of course, the discrepancy could reflect a higher quality of earnings (i.e., greater cash flow or simply more conservative accounting) for one versus another. The main reason for a discrepancy, however, probably hinges on the tenuous factor of *glamour* (yes, you read it correctly—that fleeting, volatile factor of glamour!).

My method for making maximum gains in the stock market combines qualitative, quantitative, *and* emotional elements. Before concluding, let's explore the emotional aspects of buying stocks a bit further.

23
Sex Appeal in Stocks

The past few chapters have taught us how to judge what to buy and what price to pay. It's mainly a matter of:

1. Choosing the right industry.
2. Selecting a good company in this industry.
3. Paying a price that is reasonable in relation to the company's present earning power and, most important, its potential profits.

All of this assumes that investors are completely objective in buying and selling stocks. Nothing could be further from the truth! Human beings live by their emotions, and it's tough to shut them off suddenly when investing.

Have you ever seen a movie and "fallen in love" for ninety minutes with the glamorous leading lady (or if you're female, with the handsome leading man)? Psychiatrists tell us it's not abnormal to fantasize this way, but I ask you: Did you, during the whole ninety-minute movie, even once consider whether your love of the moment could cook, fix the car, raise a family, or provide any of the countless characteristics necessary for a life of more than ninety minutes?

Stock buyers fall in love with stocks, too (though the love lasts more than ninety minutes—sometimes it lasts a lifetime). But the analogy doesn't stop there. Just as you'd gladly pay $50 to meet your favorite movie star, you might feel cheated paying $1 and only meeting her press secretary. Because of *glamour*, investors are willing to pay a premium for some stocks while others remain in the "$1" category.

Because of emotional influences, stock prices often get out of line with their growth rate. Why, for example, did Minnesota Mining and Manufacturing sell, in 1973, at around 35 times earnings (which, according even to the mathematical table that has *not* been adjusted for higher interest rates, meant the company should have been growing at a 25% yearly rate) when MMM's growth rate over the five-year period 1967–1972 averaged only 10%?

There were then, just as there have been historically and just as there are in 1987, many reputed growth stocks like MMM that sold (sell) at higher P/E multiples than their recent growth rates would seem to dictate. Going back to 1973, let me show you the astronomical premiums paid by investors for MMM and five other "thought-to-be-blue-chip" companies, adjusting the mathematical table for interest rates at that time (these were about double the levels of our computations on p. 186).

Stock	Annual Compounded Growth Rate over Five Years 1967–1972	P/E Ratio They Should Sell at Based on Growth over These Five Years on a Pure Mathematical Basis	Approximate P/E Ratio at Which They Were Selling in 1972
Corning Glass	1%	?	30
Eastman Kodak	9%	9	35
International Business Machines	14%	11½	35
Minnesota Mining and Manufacturing	10%	9½	35
Avon	14%	11½	55
Sears, Roebuck	9%	9	27

All these stocks were selling at significantly higher prices than their recent growth rates dictated. The reasons for this were:

1. Their names alone indicated strength in the minds of investors.

2. They were recognized leaders in their respective fields—all of which were glamorous at that time.

3. They had experienced growth over a long period of time, and they had proved their ability to make money "through thick and thin." In most cases, heavy depreciation charges were causing earnings to be understated (but certainly not so understated as to narrow the gap meaningfully between the "mathematical P/E" and the existing P/E.

4. They were recognized as well-managed enterprises.

5. Investors were counting on continued success in the future.

6. They were on approved investment lists of banks, insurance companies, pension funds, and other large institutional investors. They were consistently purchased by these investors for their long-term benefits and this constant demand kept their market prices higher than "normal."

Because of these six points, investors felt more confident owning these stocks than other not-so-well-known companies. Buying them seemed like buying a home with an underground bomb shelter. These stocks provided—*in the minds of their owners*—a shelter against attack from outside competition, from recessions and depressions, from all sorts of catastrophes. Buying these stocks had always proved profitable, so why not keep betting on a winning horse!

Results from these six stocks over the next ten years were, frankly, terrible. They experienced a real comeuppance because they had been overpopularized and because growth *expectations* had been far too ebullient (as a matter of fact, both Avon and Sears had serious interruptions in their growth and their fundamental outlooks are being questioned today).

These examples typify both the success and the failure that can emanate from glamour. On the success side, these six stocks—and many others—went through long periods in which they were upgraded; and this glamour produced significant gains for their holders. Failure came when the glamorization process simply went too far and/or when fundamentals deteriorated.

A sensible philosophy emerges from these examples: Avoid paying large premiums for glamour, but do not neglect it entirely. Very well situated companies, especially those in fields with bright futures, will indeed command higher P/E's than mathematical computations might suggest. In the next chapter we will discuss just how much investors might rationally expect from glamour. Now let's discuss the overall philosophy.

To begin with, there are many non–blue chip stocks that have also sold way out of proportion to their recent earnings growth experience. In these cases, the premiums paid by investors emanate mainly from an expectation that future growth will be even faster than recent growth. This projection of accelerated growth may or may not be a figment of investor imagination. Only time will tell. In the meantime, such stocks sell way above what one might expect because of their glamour status. Needless to say, overpriced stocks such as these carry substantial risks; if projections fail to materialize, these stocks can "fall out of bed" sharply and the sellers' exit can get mighty crowded.

At any rate you can see the importance of judging what kind of glamour status a stock might take on. The human mind can do strange and interesting things; it can place rockets *and* stocks into orbit.

Look, for instance, at the common stocks of Automatic Canteen (the vending machine company now known as Canteen Corp.) and Merchants Fast Motor Lines (a trucking company operating almost exclusively in the state of Texas) as they appeared in early 1961. I choose these two because five years earlier their per share earnings were almost identical. Here's how they grew from 1956 through 1960:

Year	Automatic Canteen	Merchants Fast Motor Lines
1956	$ .67	$ .61
1957	.72	.64
1958	.76	.80
1959	.91	1.18
1960	.73	1.40

Perhaps you'll be surprised to learn that even though Merchants grew more consistently and twice as fast, Automatic was selling in early 1961 for 3 times the market price of Merchants. At $45 per share, Automatic commanded a P/E multiple of about 60; while Merchants ($15 per share) sold at little more than 10 times earnings. The difference was almost solely due to sex appeal. Automatic's vending machine business had captured the imagination of the public (whose judgment, incidentally, is most often wrong), while the trucking business had no such glamour, hence the very wide disparity in price between the two stocks. This happens to be an extreme example—a case where one stock was simply *over*glamorized and the other *under*glamorized. As a matter of fact, Automatic subsequently dropped in half from 1961 to 1965, while Merchants increased some in value. Extreme as these two illustrations may seem, I could cite scores and scores more— and provide many more exciting reevaluation-upward situations than Merchants'. What the Automatic versus Merchants comparison shows, of course, is what glamour, or lack of same, can do to a stock.

A more mundane but worthwhile comparison is of two fine companies, Emerson Electric and Philip Morris. Here are the earnings and P/E multiples for the two over the 1970–1980 decade:

Year	Emerson Electric		Philip Morris	
	Earnings per Share	Mean P/E Multiple	Earnings per Share	Mean P/E Multiple
1970	$1.15	24	$ .80	12
1971	1.19	32	1.01	15
1972	1.32	33	1.17	20
1973	1.54	29	1.36	22
1974	1.66	20	1.58	15
1975	1.74	19	1.81	14
1976	2.05	18	2.24	13
1977	2.47	13	2.80	10
1978	2.93	12	3.39	10
1979	3.37	10	4.09	8
1980	3.72	10	4.63	7

You can see that Emerson sold at a higher P/E than Philip Morris in each and every year, despite the fact that Philip Morris's profit growth was vastly superior (the latter's earnings grew from 80 cents per share to $4.63 or almost 6 times, while Emerson's $1.15 in 1970 about tripled to $3.72 in 1980). The reason: Cigarettes and beer (Philip Morris) have far less glamour than the image of electrical equipment (Emerson).

It must be obvious by now that investors have to assess a *stock's potential glamour appeal as well as its expected growth rate* in determining what P/E multiple it should (or might) command in the market. By combining what we have learned in the last two chapters, we are now ready to lay out a guide for selecting the all-important "proper P/E."

BENEFITING FROM LACK OF SEX APPEAL: USING INVESTOR POPULARITY AS A REVERSE INDICATOR

Understanding how sex appeal and glamour can affect P/E multiples is crucial to your ability to buy and sell securities more efficiently and profitably. As positive as favorable industry or company image can be, too much of accepted glamour is dangerous. After all, excessive sex appeal leads to high valuations (high P/E's and high market prices), and the more of this that exists the more risk there is for the disappointment which creates lower P/E's and lower market prices.

The corollary to this is *the wisdom of so-called contrary investing.* Indeed, most of history's best investors have had an attraction for the contrary—for securities which are not highly regarded or which may be either overlooked or "despised" by most investors. Prior chapters have stressed the importance of assessing the prospects for industries and companies and emphasizing those with the best of these prospects. Remember, however, that *the price you pay is crucial, too.* In future chapters, you'll find examples of many different types of investments, all the way from owning already-recognized leaders in their fields to the uncovering of unrecognized stocks. It bears repeating that some of the very best opportunities come from the latter (unrecognized or unpopular) group.

What can you do to improve your abilities to be "wisely

contrary"? One way is to utilize computer or other screens to locate stocks which sell far more inexpensively than others based on either dividend yield, P/E, cash flow, book value, etc. (to be covered in Chapter 25). Another is to tune your sensitivities to "popularity." Are the brokerage research reports on a given company unanimously very positive or negative? Are the people around you talking mainly with similar "beliefs" or forecasts? Is there a frenzy in the market itself which suggests extreme likes or dislikes? If you can spot such extremes—such feelings of unanimity—you can normally benefit from this *if you can retain objectivity and recognize that the extremes have probably already created unrealistic and undeserved prices.* To say that extremes create excesses seems like an unnecessary truism, but this is an important principle to embrace if you are to be a successful investor. Again, most very successful investors *ARE SKEPTICAL OF EXTREME POPU-LARITY AND ARE CONSTANTLY WORRYING ABOUT THIS* (by being ready to sell) *JUST AS THEY ARE CONSTANTLY SEARCHING FOR THE UNDISCOVERED OR UNAPPRECI-ATED* (where they are tempted to buy).

As you read further, remind yourself that such contrariness is a positive. It will be difficult to build a portfolio of fine growth companies with a totally cynical attitude; but you stand a far better chance of making money and finding interesting investments if you recognize that sex appeal in stocks can be a volatile and fleeting thing. Assess the potential for glamour, but develop both the strength to buy stocks when they are out-of-favor and to sell them when they are overpopularized.

24
My Compounding Growth Guide

Since the stock market's earliest days, investors have been seeking a guide that will tell them when a stock should *definitely* be bought and when it is too high and should definitely be sold. Despite claims to the contrary, unfortunately there will never be such a *guaranteed* system! If there were, the stock market would almost cease to exist, because those stocks that showed as buy candidates by the infallible system would be bought by everyone and sold by no one—and no market would be needed. By the same token, those stocks the system signaled as sell candidates would find few buyers.

Still, investors have to rely on some methodology to determine value. To help you here, I have developed a guide that I believe will be extremely useful to you in making buy and sell decisions. I call it my Compounding Growth Guide.

My Compounding Growth Guide combines the elements described in the last few chapters. Your judgment is, of course, needed. You have to decide the approximate rate of growth expected for the company you have in mind over the next few years, and you have to determine whether the company's glamour appeal is *super, above average,* or only *average.* Once you have determined these, my guide will provide reasonable P/E ranges for you.

Let me emphasize again that this is *only a guide*. It is not a formula for guaranteed profits. The market is too fickle for such a thing. The guide makes no representation that a stock that looks too high will not go a lot higher in price. Even if you're dead right in your assessment of a glamour status and annual growth rate, you can still be wrong. Look at Studebaker stock in 1959. No line of reasoning would have prompted a sensible investor to buy that stock anywhere along the line on its rise from 10 to 29¼. And yet that's where the stock went. (Of course, it reversed itself sharply and dropped back to 8 within the next year.) Situations like this repeat themselves again and again. In 1983, for example, a raft of technology stocks sold at lofty multiples of both earnings and *sales* per share—so far beyond reasonable expectations that they were doomed to massive declines.

The guide is not all-inclusive. It is based on growth in earnings, competitive interest rates, and market psychology, but an investor has to be flexible with its use. The guide will help you to conclude what market price range is warranted for a stock, but you must remember that the general market can fluctuate substantially—sometimes to the extreme of great optimism or pessimism. In other words, the guide provides the market prices that investors should be willing to pay for the various growth rates *as an average.*

The main value of this guide is that it *will force you into organized thinking and into judgment based on value.* As I will repeat again and again in this book, buying *value* is the best guarantee for success in the stock market.

There are obviously many considerations affecting value—influencing the "proper P/E"—but let me talk about three that should be coordinated with the guide.

The first is obvious: *risk.* It stands to reason that two companies with basically similar past and future projections should sell at vastly different valuations if they carry divergent risks. Because of this, wise investors are constantly assessing the potential dangers that lurk in every stock. As you can imagine, this assessment is far from exact. The fortunes of industries and individual companies are bound to change—some positively and some negatively—and as they do, so should the prices of their securities. Our glamour-status approach is a constant reflection of this. Inherent in our Emerson Electric/Philip Morris example is the fact that investors are more apprehensive about cigarettes and the health issue than they are about electrical equipment; so the lower P/E on Philip Morris is really based on a combination of little glamour (from cigarettes) *and* the risk that the smoking hazard will curtail usage much further.

A list of risk elements to be considered would include:

1. Industry cyclicality (the more stability, the better).
2. Company stability (including management capabilities).
3. Financial structure (cash position, debt burden, amount of leverage).
4. Accounting conservatism.
5. Dividend-paying ability, cash-generating nature of the business.
6. Price volatility of the stock itself. (In recent years academicians and investors have emphasized what is known as Modern Capital Theory—part of which included a judgment of risk by what is termed "Beta," a statistical measure of a stock's volatility in price relative to the general market. Betas on individual stocks can be very deceptive, however, and the subject is too involved for discussion here. Suffice it to say that past relative market action is not necessarily indicative of the future. On the other hand, investors should include in their assessment of risk some conviction of the kind of volatility that it is practical to expect. Obviously, the more volatility there is, the more one has to weight higher risk. Let me repeat, however, that this is just *one* consideration in risk assessment—and the more "fundamental" factors, such as points 1–5 above, demand greater emphasis.)

A second consideration that should be factored into our guide is *trend of institutional ownership*. A stock that is widely held by pension funds, insurance companies, banks, and investment trusts already has attracted a lot of the demand side of the supply/demand balance that determines market price. And while such institutional support may be no more than an indication of attractive prospects for the security in mind, an investor has to play devil's advocate and query: if the stock has already attracted this large demand, what can we expect for an encore? What happens if these large holders lose enthusiasm? Wouldn't that create a huge amount of stock for sale and lead to sharply lower prices?

The answer is, of course, that a shift in the supply/demand relationship will indeed lead to lower prices. Hence we have to exercise some caution whenever we note broad institutional ownership. The corollary is that if we find what we believe is a very attractive stock and discover it is "underowned" by large holders, we can "dream a little" and postulate the positive effects on the stock if it suddenly attracts this kind of buying.

To conclude, "overownership" raises the fear of potential selling and a resulting lower P/E; and vice versa. Once again, high-quality growth companies deserve premium multiples and it would be surprising if they did not attract ownership by large investors. But you should be aware of the consequence—the unraveling of demand or an increasing supply—should the recognized qualities come into question. All of which means that you should make some sort of adjustment in your P/E figuring for the underownership/overownership situation as you perceive it.

The same sort of adjustment has to be made for our first consideration—risk. If obsolescence is a possibility, if the industry is cyclical, if the financial position of the company is weak—if there is simply a greater-than-average risk involved—then adjust the P/E downward, maybe only 5% or 10% for a slightly risky company to perhaps 50% for a very speculative venture.

Back to the institutional support overlay. You are probably wondering how you can get the proper inputs. The Standard & Poor's Stock Guide tells you how many institutions own each security and in what amounts, as do the William O'Neill service (Los Angeles, California) and *Value Line*.

Our third responsibility, already discussed, is to determine how the competition against common stocks has been altered by either higher or lower bond interest rates. For example, 1969 and most particularly 1970 brought sharply higher interest rates on fixed-income securities. Whereas a few short years before an investor could get only 5% or 6% on bond investments or from similar nonequity securities, rates of 9–10% suddenly became plentiful. This posed severe competition for common stocks. Investors had to have confidence that 12% or higher could be achieved through stocks in order to consider them attractive relative to the 9–10% "riskless" yields available from bonds. This meant that price-earnings multiples deserved to be lower than normal—something that obviously deserved some downward reevaluation of the Compounding Growth Guide. The competitive situation worsened further by 1980, with interest rates skyrocketing to almost 15%. Because of the importance of competitive interest rates, the following Compounding Growth Guide shows different "deserved" P/E multiples for three sets of interest rates: the 3½–5% area that prevailed through most of the post–World War II era; the 8–9% that prevailed from 1969 to 1975 and would prevail again in 1986–87; and the 11–15% rates prevalent from 1975–1980. The range between the three (that is between 5% and 8%, or between 9% and 11%) can be extrapolated easily by you. At any rate, here is our guide:

MY COMPOUNDING GROWTH GUIDE

THE P/E MULTIPLE YOU SHOULD PAY FOR A

Company's Expected Annual Rate of Growth in Earnings per Share over Next 3–5 Years	Super Glamour Company When bonds yield			Above-Average Glamour Company When bonds yield			Average Glamour Company When bonds yield		
	3½–5%	8–9%	11–15%	3½–5%	8–9%	11–15%	3½–5%	8–9%	11–15%
5%	18–20	9–10	6–7	15–18	8–9	5–6	10–15	5–7	3–5
10%	20–25	16–18	8–9	18–20	13–15	7–8	16–18	9–12	6–7
15%	25–30	21–24	10–12	20–25	17–20	9–11	19–20	13–16	8–9
20%	30–35	24–30	13–15	25–30	21–23	12–14	20–25	16–20	10–12
25%	35–40	30–35	16–19	30–35	25–30	15–18	25–30	20–25	13–15
30%	40–45	35–40	20–23	35–40	30–35	19–21	30–35	25–30	16–18
35%	45–50	40–45	24–26	40–45	35–40	22–24	35–40	30–35	19–21
40%	50–55	45–50	27–30	45–50	40–45	25–28	40–45	35–40	22–24
45%	55–60	50–55	31–33	50–55	45–50	29–31	45–50	40–45	25–28
50%	60–65	55–60	34–36	55–60	50–55	32–35	50–55	45–50	29–31

HOW TO USE THE COMPOUNDING GROWTH GUIDE

The guide is simple to use.

1. Look at the past record of the company you are considering and approximate its rate of growth in earnings per share over the past three to five years. (I show you how to arrive at a company's annual compound growth rate in the Appendix. I suggest you familiarize yourself with the method now.) Naturally you will want to check the growth rate over the most recent year or two, to see whether the trend is increasing or tapering off.

2. Determine if there is any reason for the company's basic trend to change.

3. Consider any new elements in the company's outlook (new products, larger production facilities, added competition in its field, etc.).

4. Decide whether these new elements will increase or decrease the company's previous rate of growth.

5. Arrive at a reasonable growth rate for the next three to five years (barring any drastic recessions in the economy).

6. Decide which glamour category the company deserves.

7. Consult the Compounding Growth Guide and see, according to its expected growth rate, competitive bond interest rates, and glamour status, what approximate P/E multiple is suitable for the stock.

8. Assess the company's approximate risk along with the stock's institutional ownership. Subtract for high risk and overownership.

9. See what P/E multiple the stock is now selling for.

10. Conclude whether the stock should be bought or not. If the present P/E is lower than the guide indicates it should be, the stock is undervalued and should be bought. If, on the other hand, the stock is selling at a higher P/E than the guide indicates, the stock is overvalued and should not be purchased.

Now let's see how effective the guide can be and go through some examples of its use.

EXAMPLE I. A. Let's look at General Foods stock as it appeared in 1960—and then in a number of years thereafter. In 1960, the company's most recent six years looked like this:

Year	Earnings per Share
1959	$2.48
1958	2.21
1957	1.99
1956	1.81
1955	1.66
1954	1.33

Following the steps outlined, here is the way General Foods could have been analyzed in 1960.

1. General Foods has shown a 13% annual compounded growth rate since 1954. (Again, see the Appendix to compute a company's annual compounded growth rate.) In this case, it is figured as follows:
   a. General Foods has shown an increase in earnings per share of 86% over this five-year period ($2.48 − $1.33 = $1.15; the $1.15 increase ÷ the $1.33 base year figure = 86%).
   b. In the Appendix glance across column A of the table till you come to "5 years."
   c. Look down the "5 years" column until you come to 84% (the nearest figure to 86%).
   d. Glance to the far-left B column and you will conclude that an 85% growth over five years amounts to a 13% annual compounded growth rate.
2. There is no reason for any change in the company's basic trend (population is still increasing, consumers are eating better and spending more on convenience foods, etc.).
3. Just as in the past, the company will introduce new products, and General Foods' established lines (Postum, Post Cereals, Jell-O, Maxwell House Coffee,

Baker's Chocolate, Calumet Baking Powder, Minute Rice and Tapioca, Birds Eye Frozen Foods, etc.) will provide consistently growing volume.

4. The rate of growth may decrease slightly because it is reasonable to assume that other food companies will enter the "convenience" market. Also, GF's heavy dependence on coffee makes it vulnerable to commodity fluctuations; and competition is building up in this area.

5. A 10% rate of growth seems reasonable for the company.

6. GF should probably command a glamour status of Above Average. While foods in general do not generally create great excitement in the minds of investors, GF's stress on convenience products, its well-regarded management, and its consistent record over the years warrant its receiving something of a premium. Result: A stature of Above Average (not as high as Super Glamour).

7. The Compounding Growth Guide shows that the high P/E for Above-Average Glamour is 20 for a 10% growth company under the 3½–5% interest rate competition that existed at that time. Therefore you will use 20 as a P/E starting point.

8. GF qualifies as a low-risk company because of its noncyclical business—so this is a plus for our table. The stock had decent, but not excessive, institutional support, with about 300 institutions then owning about 8% of its stock. This should lead to a higher multiple—by about a 2–5 increment. Thus GF stock "deserves" to sell at about 22–25 times earnings.

9. GF stock was selling around $50 per share. In 1959 the company earned $2.48 per share; therefore the stock was selling for just over 20 times earnings ($50 ÷ $2.48 = 20.2).

10. GF is selling at 20 times earnings, whereas our conclusion in point 8 was that it should sell at 22–25 times earnings. Since the stock was selling below what we deemed it should, it qualified as a slightly undervalued situation and thus we conclude that it could be purchased.

RESULT: Over the next year and a half, GF stock rose steadily. It went to 25 times 1961 results of $2.90 per share, or up to around $75. Then it proceeded to go way beyond these figures—up to the 30–35 times multiple range.

B. Now look at GF stock as it appeared in the five years following 1960:

Year	Earnings per Share	Market Prices of Stock
1965	$3.73	89⅞–77½
1964	3.44	93¼–78¼
1963	3.34	90½–77⅝
1962	3.14	96 –57¾
1961	2.90	107¾–68⅝
1960	2.69	75½–61½

Without covering all the details as shown above, the record of General Foods through this period is indicative both of how value rules in the long run and how our guide can be useful in both the purchase and sale of stocks. In 1962 the median price of GF was $78; for 1963–1965 the median was $84, $86, and $84, respectively. In other words, each time the stock rose past 25 times earnings, it ran into selling pressure. As a matter of fact, the stock's median P/E for the years 1962–1965 was as follows: 24.5, 25.2, 24.9, and 23.3.

C. And here is how GF stock looked in 1965:

Once again shortening the procedure used in A we should start with the company's growth for the latest five-year period. GF showed profits of $2.69 per share in 1960 and $3.73 in 1965. This amounted to a 39% advance or, according to our Appendix, a 7% growth rate. This diminution in growth had relegated the stock to no more than Above Average status; a look at our guide indicates that 7% growth for such a company, under the 3½–5% interest rate column, is only worth a P/E of about 18 times. The company still appeared to be low risk, which would have added to the 18 P/E. Institutional support, however, had increased some, raising fears of overownership. Thus we should cut back the 2–5 increment to around 2, giving us a P/E target of about 20 times. Multiplying this by the $3.73

earned for 1965 gives a price of only $75 (20 × $3.73 = $75). The stock looked to be overpriced in the $80 range, unless there were new developments to alter the future outlook.

RESULT: GF stock ran into considerable selling pressure through the 1965–1968 period as its growth rate diminished. The year 1966 showed only a 5½% increase over 1965; the 1967 increase was only 3½%; and 1968's was just 2%. As you can imagine, the P/E slipped along with the growth rate. Furthermore, interest rate changes would have forced an investor to shift P/E to the 8–9% column in our guide. Even if one believed GF could grow 5–10% per year, the maximum P/E for an Above-Average Glamour company would have been 15 times—and the range would have indicated a possible multiple as low as 8 times if growth rate were deemed to be more like 5%. So, whether it be a diminution of the growth rate or an increase in competitive interest rates from bonds, GF common was obviously slated to become a disappointing investment— which is just what occurred in the 1965–1980 period.

EXAMPLE II: Assessing Capital Cities Broadcasting as our firm did originally in 1975 and on through what turned out to be a very profitable ten-year holding period. Following is CCB's record as we considered the investment in 1975:

Year	Earnings per Share
1970	$0.90
1971	0.98
1972	1.15
1973	1.31
1974	1.43

1. CCB's increase from $0.90 to $1.43 was 60%, or 12½% per year compounded.
2. There was little reason to question the company's growth prospects. Management was proven and highly respected; and the outlook for broadcasting and newspapers appeared very attractive.

3. Management expressed continued interest in acquiring media properties which it planned to upgrade and improve profitability.

4. Since CCB had achieved the 12½% annual growth despite a severe economic slowdown (recession) in 1973–74, there was every reason to expect better results in the future.

5. A higher growth rate of 15–20% appeared to be very likely, especially since the company was still fairly small and the number of its shares outstanding was small, too.

6. Although Super Glamour image was certainly attainable, it was very safe to assume a minimum of Above Average Glamour.

7. In the 1975 environment of approximate 11% interest rates, a 15–20% Above Average Glamour company, according to our guide, deserved a P/E multiple range of 11–14.

8. With little debt on its balance sheet and with the media business then lacking much cyclical (downward) exposure, investors could feel quite secure with forecasts of future profitability. Institutional interest was not yet high on CCB, thereby increasing the prospect for additional buying interest in the future. This could add an additional 5 to the multiple, giving the prospect for a 16–19 P/E range.

9. CCB was selling at $15.00 per share, or at about ten times last year's E.P.S. results ($15.00 ÷ $1.43 = 10.5). Actually, profits for 1975 were expected to be around $1.65 per share—so the P/E was only 9 on this basis.

10. The stock appeared reasonably priced on all counts. It was selling below its "deserved" P/E of 11–14, even without allowing for the potential elevation of its Glamour image or increased institutional demand. CCB stock, therefore, certainly looked undervalued.

RESULT: The company exceeded all earnings expectations over the next five years, with E.P.S. rising from 1974's $1.43 to $4.68 in 1979. This 274% increase amounted to an astounding 30% compounded annual rate; and yet, despite the stock's advance from $15.00 per share to almost $50.00, the P/E was still around 10 times. Interest rates had risen over this period, but our guide continued to signal how attractive it might be. Six years later, in 1985, E.P.S. had more than doubled from 1979's $4.68—to $10.82— and the stock price had risen above $200.00 per share. At long last, it was accorded a P/E of almost 20 times. Fortunately, therefore, CCB investors were able to feel confident throughout eleven years of ownership; at no time had the stock exceeded the top part of the 16–19 P/E range, despite the fact that both Glamour image and institutional demands increased significantly over this period. All these factors, along with higher growth than forecast, allowed us to be relaxed holders even though our original purchase price was multiplying (with the stock eventually up more than ten times over cost).

EXAMPLE III: An analysis of Hewlett-Packard Company common stock in mid-1961. Here is Hewlett-Packard's record from 1956 to 1960:

Year	Earnings per share
1960	$.11
1959	.10
1958	.07
1957	.07
1956	.05

Now we will evaluate Hewlett with the use of our guide.

1. Hewlett's earnings per share had grown 120% over this four-year span ($.11 − $.05 = $.06; $.06 ÷ .05 = 1.20 or 120%). The four-year-column for a 120% growth (see Appendix) shows a figure of 22%. Thus Hewlett-Packard grew at a 22% compounded annual rate over this period.

2. The company's basic trend should not change. Demand for electronic measuring instruments should continue to increase and Hewlett's reputation for quality is almost unchallenged.
3. The company will continue to bring out new products. In addition, Hewlett is interested in making acquisitions, any of which will no doubt increase its earnings per share.
4. Balancing these elements against the realization that as a company gets larger it is more difficult to sustain very high growth rates, one might conclude that H-P's rate over the next three to five years will approximate the past.
5. A growth rate of 20–25% seems attainable.
6. The company certainly deserves a Super Glamour rating.
7. A 20–25% Super Glamour company is entitled to a P/E of 30–40.
8. Risk was about medium for the company. H-P seemed to be advanced over its competition, but one had to assume potential obsolescence. Hewlett was at that time gaining institutional support—something that was fostered by a recent listing on the NYSE. This support, from a low base, might add an extra 5 to the multiple. Thus the stock should command a 35–45 P/E.
9. At the then-current price of $12, H-P stock was selling at an astronomical 110 times earnings ($12 ÷ $.11 earnings = 110).
10. It should be obvious that the public had inflated H-P stock. Despite the conviction that the company represented a solid and exciting vehicle in a rapidly growing field, the present price was simply "too rich."

RESULT: Certainly we did not need any guide to tell us that the stock was overpriced at that time and that it should be sold. Perhaps the thinking *process* described here, however, would have corrected the dangerous emotionalism that had obviously led to an overvalued stock.

A better proof of the value of our guide comes from an appraisal of its use in years subsequent to 1961. Just to trace the facts, H-P stock dropped from the $12 level to around $8 in a six-month span. Quite interestingly, a full five years after 1961 the stock was selling at $9. By that time the company's earnings had risen to 28 cents per share—for a 21% annual growth rate (over the five years). The then-$9 market price amounted to 34 times the 28-cent profit. Finally the stock had hit buying levels according to our guide (which concluded that it deserved 35–45 times earnings). And from there the stock proved to be a good value as it advanced to the equivalent of $22 in 1968, and on to almost $50 in 1973.

This $50 price was more than 50 times the 95 cents H-P earned in 1973, once again signaling that the stock was overpriced. According to our guide, we should have been a seller of H-P as it rose past $40. It subsequently fell to $28 in the 1974 bear market, then rose to $60 in the ensuing recovery in 1975, and then declined again to $30 in 1978. Let's see whether this $30 price looked like a bargain in that year.

Here is H-P's record from 1973 to 1978:

Year	Earnings per Share
1973	$0.95
1974	1.54
1975	1.51
1976	1.62
1977	2.14
1978	2.64

Company growth from 95 cents to $2.64 per share amounted to 178% over the five years, or (according to the Appendix table) a 22½% annual growth. Interest rates had, however, risen to about 10% in the United States, which according to our guide would have justified about a 17 P/E. (Remember, the higher the competitive interest rates the lower the "deserved P/E"!) Multiplying the $2.64 earnings per share by 17 indicated an approximate value of $45. Thus H-P stock looked (very) attractive once again—which is exactly what it turned out to be. Over the ensuing five years from 1979 through 1983, H-P stock price (adjusted for splits) rose sharply. The company's earnings jumped over 33% in 1979 and then progressed steadily over the next few years, finally slowing to 10% growth in 1983—as shown:

1979	$0.86
1980	1.12
1981	1.28
1982	1.53
1983	1.69

The 1983 investor had cause for real skepticism. The company's five-year increase of 96% meant an 18% compounded growth rate and the latest year was experiencing an increase of only half that. Competition in the computer markets and a shortening of product life cycles had begun to crimp earnings growth. With interest rates in the 11–15% range, even an optimistic 18% growth company "deserved" only a 12–13 P/E range. H-P stock, trading at $40, appeared overvalued with a P/E of well over 20. At the time of this writing (1987) H-P stock had exceeded its 1983 levels, despite a strong rally in the general market. In other words, the stock was overvalued (priced too high) in 1983 even though its P/E was well below its historical standard.

EXAMPLE IV. Here is an analysis of one of my favorite growth companies of the past, Bristol-Myers, using as a base the year 1961, which was a top for the general market over the next few years:

Year	Earnings per Share
1960	$1.03
1959	.85
1958	.73
1957	.68

1. Bristol-Myers earnings grew from 68 cents in 1957 to $1.03 in 1960; this increase of 35 cents amounted to a 51% increase over this three-year period ($.35 ÷ $.68 = .51 or 51%). The Appendix shows that a 50% growth over three years (Column B) amounts to a 14½% annual compounded rate.

2. There is no reason for any change in the company's basic trend.

3. A flow of new products, plus continued strong demand for existing lines, plus steadily rising product prices, equals a good outlook.

4. Conclude that these elements will at least retain—and possibly enhance—the growth rate.

5. A 15% rate of increase is a reasonable expectation over the next three to five years.

6. Management image of this company is supreme; thus it is a Super Glamour stock.

7. A Super Glamour company with a 15% growth rate deserves 25–30 times P/E under prevailing (low) interest rates.

8. The company's business seemed to carry very low risk. Its institutional support was medium (193 owning about 11% of the company) but seemed to be growing. The combination of low risk and accumulation by large holders was enough to add perhaps a 5 P/E to the 25–30, giving a 30–35 "deserved" multiple.

9. Bristol-Myers stock is selling for $35 per share. In 1960 the company earned $1.03 per share. Dividing this $1.03 into the $35 market price gives a multiple of 34, right in line with our conclusion of 30–35 times above. Therefore the stock can still be purchased with the expectation that appreciation percentages will about parallel the company's earnings growth from here on.

RESULT: Four years later the company's net income had risen from the $1.03 figure to $2.65 per share. This increase of 157% over the five years was actually slightly above a 20% compounded gain. Over this period BMY stock rose from the $35 figure of 1961 to $95, an increase of 171%. The P/E based on 1965 earnings was 35.8, a slim premium over the 30–35 times range that our guide would have indicated a full five years earlier. Purchase of Bristol-Myers stock did work out well—and it did about parallel the company's profit growth.

EXAMPLE V. Let's see whether our approach would have helped in the buying or (all-important) holding of what was once one of the nation's great growth companies, Xerox. Assume we were considering the stock sometime *after* the introduction of the 914 office copier in mid-1963. In the case of Xerox, it would be deceptive to go way back in the company's history and establish a growth rate; obviously the 914 precipitated a new pattern. In 1962, the first year of sizable deliveries of the 914, Xerox earned 72 cents per share. By 1963 quarterly results indicated that profits would rise to the $1.10–$1.20 range, up almost 60% over the previous year. Thus:

1. Xerox was apparently growing at a fantastic rate; many analytical projections pointed to a 50–60% compound growth rate over the next three to five years.
2. The above projections were feasible to substantiate because of the rental nature of Xerox's business.
3. New elements would obviously come into the Xerox scene (i.e., extensions of the 914, new products based on Xerography, etc.).
4. Certainly it would be difficult to anticipate a greater average rate of growth than 50–60% compounded because competition would no doubt build up.
5. Keeping our fingers crossed, we might have concluded that a figure of 50% was possible, realizing, however, that this high a rate could never be sustained for a very long period of time.
6. No question about glamour status for this company: Super.
7. 50% growth with Super Glamour allows multiples in the 60–65 range when interest rates are very low.

8. Despite the technological nature of Xerox's business, risk appeared to be quite low, because of the company's very advanced position vis-à-vis its competition. On institutional support, I could not determine figures for 1963—but 223 institutions owned about 16% of Xerox's outstanding shares a full three years later in 1966. So the stock was probably in its early stages of accumulation—especially since Xerox was "the only game in town" for an investor who wanted photocopy exposure in his portfolio. Conclusion: Could add a 5 P/E to 60–65 range.

9. Xerox stock at $60 per share was selling at 50–55 times the $1.10–$1.20 per share earnings forecast for the current (1963) year.

10. Despite the apparently astronomical multiple, Xerox stock was still within buying range and actually cheaper than our guide would indicate it deserved to sell at the moment.

RESULT: Xerox stock was, of course, a profitable performer over the next few years. In the following year (1964) profits rose from the $1.13 reported for 1963 to $1.88—an advance of over 66%. The stock proceeded to sell as high as almost $132 during the year; high as this looks, the resulting multiple of 70 times was still in the ball park of our 65–70 P/E conclusion in point 8 above. The year 1965 saw Xerox earnings rising to $2.78 per share, up 48% over the previous year; during this year the stock jumped to the $200 range—but once again the multiple was around 70 times.

Obviously the assessment of a company such as Xerox involves considerable guesswork. The risks of being wrong about growth rates are large, as evidenced by what happened to Xerox stock over the past ten to twelve years as the company's dominance in the copying field diminished. Our guide would have dissuaded you from owning Xerox over this period, just as it encouraged ownership through some very profitable early years (despite the stock's carrying what looked like a very rich P/E to many). Actually, the history of Xerox stock since 1965 is rather interesting. Although it doubled between 1965 and 1972, this was due to the enthusiasm (overenthusiasm) for a select number of growth-type stocks that rose in 1971 and 1972 to exorbitant P/E's *relative to their growth rates*. Our guide would not have allowed us to stay aboard for this "ride" since the very maximum P/E for a Super Glamour 15% growth company (which Xerox had become by the early 1970s) would have been 21–24 under the then-prevailing interest rates. Even adjusting to a 25–30 range would have forced you out in the late 1960s. In getting out then, you would have missed a 30–40% move in the stock—but this kind of move to unrealistic prices is something not to rely on in stock ownership. Actually, Xerox stock sold in 1986 at about the same level it did back in 1965!

Thinking of P/E's anywhere near 60 or 70 seems ludicrous today. Interest rates (even the 7½–9% levels of mid-1986) are approximately double those of the mid-1960s; and extraordinary growth rates are much harder to come by, due to slower economic growth and greatly heightened foreign competition. Only a tiny minority of stocks command P/E's exceeding 25—which frankly is the way it should be. High P/E's obviously leave little room for disappointment—and they should be accorded sparingly.

Time now for some additional and very pertinent comments about the use of our Compounding Growth Guide.

First of all, as the examples indicate, be sure to key into your thinking the level of earnings expected for the *coming* year or two. Last year may well be an indication of the future, but it is ancient history as far as the stock market is concerned. Be sure to relate the present P/E to the immediate future—not to the past.

Second, you must continuously reassess your stocks against this guide (or any other). Time flies and conditions change; and your success hinges on staying current and anticipating the future. This means monitoring your earnings estimates continuously—and reassessing market prices and their potentials according to the new figures. Most important, it is your responsibility to determine whether your growth rate expectations are on the beam or whether the company's pattern is changing.

Third, you can see from the examples that our guide is

valuable mainly in evaluating *growth companies*. The next chapter will show the guide's usefulness in four specific money-making areas in the stock market, but many areas defy analysis by our guide. Nongrowth stocks, for example, generally sell on a basis of either yield or asset value (since there is no definable growth rate). In addition, typical cyclical stocks are difficult to evaluate with a guide such as this; and certain industries have a heavy bias toward some deeply entrenched historical basis and do not generally sell at prices that reflect annual growth rates.

Last, I want you to realize that there is method in my madness of choosing very high P/E stocks as examples in this chapter. I did so because the premium multiple equities are often the most difficult for people to buy (their fear that the premium might disappear inhibits them). Stocks that are cheap on earnings (i.e., 5–8 times earnings) do not pose the same "psychological block" as those that were in the 25–30 range when interest rates were low, or are in the 10–20 range when there is much greater fixed-income competition. Obviously, it would have been simpler for me to present a raft of examples pinpointing the wisdom of purchasing stocks at 5–8 times earnings (as a matter of fact, I provide such examples in the next chapter). By outlining the right procedure for buying growth companies, which unfortunately are rarely found at dirt-cheap multiples, and by understanding how money can be made in stocks that carry relatively high P/E's, too, I believe I have given you a well-rounded and sophisticated approach.

Needless to say, this approach requires judgment on your part. But then, what successful endeavor does not! Furthermore, remember (again) that the stock market is not as precise as any formula or guide might make it out to be. I have felt it essential, however, to prove the point that the key to long-range success is in *paying the right price for what should be reasonably expected to occur in the near future*—and this is what my guide helps you to do. Over the long term, your largest stock market profits should come from companies that *are* growing, and the Compounding Growth Guide should be very valuable to you in assessing these growth companies correctly.

PART VII
How to Make Money in the Stock Market

25
Five Paths to Big Profits

The Compounding Growth Guide will help you to consider a company's growth rate against various interest rate conditions, and show you the effect of public psychology and institutional support on a stock's price. The guide will allow you to analyze companies of differing qualities and quantities.

Correctly used, the guide will help you to buy good values and to sell those stocks that have run up beyond a logical judgment of their intrinsics. The guide revolves around value, and in the stock market value will eventually prevail.

Let me show you five major ways to make money in the stock market and indicate how the Compounding Growth Guide is useful in all but one of these approaches. Let's consider these five paths to big profits separately.

PATH NUMBER ONE: CYCLICAL STOCKS

Buying "cyclical" stocks when they're at the bottom of their cycles.

Most industries go through definite cycles over the years. They have several years of very good business and then fall into the doldrums for a few years. Most cyclical industries parallel the business cycle: when the economy is rolling along at high speed, they prosper famously, but when the country's output starts slipping, they face sharp cutbacks. Automobiles, heavy machinery, copper, steel, and airlines are some of the foremost industries that follow the economy in this way.

Other industries have their own cycles—not necessarily in line with business in general. Building (which can get a boost when *lower* business activity forces the Federal Reserve to promote easier money and lower interest rates), farm equipment, and insurance (fire and casualty) are a few cyclical industries that fluctuate in their own way.

All of these cyclical industries lack a strong enough growth trend for their products to overcome this sensitivity to ups and downs. You can be pretty certain that when business is booming, it will not be too long before the cyclicals are slipping once again. Automobiles are a perfect example! Autos are "durable goods"—they can be made to last a long time if necessary by their owners. When you run out of food, you have no choice but to buy more, but when your car runs down, you can make it workable by a motor overhaul, new brakes, and a set of tires. Thus, people are not compelled to buy new cars. They do so in vast quantities when times are good, but when business and/or employment sloughs off, new purchases can be deferred. You can see from this that new car sales may enjoy one, two, or even three good years in a row, but it is almost inevitable that the booming sales will be followed by a decided dip, at least temporarily. Auto sales, then, are extremely sensitive to the changes in the business cycle and auto stocks must be classified as "cyclical."

This gloomy picture does *not* mean that people cannot make money in auto or other cyclical stocks. They can. Stock prices will respond to these cycles. Take steel, for example. When production is falling, steel stock prices generally go lower and lower and lower. Then it's only a matter of guessing how low steel production will go and *buying* a steel stock sometime *before* production improves drastically. (Remember, the stock market is always looking ahead. If you wait for production to rebound sharply, steel stocks will already have experienced a good part of their rise.)

The trouble with cyclical stocks is that you *do* have to plan to sell them, frequently, for maximum profits. Steel stocks are a buy when production is at very low levels, but they should be sold when the operating rate is very high. After all, what more can you expect when the industry has attained an operating level of 90–100% of capacity? Certainly not 150%.

Our Compounding Growth Guide will *not* help you in buying and selling cyclical stocks because the growth rates are so erratic that they cannot be depended on. Instead, you have to approach cyclical stocks by acting directly opposite to the way business is. You assume investors are not trained to buy when things are bad (on the contrary, they are probably selling their stocks in a state of panic), and then you have to fight your own emotions and *sell these stocks when things look their very best*.

This takes flexibility and strong convictions—and a special sophistication. After all, just as the most opportune time to buy cyclicals is when they are at high P/E's (when their business is soft and profits are almost nonexistent), cyclicals usually have to be sold when their P/E's are low in relation to expected, but peak, results. It is not easy to buy stocks when the news is bleak and P/E's look high, and it is even more difficult to sell them when everything looks rosy and they look cheap.

The other negative about cyclicals is that a person will probably do better to buy companies with stronger inherent growth trends which you don't have to be so nervous about selling at the first blush of prosperity. Your chances for big gains are enhanced, especially in contrast to the smaller after-tax profits generally made by buying and selling cyclical stocks.

PATH NUMBER TWO: MANAGEMENT "PLAYS"

Buying companies that have new, more aggressive, more efficient management.

Many companies are held back by poor management. With an infusion of new blood, the profit picture can change tremendously. Safeway Stores (see Chapter 19) was a good illustration of this, although not nearly so dynamic as Crown Cork and Seal, Toys R Us, and some others over the past few years.

Beckman Instruments is another example. Here was a strong research company with many glamorous products. Management made the mistake of becoming so interested in research that it neglected the backbone of success—profits. Earnings in 1956 were $1.36 per share; by 1957 they had slipped to 16 cents per share, and by the end of that year the company was operating at a loss. Beckman stock had followed this trend: from a high of 47¾ in 1957 the stock had sunk to a low of 18⅛. The time had come for a change in managerial philosophy, and Beckman's board of directors set about to make just such a change. Some personnel changes were made and a complete housecleaning was accomplished. While these changes were being made, Beckman remained in the red and ended up the 1958 year with a loss of 70 cents per share. By the end of this year, however, the company started "turning the corner" and profitable operations were foreseen. In 1959 Beckman earned $1.30 per share and in 1960 net income was a fat $2.25. By that time, Beckman common stock had soared to over $100—a wonderful 5 times higher than its low of just two years before.

Our Compounding Growth Guide will help you to decide what price to pay for these "new management" companies. *In these cases, however, the past record is not a reliable indication of what lies ahead, so the proper procedure is to pick a normal earning power for the company and project a growth rate ahead for it in determining what price to pay.*

Let's look at International Telephone and Telegraph in 1960. This old established company had embarked on a management change (Mr. Harold S. Geneen, who did such a good job at Raytheon, joined ITT in 1959). ITT's earnings over the previous five years (1955–1959) averaged 83 cents per share, with 92 cents being the average for the last two years (1958–1959). The company had announced that it expected sales to double by 1965, and since Mr. Geneen's forte had been the improvement of profit margins, you could have assumed a 20% annual growth rate over this period. ITT would be a Super Glamour company but for the risk of its large overseas operations. Thus we might have concluded that it deserved an Above-Average rating. Consult our guide and you can see that a 20% Above-Average growth company should have sold, in those days of low competitive interest rates, at 25–30 times earnings. Multiply this 25–30 P/E times last year's 90 cents earnings and you come up with a price of $22–$27, compared to a market price at that time of about $18. Obviously this "management-change" stock was very reasonably priced at that time, according to the guide. Interestingly, only a year later

ITT stock was selling in the $25–30 price range, in line with our projection. Later ITT's growth rate diminished, and in 1973 and 1974 the company experienced earnings declines. You can imagine what happened to the P/E. The combination of higher interest rates, a reduced growth prospect, and the label "cyclical" drove the stock's multiple well below 10 times earnings.

PATH NUMBER THREE: RECOGNIZED STOCKS

Buying a company that is correctly priced according to both glamour and growth rate and holding it for continued gains over the years.

On pp. 211–213 I discussed the stock of Bristol-Myers and concluded that it was selling about where it should considering its glamour status and expected growth rate. In such a case, I concluded, the stock should be bought for consistent gains— about in line with the company's earnings progress over the years. There are many stocks like Bristol-Myers—stocks that are already selling at P/E multiples that correctly evaluate their glamour status and growth rate. So long as they continue to increase their earnings and retain their glamour, investors can make money owning them.

Take the case of duPont (E. I. duPont De Nemours, to be exact) stock. Back in 1946, duPont was recognized as a blue chip growth issue. The stock had a median price of $50 during 1946; it earned $2.36 per share that year and thus had a median P/E of 21 ($50 ÷ $2.36 = 21.2). As of 1960 duPont was selling for $195; the company earned $8.92 per share in 1959, so the P/E was 21.8 ($195 ÷ $8.92 = 21.8). Here's what had happened to duPont's earnings and to the market's evaluation of duPont stock over this fourteen-year period:

Year	Earnings per Share	Median Market Price	P/E Multiple
1946	$2.36	$ 50	21.2
1959	8.92	195	21.8
% INCREASE 1946–1959	277%	290%	

The stock market gave the same overall rating to duPont in 1960 as it did in 1946—a P/E multiple of around 21. Because of this, the growth in duPont stock *came mainly from the growth in earnings:* these earnings grew 277% and duPont stock grew 290% over this fourteen-year span.

For a more recent example, look at the case of Anheuser-Busch. Over the nine-year span from 1977 through 1985, here is what happened to the world's largest brewer:

Year	Earnings per Share	Median Market Price	P/E Multiple
1977	$0.68	$ 7.37	10.9
1985	2.84	33.75	11.9
% INCREASE 1977–1985	318%	358%	

Anheuser-Busch stock appreciated about in line with the company's solid growth. Apparently, investor perception of the company changed little—the P/E in 1985 was just slightly above the P/E nine years before. Yet investors gained over 18% annual appreciation (plus dividends which added approximately 3% per year) with their Bud stock. Again, as with duPont, the growth came primarily as a reflection of growing earnings.

At any rate, you can see how much money can be made from owning companies that produce rising profits—you can prosper handsomely even without any change in P/E.

A few generalizations are appropriate here:

1. Whenever you pay a very high multiple for a stock, you probably should assume that your investment will increase at best about in line with its increase in earnings per share. Thus when you buy the equivalent of our duPont, Bristol-Myers, or Anheuser examples, be satisfied with more gradual but consistent gains as time goes by.

2. When you own securities that seem to be anticipating lower growth than might be expected, you may well get a "kicker" as investors recognize the fundamental improvement. Although our Anheuser example was not

one where a higher P/E developed from a fairly low base, shareholders did fine without this; but just imagine the gains that would have been made if the P/E had risen, too.

Let's look now at opportunities that present themselves when you get either improved image alone or the great combination of higher glamour status and excellent earnings growth.

PATH NUMBER FOUR: GLAMOUR PLAYS

Buying companies when you can foresee an improvement in their glamour status.

In Chapter 23 we discussed the importance of sex appeal in stocks. If you can foresee an improvement in a company's glamour status, you can make big money without any appreciable growth in earnings. Many times an industry will lack appeal to investors for years on end. Then, suddenly, investors will fall in love—either with the industry or the company's growth prospects—and go on a buying spree that will hike market prices. Stocks may double or triple in a short time despite the fact that actual growth prospects may not be much better than before.

Consider the stocks of B. F. Goodrich Company in 1946 and Crown Zellerbach in 1950.

At the end of World War II the rubber stocks had little following. Investors were concerned about the fluctuation of natural rubber prices in the world market and the industry's dependence on new car sales for growth. Because of this, rubber stocks were "cheap": Goodrich for one was selling around $11.00 with earnings of $2.95 per share, for a P/E of less than 4. A person with foresight could easily have become enthusiastic over the industry because: (a) synthetic rubber plants built during the war had lessened the dependence on natural rubber; (b) a large replacement demand for tires would build up as more autos were put on the road.

Thirteen years later (1959), Goodrich's earnings had grown only 42% (from $2.95 to $4.18), yet its stock had climbed from $11.00 to $90.00—an increase of over 8 times. *Despite very limited growth in earnings, Goodrich stock had advanced greatly because its glamour status had improved.* (This improved glamour status was aided by an upward reappraisal of the general market, but Goodrich's reappraisal was unusually positive— even though earnings hardly improved.)

The case of Crown Zellerbach is similar. In 1950 paper stocks were not regarded as growth vehicles. Crown Zellerbach earned $2.73 per share in 1950 and sold for around $13.00—at less than 5 times earnings. Nine years later Crown's earnings were still at the 1950 level—$2.76 to be exact—and yet Crown Zellerbach stock was now selling at $55.00. *Despite the lack of earnings growth, the stock had more than quadrupled.* Obviously this appreciation was due to an increase in the company's glamour status because net income had failed to advance.

A more recent example is that of Pneumo Corporation (which merged with IC Industries in 1984), a conglomerate-type company with interests in food distribution and retailing but with its greatest apparent potential in the expanding aerospace field. Here is what occurred to Pneumo from 1975 through 1979:

Year	Earnings per Share	Median Market Price	Median P/E Multiple
1975	$ 0.71	$ 1.89	2.6
1976	0.79	3.11	3.9
1977	0.73	3.83	5.2
1978	0.50	5.22	10.4
1979	0.72	8.33	11.5

Despite the lack of progress in earnings per share over the four years, the stock more than quadrupled and ended up at a P/E that seemed totally unjustified by its recent record. Excepting the extremely low evaluations of 1975 and 1976 (multiples of 2½–4 times), it is hard to understand why Pneumo share-holders fared so well. One might assume that investors were anticipating the future would be much, much brighter than the recent past—and this turned out to be the case. In 1980, Pneumo earned $.97 per share, and earnings continued to grow rapidly thereafter, reaching $2.53 per share in 1983. The median stock price in 1983 was $24.50, making the P/E multiple 9.7. Our guide shows that justifying P/E's of 10 or 11 in an 11–15% interest rate environment "demands" growth rates of 20% or 25% per year. Pneumo grew at more than a 35% pace from 1979 to 1983, and investors were well rewarded. So it is obvious that well before any such progress, investors were assigning a higher glamour status to the company.

Speaking of glamour status, let's turn to a fad of the late 1950s—the vending machine stocks. With the introduction of an automatic bill-changing device in 1959, investors literally fell in love with this industry and two companies in particular, Automatic Canteen and Universal Match (both of which are known by different names today), became star performers through 1959–1960.

Early in 1959 Universal Match stock was selling as low as $12.00, or at about 10 times the year's expected earnings of $1.20 per share. The company had shown a growth rate of about 13% over the 1955–1958 period. According to our guide, a 10–15% growth company should have sold, under conditions then, as follows:

	Super Glamour	Above-Average Glamour	Average Glamour
10%	20–35	18–20	16–18
15%	25–30	20–25	19–20

It is obvious that the market felt Universal Match (at 10 times earnings) had only *below*-average glamour. As an investor in 1959, you only had to say to yourself: "Universal is engaged in an industry that should have at least Above-Average Glamour and possibly Super Glamour—because of its potentials."

On this basis alone, you could have bought Universal. After all, an above-average multiple of 18–25 (times the $1.20 earnings) makes the stock worth $22–$30, and a Super Glamour multiple of 20–30 makes it worth $24–$36 *without any increase in the growth rate at all.*

Thus our guide would have provided a go-ahead to buy, even if you took the most conservative approach and figured no increase in the growth rate. Had you allowed for an increase in the growth rate, too, you could have looked for spectacular results from the stock.

As it turned out, Universal ran into some severe operating problems in 1961 and earnings declined sharply. Before that, however, the stock had experienced the kind of gain the guide showed possible. I have used Universal to illustrate how stocks will advance or decline on the basis of what people *think* may occur. Long-term results, however, depend on what actually happens—hence, one hopes for actual performance from a company (not just image alone) for maximum results.

This leads us to the ultimate.

PATH NUMBER FIVE: THE ULTIMATE—GROWTH AND GLAMOUR

Buying companies when you can foresee an improvement in both their growth rate and glamour status.

Here's the way to make really *big* money in the stock market. Find a company or an industry in which you can visualize both a stepped-up growth rate over the next few years *and* a reevaluation of the glamour status (upward, of course). This double-barreled effect will lead to explosive profits for you.

Let's look at one stock that captured my imagination many years ago, American Photocopy Equipment.

Back in 1957 American Photocopy sold stock to the public for the first time (it had been a privately held company until then). The company's record of earnings from 1954 to 1956 and its 1957 earnings were as follows:

Year	Earnings per Share
1957	$.26
1956	.23
1955	.17
1954	.13

Apeco's earnings over the 1954–57 period had increased at an average annual rate of about 25% (a 100% increase over a three-year span equals a 26% compounded rate—see Appendix table). Going through the procedure explained in the last chapter, you might have concluded that the company's growth rate would continue at this 25% figure, based on the development of decent products and hard-driving marketing. In addition, each photocopy machine sold "built-in" an ever-increasing demand for photocopy *paper*—and this replacement demand was an extremely profitable item for Apeco.

Apeco stock was brought to market at a price—adjusted for subsequent stock splits—of $1.50 per share. While a very limited supply of Apeco stock was available at this $1.50 price, I found there was a considerable supply of stock available around $2.50 per share, which was about 9 times the 26 cents per share earnings Apeco had achieved in 1957.

Now let's see what our Compounding Growth Guide shows you might pay for a 25–30% growth outfit like American Photocopy:

	Super Glamour Company	Above-Average Glamour Company	Average Glamour Company
25% Rate warrants	35–40 times earnings	30–35 times	25–30 times
30% Rate warrants	40–45 times earnings	35–40 times	30–35 times

The guide would have shown you how very cheap Apeco stock was at only 9 times earnings. Even if the stock had only Average glamour, it might deserve 25–35 times earnings; as a Super Glamour company, the stock might sell at 35–45 times earnings, or at between $9 and $12 per share at that time (35 times $.26 = $9 and 45 times $.26 = $11.70), compared with the then-existing price of $2.50.

The results for Apeco stock were startling. The double-barreled effect of *increasing earnings and a higher glamour status* (as reflected by a rising P/E) brought the following results:

Year	Earnings per Share	Median Market Price of Stock	Median P/E Multiple
1957	$.26	$3	12
1958	.30	5½	18
1959	.47	12	25
1960	.57	21	36

At the close of 1961 Apeco stock was selling around $38 per share, which amounted to over 57 times the 66 cents earned for the year that ended in November. This very high multiple was the result of the public's expectation of even faster growth in 1962. The combination of a multiple that greatly exceeded the range indicated by our guide plus my fears about the advent of dry-process (Xerox-type) copiers caused me to alter my opinion of Apeco. By April of the following year all of my people had sold their shares in this company, most with gains of 10–20 times their original investment.

Aside from the fact that our Growth Guide would have prompted us to buy Apeco stock in 1957 *and in every year thereafter (through 1960),* there are other lessons to be learned from this success story. First of all, the reevaluation, or upward revision, of the P/E did not occur overnight. As a matter of fact, it took a full three years for the P/E to get to the 35–45 level that the guide indicates it could have commanded right from the start. Therefore the investor had to have patience to realize the maximum gains on this stock.

Second, you can't expect the same rate of growth in earnings every year. For example, Apeco's 1958 earnings of 30 cents per share were up only 15% over the 26 cents earned in 1957; but 1958 was a recession year in the United States and a 15% increase under these conditions was remarkable (when business returned to normal in 1959, the company experienced a 57% increase in profit).

Third, the fact that Apeco had doubled or tripled or quadrupled in price over the two years from 1957 to 1959 did *not* mean that it had reached its maximum potential. Too often investors are scared away from buying a stock solely because "it already has tripled in the last _____ years." Despite a quadrupling in price to $6 per share in the latter part of 1958, Apeco was still a great buy. This is a perfect example of how you should appraise a stock on the basis of its merits rather than on the basis of where it has been in price.

Fourth, *you must constantly reassess your stocks. Industries and companies obviously change their spots and you cannot assume they'll maintain their status quo.* Apeco was a classic example of an enterprise that lost a competitive battle—and investors had to be sensitive to this. Countless stocks become overglamorized and have to be sold, hopefully well before their fundamentals deteriorate.

The private airplane industry affords another illustration of an improvement in growth rate and glamour status. In 1955 the private airplane stocks in general—and Cessna Aircraft in particular—could be purchased at about 6 times their earnings. The group had little glamour appeal! Over the next few years the net income of these manufacturers increased (Cessna outperformed the group) and suddenly investors took notice and began paying higher and higher P/E multiples for the stocks. Look what happened to Cessna:

Year	Earnings per Share	P/E Median Multiple	Price Range of Cessna Common Stock
1955	$1.12	5.7	8¼– 4⅝
1956	1.66	6.0	13¼– 6¾
1957	1.53	6.3	13¼– 5⅞
1958	1.87	6.3	16⅜– 7⅛
1959	2.47	9.9	34⅝–14⅝

Because of an improvement in growth rate and glamour status, Cessna provided gratifying results for its owners. Over this five-year period its common stock went from an average price of 6 in 1955 to a high of 34⅝ in 1959, and up to 40 in 1960.

Zenith Radio is another case in point—one that brought some worthwhile profits for my clients. Despite the company's then top management, quality product, efficient distribution system, strong financial position, and some interesting "kickers" from pay-TV and the advent of color TV, I found that Zenith stock in 1958 was selling at only 9 times its previous year's earnings. I strongly recommended the stock, which was then at only (adjusted for subsequent splits) $4.50 per share. In 1958, despite a recession in the United States, Zenith reported record profits of 68 cents per share and investors were attracted by this amazing performance. The year 1959 saw new highs in earnings, and the stock was spectacular. Here's what happened to Zenith in a period of less than two years:

Year	Earnings per Share	Median P/E Multiple	Price Range of Zenith Stock
1958	$0.68	11.2	11⅝–3⅜
1959	0.94	17.4	22⅞–9⅞

The combined effect of increasing earnings and a higher P/E multiple had shown Zenith stockholders a fast quintupling in market price. But that was not the end of this success story. The next year (1960) Zenith had a minor dip in earnings, but 1961 was on the up trend again and the stock proved to be a dynamic performer:

Year	Earnings per Share	Median P/E Multiple	Price Range of Zenith Stock
1960	$0.85	21.5	21⅝–14⅞
1961	1.00	28.9	41⅜–16⅛

In a period of just three and a half years (from May 1958 to November 1961) my Zenith owners had seen their stock rise from $4.50 to $40.00 per share. This increase of almost 9 times their original investment was brought about by a combination of advancing earnings and a higher P/E multiple. Of additional interest is the fact that the person who bought Zenith stock through most of 1958 was taking very little risk. He had the confidence that he was buying the stock at a very reasonable price in relation to earning power; he knew that if Zenith's profits merely held around their existing level, the stock should not fall very far in price. Contrast this with the situation of a person who buys a stock selling at 40 or 50 times earnings. The latter certainly cannot expect any upward revision of the P/E; and if earnings fail to advance or if profits begin to trend downward, there will be lots of "air" in the stock (having small earnings to begin with, the stock could retreat a long way before it becomes reasonable on a P/E basis).

More recent, interesting examples are two stocks—John Harland and General Cinema—owned for clients by my firm. Here are the records for these two from 1979 through 1986:

Year	Earnings per Share	Median Market Price	Median P/E Multiple
John Harland			
1986	$1.05	21½	20.5
1985	0.89	15⅝	17.6
1984	0.74	10¼	13.9
1983	0.62	10⅜	16.9
1982	0.51	6⅝	13.0
1981	0.42	5⅜	12.6
1980	0.34	4	11.9
1979	0.28	2½	9.4
General Cinema			
1986	$3.43	47⅞	14.0
1985	2.43	33⅜	13.7
1984	1.98	22½	11.4
1983	1.53	18⅜	12.0
1982	1.19	11⅜	5.7
1981	1.00	8¼	8.3
1980	0.76	5¼	6.9
1979	0.70	5¼	7.5

What happened at John Harland and General Cinema typifies what we all like to find for our investment dollars. Six or seven years ago, Harland's check printing business was hardly considered glamorous—despite a consistent record of very fast growth in both sales and E.P.S. Investors worried about the effects of electronic transfer of funds on check writing. This may someday slow this industry's growth, but "E.T.F." has not made an impact on demand as yet (actually, the introduction of check-writing privileges against money market funds and mutual funds of all sorts has increased demand). Furthermore, investors had overlooked the oligopolistic nature of this business; very few companies dominate this field, and firm pricing (leading to high margins and steadily advancing profitability) has been the result.

General Cinema's record was equally impressive. The company prospered from soft drink bottling and distribution, movie theaters and related consumer markets—and investor expectations rose along with sharply rising E.P.S. Like Harland, General Cinema was not fully appreciated in the late-1970's, despite having had a stellar record of earnings gains for at least five years beforehand.

A more recent example is that of Wal-Mart Stores, a wonderful growth story in the past decade. This well-managed retailer operates discount department stores, primarily located in small towns. Wal-Mart has fostered a great allegiance of both customers and employees . . . and more recently of the investment community. The stock has been a marvelous performer, as illustrated below.

Year	Earnings per Share	Median Market Price	Median P/E Multiple
1979	$0.17	$2.00	11.8
1980	0.22	2.80	12.7
1981	0.32	4.37	13.7
1982	0.46	9.12	19.8
1983	0.70	17.12	24.4
1984	0.96	19.37	20.2
1985	1.16	26.25	23.1

Earnings growth at Wal-Mart has continued to please and practically amaze most investors. Whereas the Wal-Mart "story" was not widely known back in 1979, the company's success attracted attention and promoted Wal-Mart's status as a "super glamour" company. In the process, Wal-Mart's P/E more than doubled from around 12 to over 26. Looking back to 1979–80, with interest rates in the 11–15% range, justifying a 12 or 13 P/E would have demanded 20% growth. Wal-Mart was growing at above a 35% rate! Wal-Mart continued this growth pace and in 1983, again looking at our Compounding Growth Guide, with 11% interest rates, a P/E of about 24 times earnings (for a

Super Glamour company) was justified (precisely where Wal-Mart traded at this time). Thus, the stock appeared to be "correctly valued" according to our model, despite the tremendous gain in market price. In early 1986, security analysts were estimating about $1.50 in earnings and projecting Wal-Mart's growth at about 25%. With interest rates at about 9%, our model would have suggested a P/E multiple of 30–35 times earnings (though we might have wanted to adjust this downward because of high institutional ownership). Thus, a target for Wal-Mart stock of around $45–53 seemed justified versus a market price, at that time, near $40. At the time of this writing (early 1987) Wal-Mart was trading at about $54 per share.

This story typifies what investors like to find: earnings progression and an expanding P/E multiple (glamour image).

So you can see the potentials of path number five—of having a double-barreled profit-making effect working for you.

In all these examples our Growth Guide would have shown the value that existed in these stocks and given us a definite "buy" signal. Apeco, Cessna, Zenith, John Harland, General Cinema, and Wal-Mart were obviously not correctly valued relative to their growth rates or glamour status at the beginning. The important thing is that the guide would have given us the confidence to buy them *right along their upward trend.*

CONCLUSION

The Compounding Growth Guide gives you a tool to use in four of these five paths to big profits. You should find it valuable in assessing future profitable ventures in the stock market, though your imagination will certainly play a big role in selecting the star performers of tomorrow. The next two chapters will give you some food for thought and some ammunition to use in making such selections.

26

Spotting Growth (and Other Attractive) Companies

So-called growth stocks have been in fashion for many years now. They have done far more than provide a hedge against inflation—they have built up small and large fortunes for their owners. The success of growth stocks has changed the theory behind investing in the stock market.

Years ago investors were advised to buy stocks mainly for their yield—for the high current dividends they paid to their holders. The stock market represented a medium for achieving higher current returns than were available from various other investments. Buy stocks that yield 6%, 7%, or more! After all, a 6% return compounded (that is, with the dividends added to the investment each year) will double your capital in just twelve years.

Suddenly in the early 1950s many investors woke up to the realization that capital appreciation could produce higher returns than dividends; and that it was better to buy a growing company with a lower yield than to buy a nongrowth company with a high yield. One startling fact became apparent: Stocks of growing companies not only gained more in market price over the years, but *they actually provided more dividends for their owners over the long run.*

Remember our comparison of supreme and normal

growth companies with stable and stagnant companies? To save you looking back, here is a repeat of the table comparing growth of the Supreme (30% growth rate) company with the Stable (no growth). For the sake of this discussion, though, let's see what might have happened to *dividends* of these two companies over the ten-year period. We'll assume that Supreme pays out one-quarter (25%) of its earnings to its stockholders in the form of dividends, while Stable pays out three-quarters (75%).

| | Supreme Growth Company | | Stable Company | |
Year	Earnings per Share	Dividends per Share	Earnings per Share	Dividends per Share
Base Year	$ 1.00	$ .25	$1.00	$ .75
1st	1.30	.33	1.00	.75
2nd	1.69	.42	1.00	.75
3rd	2.20	.55	1.00	.75
4th	2.86	.72	1.00	.75
5th	3.72	.93	1.00	.75
6th	4.83	1.21	1.00	.75
7th	6.28	1.57	1.00	.75
8th	8.16	2.04	1.00	.75
9th	10.61	2.66	1.00	.75
10th	13.79	3.45	1.00	.75

| TOTAL DIVIDENDS RECEIVED OVER 10-YEAR PERIOD | $13.88 | | | $7.50 |

Supreme's growth allowed it to increase its dividends consistently over these years. By only the fifth year, this growth had brought the dividend rate to a level surpassing Stable (93 cents for Supreme versus 75 cents for Stable). Note that Supreme stockholders received $13.88 in dividends over the ten-year span compared to Stable's $7.50. Of even greater importance is the annual dividend rate of Supreme in the tenth year: the $3.45 dividend is more than 4½ times Stable's 75 cents.

Supreme stockholders indeed received supreme benefits. And chances are they will continue to do so in the future. After all, Supreme in the tenth year looked like this:

Earnings per share	$13.79
Dividends paid out	3.45
Money left to be reinvested in the business	$10.34

By comparison, Stable is still earning $1, paying out 75 cents, and still has a measly 25 cents per share to reinvest in the business.

You may think this theoretical example extreme, but I could cite countless cases to verify the point. To illustrate, let me show you how a $5,000 investment in 1958 in then-stable Consolidated Edison and Wrigley Company compared ten years later with normal-growth Sterling Drug, above-average-growth Bristol-Myers, and with (then) supreme-growth Xerox.

A $5,000 Investment in 1958 Would Have Bought	Which Would Have Paid You the Following Dividends in 1958	Here's What Your $5,000 Investment Was Worth in 1968	Your Yearly Income in 1968 Was
185 Con Ed at $27	$249.75	$ 6,100	$ 333.00
60 Wrigley Co. at $84	270.00	6,900	330.00
500 Sterling Drug at $10	170.00	19,000	350.00
900 Bristol-Myers at $5.50	162.00	61,200	1,080.00
1250 Xerox at $4.00	50.00	323,750	2,000.00

Despite the fact that both Con Ed and Wrigley paid (by far) the highest dividends in 1958, the growth of the other companies brought a sharply *higher yearly rate* in 1968. Actually, their dividends exceeded the stable Con Ed/Wrigley payouts well before 1968. It is obvious, too, how much more successful Sterling, Bristol-Myers, and Xerox were, market-wise. The $5,000 investment in Xerox, for example, was worth some $316,000 more than the same investment in Con Ed and Wrigley; at the latter two's current dividend rate it would take almost a thousand years to amass this amount. While Xerox is hardly a typical example (and the company was unable to sustain growth for most of the 1970s and through 1987), the experience of Bristol-Myers is not so unusual even though it is startling. And even conservative-growth Sterling experienced market appreciation of around triple that of the two stable companies—and with more dividend return than either of them at the end of the tenth year.

History has proved over and over how profitable it is to buy growth companies. As I've pointed out before, investors are generally willing to pay premiums for growth stocks.

Corporate managements have reacted accordingly. Most companies take great pains to point out to stockholders, security analysts, and the general public why their company qualifies as a growth vehicle—hoping the label will stick and the company's stock will be better received (and qualify for a higher P/E) in the market. For this reason, many people are confused as to which companies are true growth vehicles.

Professional investors have found that there are certain fundamental elements that enable one company—and its stock—to outperform others.

Here's a checklist to enable you to distinguish a growth company on your own:

1. Growth companies have top management, which shows up as follows:
   A. They possess records of better-than-average increases in sales and earnings over the years.
   B. They have records of introducing new products over the years and these products develop larger markets and good profits.
2. Growth companies spend greater portions of their sales dollar on research and development than their competitors.
3. Growth companies earn high returns on their invested capital.
4. They plow back a good part of their earnings into expansion (new plant and equipment, etc.). This means that dividends paid out to stockholders may be very small at the beginning.

5. They have some great advantage over competition—
something "proprietary" like strong patent position,
manufacturing know-how, low-cost natural resources,
strategic geographical location.

Whenever you find these characteristics in a company, you
will probably have to pay a premium for it in the marketplace.
*Timing is not quite so important in buying a growth stock as with
nongrowth companies: the inherent trend of the growth company will
usually bail you out even if (within reason) your timing is wrong.*
Let me warn you, however, that growth stocks are by no
means resistant to declines. As a matter of fact, when investor
psychology changes and becomes pessimistic, growth stocks
may well decline faster than the average, which means that you,
as an owner, may have some uncomfortable months or years.
The onus is on you, therefore, to feel reasonably confident that
the company's growth is sufficient to give you profits *in the
future*. Likewise, be careful not to overpay for growth. Once
again, let me stress the value of our Growth Guide. Value will
win out in the long run, and the guide allows you to make a
value judgment for each stock.

PART VIII

Looking Ahead: A Forward View Toward Future Success in Stocks

27
Food for Thought

We have already determined that one logical approach to investing is to believe in *the industry* in which a company is engaged. One excellent discipline, therefore, is to know the basic characteristics of the major industries of our country and to be able to make relative judgments of them. Look at the pros and cons as they appear today. Keep in mind that there may be some "sleeper" industries—ones that are not highly regarded today but that may turn out to be the Super Glamour babies of tomorrow.

Following is a summary of practically all the industries available for investors today. I have tried to be objective in giving you both sides of the coin. I've also tried to plant some seeds along the way. Let your imagination bring them to blossom.

Follow this procedure:

1. Read over the pros and cons of the industry.
2. Argue these points and conclude just how much the pros outweigh the cons, or vice versa.
3. Decide what glamour status you would objectively assign to the industry and what kind of growth you might expect *in the future*.
4. Look at the approximate absolute and relative (to the S&P 500) P/E multiple the industry sells for in the market (which I have shown after the pros and cons).
5. Conclude that the market is undervaluing or overvaluing the group (or valuing it about the way you would). Of course, you should be especially attracted to any industry group that is selling at a lower P/E multiple than you think it should. To help you here, I have provided absolute P/E ranges for each industry group at

the (1986) time of compilation—when the general market's average P/E was about 12 times "normalized" earnings (adding back the many extraordinary write-downs taken by companies at that time). Further help has been provided by giving the approximate range multiples relative to the S&P 500 Stock Index. A 1.00 means the group's P/E is about equal to that of the S&P; 0.80 means the P/E is about 80% of, or about a 20% discount to, the S&P; 1.20 means a premium of about 20% above the S&P; etc.

6. Start investigating individual companies within the groups you like, particularly the ones which appear undervalued.

Here we go!

PRO   CON

AEROSPACE

Companies also heavily engaged in more glamorous electronic and other technological projects. Less chance of contract cancellation than in prior years (i.e., no duplicate programs awarded to more than one producer). Government incentive contracts can mean greater profitability.
Awareness of needs for military strengthening of U.S. (now reflected in federal budgets).

Remote possibility of world disarmament or reduced tensions in cold war. Heavy dependence on government spending.
Possibilities of contract cancellations.
Profits subject to renegotiation by government.
Massive R&D expenditures required.
Heavy labor factor.
Federal budget constraints should lower spending in this area, perhaps dramatically.

Average P/E Multiple: 8–12
Relative P/E's: 0.80–1.00

| PRO | CON |

AIRLINES

Tremendous growth in revenue since World War II.	Companies need huge capital to pay for new equipment.
Low saturation point (still very low percentage of adult population use the airlines).	Companies carry large debt.
	Operating earnings have been erratic.
Air freight in its infancy.	Costs very difficult to control.
Increasing leisure time.	High labor costs.
Deregulation allows more business flexibility.	Very competitive pricing.
Some companies control interesting real estate (hotels).	
Smaller airlines experiencing difficulties, and many dropping by the wayside.	
Mergers shrinking the numbers of participants.	

Average P/E Multiple: 10–12
Relative P/E's: 0.80–1.00

ALUMINUM

Lightweight, durable metal, easy to fabricate.	Sensitive to level of industrial and construction activity.
Making inroads with many new uses.	Industry temporarily plagued by oversupply.
Tremendous potential demands exist from aluminum engine blocks, food packaging.	Government no longer buying for stockpile.
Dominant producers in North America.	Metal subject to price cutting on occasion.
Major companies are aggressive marketers.	Government looks upon metals as inflation scapegoat.
Use cuts down on weight and can be an energy saver.	Substitution by plastics occurring.
	Increasing Third World capacity.

Average P/E Multiple: 7–9
Relative P/E's: 0.50–0.80

| PRO | CON |

AUTOMOBILES

Moving toward three-car households. Increased affluence leading to purchase of upscale (higher margin) cars. Greater differences in style changes. Cars are a "status" symbol in U.S. (new car is a sign of success). Excellent highway system. Fairly "blind" price item (gives manufacturers firm price structure). Production costs declining due to better engineering and factory automation. Weaker dollar.

Autos are being built better and will last longer, delaying new purchases. Sales very sensitive to consumers' personal income, personal debt, savings, etc. Style changes expensive for producers. Hard to gauge which manufacturer's style will be popular. Foreign car competition is severe. More frequent style changes occurring.

Average P/E Multiple: 6–9
Relative P/E's: 0.60–0.80

AUTOMOTIVE PARTS

Those companies selling to replacement market benefit from increasing number of vehicles on the road. Lower oil prices lead to more driving and more demand for parts.

Suppliers to Big Four forced to operate on low profit margins, are subject to fluctuations in new car sales. Always the risk that Big Four may manufacture parts for themselves. Possibility that new developments might outmode certain parts. Higher gasoline costs mean less driving and correspondingly low need for replacement. Growing foreign competition.

Average P/E Multiple: 6–8 (for parts manufacturers)
9–14 (for distributors)

Relative P/E's: 0.60–0.80 (manufacturers)
0.90–1.10 (distributors)

BANKS

Services being expanded. Mergers reducing overhead expenses. Most have shown consistent growth over the years. Mechanization of work is increasing. Disinflation raises value of financial assets. Interstate Banking creating "buyout" valuations. Creation of "super-regional banks."

Competition from savings and loan associations and other financial institutions. Loan volume depends on business conditions. Labor costs are sizable percentage of expenses. Most employees earn less than in a comparable job in another industry. Heavy loan losses; question of adequate reserves. Apprehension about questionable energy, agriculture, and foreign loans. Money market funds are tough competition.

Average P/E Multiple: 7–9
Relative P/E's: 0.60–0.80

| PRO | CON |

BROADCASTING

PRO	CON
Growing use of TV advertising. Home entertainment the most convenient; should grow in usage. A strong cash flow business. Low labor costs.	Have to operate within FCC requirements—which can mean nonincome guidelines. Advertising bound to be affected by general economy. Audience fragmentation due to growth of CATV, independent stations, and VCRs.

Average P/E Multiple: 10–20
Relative P/E's: 0.80–1.60

BUILDING

PRO	CON
Affordability much improved. Represents an important segment of economy and thus government tries to avoid drastic declines. Much potential in modernization of older buildings. Experience of homeowners has been favorable. Home ownership still a major desire. Less cyclicality because of adjustable rate mortgages.	Easily postponed by consumer if he chooses. Been subject to ups and downs over the years (no steady growth). Labor rates are expanding sharply. Most materials lack uniqueness; this leads to excessive price competition. Question whether high construction costs make new dwellings out of reach of consumers. High interest rates hurt.

The building industry has many distinct segments (asphalt, cement, gypsum, plywood, paint, plumbing, etc.), and each requires a separate study.

Average P/E Multiple: 7–10
Relative P/E's: 0.80–0.90

CHEMICALS

PRO	CON
Lower oil prices mean lower costs. Strong research continues to bring out new products and uses. Engineered plastics are making inroads into countless markets. Takes considerable capital and know-how to operate—which excludes small competition. Many companies develop proprietary products for consumers. Product mix shift toward higher value products.	Ample capacity in most lines. Subject to severe price competition. Middle East competition building up. Somewhat sensitive to business cycle. Pollution and other environmental costs are a real problem. Oil companies and producers have integrated forward into chemicals.

As in the building field, there are many distinct areas, which have to be looked at separately.

Average P/E Multiple: 12–16
(Specialty chemicals 15–20)
Relative P/E)s: 0.90–1.20
1.20–1.80 (specialty)

PRO	CON

COMPUTERS

Decreasing costs result in expanding use and new uses.	Heavy research and plant expenditures are required.
U.S. has worldwide leadership.	Rate of new products is increasing.
Base of programs written by customers results in strong vendor loyalty.	Worldwide competition is strong.
Industry is diverse and growing, allowing many companies to prosper.	IBM is the largest company and is a fierce competitor.
	Maintenance of older programs is using steadily more of the customer's resources.

Average P/E Multiple: 12–20 (hardware)
15–25 (software)
Relative P/E's: 1.30–1.70 (hardware)
1.50–2.00 (software)

CONTAINERS

Attractive packaging an important sales medium.	Plastics replacing paper & glass.
Trend to supermarkets makes good packaging essential.	Possibility that customers might manufacture own materials.
Glassplants sold out.	Few proprietary products.

Average P/E Multiple: 12–15
Relative P/E's: 1.00–1.25

COPPER

Most of the world supplies are controlled by a small group.	Demands are very sensitive to economic conditions.
Widely used in some attractive industries (i.e., electronics).	Aluminum and fiber optics are making inroads.
Industrializing world use growing (i.e., China).	Prices fluctuate widely.
Labor givebacks and cost cutting reducing breakeven points.	Persistent labor troubles and foreign government interference.
	No control over prices because of sensitivity to world metal conditions.

Average P/E Multiple: 7–9
Relative P/E's: 0.60–0.80

COSMETICS

Expanding middle-income population.	Heavy advertising programs necessary.
No severe price competition.	Promotional expenses large.
Increasingly vanity-conscious population (both men and women).	Some products have seasonal patterns.
High return on invested capital.	Consumer buying patterns can be fickle; may also be more reluctant to pay very high prices.
Usage commencing at earlier ages.	

Average P/E Multiple: 10–20
Relative P/E's: 0.90–1.60

| PRO | CON |

DISTILLING

PRO	CON
Strong brand loyalty. Development of lighter and lower-alcohol products.	Rising social and legal pressures against alcohol consumption. Possibility of excise tax increases. Beer pretty much a nondifferentiated product. Little increase in per capita consumption over past 10 years. Industry has excess production capacity. Many institutional investors will simply not own liquor stocks.

Average P/E Multiple: Beer: 13–17   Liquor: 12–15
Relative P/E's: 1.10–1.40   1.00–1.25

DRUGS (ETHICAL)

PRO	CON
Drugs protected by patents have firm pricing. Huge volume can be generated from new products. Breakthroughs in heart disease, cancer, common colds, etc., yet to come. Expanding old-age group will use more and more drug remedies. Expanding markets overseas. Labor costs insignificant. Not affected by fluctuations in general economy. Generally strong cash flows and excellent balance sheets. Long product life cycles with strong patent protections.	Heavy research expenses are necessary for company survival. Subject to occasional government investigations and criticism of high profit margins, both U.S. and abroad. Threat from greater use of generic drugs encouraged by most insurance companies. Medicare and Medicaid could lead to more governmental intervention. Subject to currency exchange rate fluctuations (both a plus and a minus). Subject to regulatory approval delays.

Average P/E Multiple: 12–20
Relative P/E's: 1.00–1.75

DRUGS (PROPRIETARY)

PRO	CON
Public now more "drug-conscious." Like ethical, have expanding old-age group and potentials overseas. Low labor costs. Products have little obsolescence. No price cutting. Not affected by recessions.	Heavy advertising outlays necessary. Little prospect for dynamic breakthroughs.

Average P/E Multiple: 10–20
Relative P/E's: 0.90–1.60

PRO   CON

ELECTRICAL EQUIPMENT

Consumers using more and more elec-   Growing foreign competition for heavy
trical appliances, which in turn con-   electrical equipment and small
sume more electricity.   appliances.
Proliferation of small, efficient cogen- Occasional price wars in heavy electri-
eration facilities.   cal equipment and so-called white
                                        goods.
                                        Appliances sensitive to business cycle;
                                        heavy equipment subject to own cycle.
                                        Nuclear problems.

Average P/E Multiple: 10–16
Relative P/E's: 0.90–1.30

ELECTRONICS

Countless new discoveries to be   Heavy research expenditures a
achieved in the future.   necessity.
Fits in with definite trend in missiles, Obsolescence can be rapid.
space, automation, miniaturization, etc. Like most young industries, it is
Usage still at low saturation.   flooded with many small companies.
One of our country's greatest strengths. Growing foreign competition, espe-
                                        cially from the Far East.

This industry is highly fragmented. There are tremendous
disparities from company to company.

Average P/E Multiple: 12–25
Relative P/E's: 1.00–2.00

FIBERGLASS

Constantly expanding uses.   Reliance on textile and building
Very flexible material with excellent   industries.
qualities.   Has been sensitive to business cycle
Growing use in autos.   (particularly the building cycle).
An energy saver.

Average P/E Multiple: 9–12
Relative P/E's: 0.80–1.10

FINANCE AND SMALL LOANS

Buying with credit now an accepted   Amount of consumer credit now very
practice in U.S.   high in relation to historical pattern.
Former "luxuries" become "necessities" Fluctuating auto and appliance sales
and people will borrow to buy these.   represent large part of business.
Unemployment and medical insurance   More competition from banks and
make people better credit risks.   S&L's.
                                        More "captive" companies competing
                                        (i.e., auto companies, retailers).
                                        Credit cards taking away business.

Average P/E Multiple: 7–10
Relative P/E's: 0.60–0.80

PRO	CON

FOOD CHAINS

Chains still eliminating smaller, marginal stores.
Taking on more profitable nonfood lines.
The "traffic center" for housewives.

Most areas now have ample supermarkets and thus it will be more difficult for the chains to achieve the rapid penetration they have had in the past ten years (many areas overstored).
Profit margins under pressure.
Independents have more flexibility to compete.
A low-margin business.

Average P/E Multiple: 8–14
Relative P/E's: 0.70–1.20

FOOD PRODUCTS

A stable business—not subject to wide fluctuations.
Trend to convenience and healthier foods; the microwave phenomenon.
Lower than average labor costs.
Brand extensions increase profitability.
Pricing flexibility in low inflation economy.
Recurring crop surpluses keep costs low.

Large advertising outlays necessary.
Sizes of crops vary, which affects prices of raw materials.
Difficult to achieve dynamic product breakthroughs.

Average P/E Multiple: 12–17
Relative P/E's: 1.00–1.60

INSURANCE (FIRE AND CASUALTY)

Everyone needs insurance.
Have large investment income, which is growing steadily for some.
Investment income has made dividends more secure.
Tort reform.

Some rates are regulated.
Lag in receiving rate increases harmful.
Profits from insurance underwriting have been cyclical; most often, large losses occur.
Inflation not to their benefit.

Average P/E Multiple:
Top operating companies: 10–13
More marginal companies: 7–10
Relative P/E's: 0.80–1.00 (top)
0.60–0.80 (marginal)

PRO	CON

INSURANCE (LIFE)

PRO	CON
Growing recognition of its importance by public.	Trend to group coverage means lower premiums per $1,000 of coverage.
Companies have aggressive sales forces.	People becoming more conscious of equity (rather than fixed dollars) for their future.
Prospects for broadening product line (i.e., mutual funds, variable annuities).	Universal Life margins under pressure.
Longer life expectancy means more premiums and profits.	Tax advantages under attack in Congress.
Investment income growing.	
Enjoy favorable tax shelter.	
Higher interest rates help.	

Average P/E Multiple: 8–12
Relative P/E's: 0.70–1.00

MACHINE TOOLS

PRO	CON
Possibility of more governmental stockpiling.	A function of capital spending; sensitive to business cycle.
More sophisticated equipment a necessity for business.	Heavy competition developing as large companies pushing hard to get in N/C business.
Numerical control (N/C) tools revolutionizing industry.	Foreign competition has taken big share of U.S. markets.
No developed second-hand market for N/C tools.	U.S. manufacturing building more plants abroad.
Retooling of auto industry helps.	

Average P/E Multiple: 8–10
Relative P/E's: 0.70–0.90

MACHINERY (FARM)

PRO	CON
More large farms now, which become mechanized and need more machinery.	Sales have been cyclical—according to farmers' income.
Government subsidies have favored farmers.	Public concern over huge subsidies to farmers.
New kinds of machinery being developed.	Profit margins have varied widely.
Increasing labor costs force farmers to more mechanization.	Fight over control of farming by big business—attempts through proposed legislation to break up ownership.
	Farm equipment has very long useful life.
	Greater food production overseas means lower commodity prices in U.S.
	Heavy supply of foodstuffs exists.

Average P/E Multiple: 8–10
Relative P/E's: 0.70–0.90

PRO	CON

MACHINERY (INDUSTRIAL)

PRO	CON
Highway programs require large equipment needs. Tremendous potentials for mass rapid transit—and equipment needs for this. Foreign nations have large equipment needs (i.e., dams, highways). Sales subject to strong cycles.	Machinery quite durable and can be made to last (style not important). Attempts to cut governmental spending may impact this group. Increasing foreign competition. Slowdown in Third World infrastructure development.

Average P/E Multiple: 10–12
Relative P/E's: 0.80–1.00

MOVIES

PRO	CON
Film libraries great asset. Getting higher prices at box office. Many companies have valuable real estate. Industry's financial management improving.	Lower theater attendance because of competition from television, cable, VCR, etc. Overseas markets will eventually get widespread television. Risks of producing high-cost films. Management often more concerned about awards than profits. A "hit or miss" business.

Average P/E Multiple: 8–12
Relative P/E's: 0.70–1.00

NEWSPAPERS

PRO	CON
Tend to be natural monopolies, especially in smaller markets. Strong cash flow and balance sheets. Excellent control of pricing. Excellent cost control. Long-lasting franchises. Less prone to audience fragmentation than broadcasting.	High labor costs (though technology constantly being adopted). Low unit volume growth. Cyclicality of ad rates.

Average P/E Multiple: 15–20
Relative P/E's: 1.25–1.75

PRO	CON

OIL

PRO	CON
Fully integrated companies have shown reasonable growth over the years. Profitable byproducts exist (chemicals). Improved demand outlook now that prices have dropped.	Price structure not firm due to OPEC's excess production capacity. Risk of owning large reserves overseas for international companies. Increasing foreign pressure on royalty, tax structure.

Average P/E Multiple:
Fully integrated companies: 6–12   Refinery companies: 8–11
Producing companies: 10–15
Relative P/E's: Integrated companies: 0.50–1.00
Refinery companies: 0.70–0.90   Producing companies: 0.80–1.25

PAPER

PRO	CON
Consumer paper products showing steady growth. Limited foreign competition. Paper an expendable item that is used up rapidly. Per capita consumption overseas increasing rapidly. U.S. is low cost producer.	Historically a poor "price discipline" industry (but improved now). Industrial uses somewhat sensitive to business cycle.

Average P/E Multiple: 10–14
Relative P/E's: 0.80–1.20

PHOTOGRAPHY

PRO	CON
Benefits from increased leisure time activity, expanding middle-income group. Film an expendable item—rapidly used up. The more cameras owned, the more film sold. Trend to more easily operated cameras.	A luxury item that could be affected by a drastic business depression. Profitable processing business being proliferated with local competition. Silver prices squeezing profit margins. Growing threat from electronic imagery.

Average P/E Multiple: 10–12
Relative P/E's: 0.80–1.00

PRO | CON

PUBLISHING

Expanding "middle class" in U.S.	Television detracts from reading.
More and more adults with greater education (more "readers").	Magazine publishing very difficult to make profitable.
Firm price structure for successful hard-cover books.	Paperback book field crowded and difficult profit-wise.
Growing need for reference books.	Possibility of more paperbacks cutting into hard-cover sales.
Mini baby boom.	Retailers can return unsold copies.
	Demographics working against higher school enrollments in the short term.
	Electronic publishing: distribution of information.
	Proliferation of PCs.

Average P/E Multiple:
Magazine Publishers: 10–15   Textbooks, Business Services: 8–15
Normal Hard-Cover Publishers: 7–10

Relative P/E's: 0.80–1.25 (magazines)
0.70–1.25 (business services)
0.60–0.90 (hardcover)

RAILROADS

Vital part of our country's transportation system.	Inroads made by air freight and trucking.
Mergers should eliminate duplication of equipment, facilities, etc.	Huge upkeep costs.
Staggers Act beneficial to railroads.	Need large amount of equipment to remain in business.
Advent of "piggyback" very helpful to rails.	Business very sensitive to general economy—very cyclical.
Possibility that unfair labor practices will be reduced.	Burdened by unrealistic labor practices (feather-bedding, etc.).
Incentive freight rates and contracts have attracted considerable business.	Earnings records quite erratic.
Many companies control extremely valuable assets (land, resources).	Competing forms of transportation get direct and indirect subsidies that railroads do not enjoy.
Many companies have diversification of assets.	High labor factor industry.
	Regulated by ICC.

Average P/E Multiple: 8–12
Relative P/E's: 0.80–1.10

PRO	CON

RESTAURANTS AND LODGING

PRO	CON
Restaurant business now being approached in more scientific way to save labor, lower food costs, etc.	Franchising has led to a proliferation of outlets.
Affluent society eating out more and traveling more.	Food, lodging should be sensitive to general economy.
Changing eating styles including salad bars, lighter (fish and poultry) and healthier foods.	Higher labor content industries and labor shortages in some areas.
Low-cost travel packages increasing demand for hotels.	Competition from the VCR, the microwave, and frozen food encourages eating in.
Hotels, restaurants going into fewer and stronger hands.	

Average P/E Multiple: 12–20
Relative P/E's: 1.00–1.75

RETAIL TRADE

PRO	CON
Government payments make personal income more reliable.	Sales sensitive to change in disposable personal income, stores with large durable goods sales subject to wider fluctuations.
Consumer has been a reliable spender over post–World War II period.	Competition from new discount formats and a specialty retailing revolution.
Some automation procedures to help industry.	Highly seasonal business.
	Hard to increase productivity of labor.
	Many new entrants coming into discount field, which is a low-margin business.

Average P/E Multiple: 9–14 (retail chains)
10–16 (specialty stores)
15–25 (off-price merchants)
Relative P/E's: 0.80–1.20 (chains)
0.90–1.40 (specialty)
1.30–2.00 (off-price)

PRO   CON

RUBBER

PRO	CON
More cars on road lead to more replacement demand. Numerous plant closings now taking place. Consolidations under way.	Foreign competition fierce. Sales to auto manufacturers fluctuate with new car sales. Compact cars, light in weight, use smaller tires and do not wear out so fast. Have occasional price cuts. High energy costs.

Average P/E Multiple: 8–10
Relative P/E's: 0.70–0.90

SAVINGS AND LOAN

PRO	CON
Industry basic to all-important building industry. Many companies in fast growing geographical areas (California in particular). Prospect for broadening lending areas. Enjoy favorable tax treatment. Adjustable rate mortgages decrease volatility. Interstate and interindustry acquisitions.	Have to offer higher interest rates. Banks getting more competitive. Possibility of more normal taxation in future. Some companies engage in risky land and construction loans. Need for some sophisticated management. Money market funds attracting time deposits.

Average P/E Multiple: 6–9
Relative P/E's: 0.50–0.70

SEMICONDUCTORS

PRO	CON
Costs are declining as fast as any industrial product, generating many new uses. U.S. has a strong position. Many companies use this technology to build more valuable products. Some niches are well protected. Growing strength of industry, trade, and patent protection.	Worldwide competition is intensifying. Products have commoditylike attributes. Business is increasingly capital intensive. Japanese are gaining world-wide leadership. Industry is very cyclical and earnings are very volatile.

Average P/E Multiple: 13–18
Relative P/E's: 1.10–1.50

| | PRO | CON |

SOFT DRINKS

PRO	CON
Strong domestic and foreign demand outlook. Evolution of diet and fruit-juice-based soft drinks. Very firm price structure on part of syrup manufacturers. Companies have strong balance sheets. A few firms enjoy exceptional brand loyalty. Recession-resistant. Low labor factor.	Need for heavy advertising. Weather can be a factor (e.g., cool summer a negative). Expensive to launch new products. Companies competing more on a price basis.

Average P/E Multiple: 15–18
Relative P/E's: 1.30–1.60

STEEL

PRO	CON
Efficiency improvement possibilities large. Large earnings leverage when business good. Plant closings now taking place. Labor making some concessions. Quality is improving.	Closely tied to autos and construction and other cyclically sensitive industries, thus quite sensitive to economy. Meeting stronger competition from other materials. Foreign competition. Small per capita growth in consumption. A very mature industry. Unfunded pension liabilities.

Average P/E Multiple: 5–8
Relative P/E's: 0.40–0.70

TEXTILES

PRO	CON
A basic industry. Companies modernizing plants and getting greater productivity. Industry has gone into fewer, stronger hands. Industry trying to get more tariff protection. U.S. producers may be lowest cost now. Low labor content now.	Foreign competition is severe. Hard to control inventories. Wide swings in prices. Excess capacity exists. Shifts in fashion.

Average P/E Multiple: 10–12
Relative P/E's: 0.80–1.00

| PRO | CON |

TOBACCO

| Companies have reduced their costs substantially; low labor costs. | Product lacks growth potential. |

Companies have reduced their costs substantially; low labor costs.
Sales are really depression resistant.
Disciplined price structure.
Most companies diversifying into other consumer products.
Ability to pass along costs, including excise taxes.

Product lacks growth potential.
Heavy advertising and promotional expenses necessary.
Companies introducing many new brands—including lower-price cigarettes.
The health and social issues.

Average P/E Multiple: 7–12
Relative P/E's: 0.80–1.00

TRUCKING

Short-haul business cannot be replaced by other means.
Can depreciate trucks rapidly and usually make capital gains when equipment is sold off.
Improved highways beneficial.
Full tax payer.
Deregulation leading to consolidation.

Regulated by the ICC.
Continuous labor difficulties in the industry.
Business very cyclical.

Average P/E Multiple: 10–15
Relative P/E's: 0.80–1.25

WASTE MANAGEMENT

Few companies in industry.
Waste problems (demand) increasing geometrically with increasing public concern and government enforcement.
Large sums available (Superfund) to pay for clean-ups.
Disposal capacity shortage.
Great price flexibility.
Increasing use of off-site treatment and disposal by waste generator.

Potential liabilities are large.
Poor public image.
Industry subject to constant government scrutiny which is increasing costs.
Liabilities are long-lived.

Average P/E Multiple: 20–28
Relative P/E's: 1.50–2.20

Naturally a listing such as this cannot be all-inclusive. I have tried to list basic industries as they are normally shown. It is my hope that you will refer to this chart whenever you are considering a purchase or sale in the market. As you can see, there are arguments for and against *every* industry. The main advantage of these summaries is that they force you into objective thinking—into the "vacuum" approach I talked about earlier. You will no doubt come up with some positives and negatives not listed (this is where your own imagination comes in). Then it's a matter of determining how much the pros outweigh the cons (or vice versa) and relating this appraisal to the P/E multiple investors have assigned to the industry.

PART IX
Utility Stocks

28
Making Money from Utilities

The other day I returned home from a short vacation. On entering my house, I activated four conveniences we all take for granted—I turned on the lights, flipped on the heat, turned on the water, and picked up the telephone and made a call. All of us spend a sizable amount of money each year on these conveniences, which in investment circles are lumped together under the title "utilities."

In the last chapter I gave you some food for thought about the many industrial fields that exist today. Aside from railroads, which constitute a separate and distinct field, the others are termed "industrial stocks." I didn't include utilities in that chapter because this group of stocks deserves a discussion of its own.

Although investors in utility stocks fared very poorly over the 1970–1980 decade, there have been periods in which they have been very rewarding stocks to own (including most of the 1981–1986 span).

UTILITIES AS A GROUP

As you already gathered from the first paragraph, utilities are the companies that supply us with electricity, telephone service, natural gas, and water. While there are some basic differences among these four utility services, they do have certain common characteristics:

1. *All are noted for their stability of revenues.* Regardless of what happens to the general economy, you and I are

going to heat our homes, stay clean, turn on the lights, and talk to our friends. In short, we're going to continue to use the utilities; therefore these companies can count on *stable revenues* (profits are not so reliable because of inadequate rates or the lag between the time when costs are incurred and when rate relief is granted).

2. *All the companies are regulated. The rates they charge are set by a regulatory body.* Utilities that operate within one state have their rates set by either their state public utilities commission or a local body; those that operate interstate are regulated by federal bodies (gas and electric companies by the F.E.R.C., the Federal Energy Regulatory Commission, and telephone companies by the Federal Communications Commission). Naturally, regulation is a negative for the industry, and it is doubly so in our era of consumerism.

3. *Utilities are granted franchises, which prohibit identical competition in their operating area.* The electric utility in your area has been granted a franchise to supply electricity to you, and no other company can offer you this service. Your utility may or may not also have the franchise for supplying natural gas, which, of course, is competitive for the home heating and cooking market. *If the utility supplies both electricity and gas, then it has very limited competition.* Competition, however, has been introduced into the long distance phone business.

4. *All utilities have to install expensive equipment to serve you* (huge generating equipment, extensive pipelines and storage facilities, etc.), but *these expenditures can be financed through heavy borrowing because of the industry's stability.* A utility that is not heavily leveraged with debt and/or preferred stock is a rare exception.

5. *Utilities don't need as much cash on hand as industrial companies.* I mentioned earlier that utility companies get by with a current ratio of slightly over 1 to 1. This is because the companies have money coming in every month without fail. Their accounts receivable (the monthly bills mailed to you every month) are paid fairly promptly because if customers avoid their bills too long,

the utility can shut off its service—a devastating prospect.

6. *Utilities don't have the problems of carrying inventories or of product obsolescence.* Whereas General Motors has a sizable inventory of this year's cars—which are worth far less if they're not sold this year—a utility has no such problem. Electricity, for example, doesn't have to be produced far in advance of its sale and it never goes out of style.

7. *Utilities have pollution and other environmental problems, as well as fuel problems.* None of these problems is easily overcome.

8. *The quality of utility earnings is not always as high as that of industrials.* Without going into accounting details, the fact is that many utilities report "bookkeeping" profits that are overstated relative to "cash" profits. (In some cases, this accounting has been forced on the utility companies by the regulatory commissions and thus it is not deceptive on their part, but merely in conformance with regulations.) With plant-building programs winding down, many utilities are now becoming "cash cows" and thereby qualify as possessing higher, rather than lower, quality of earnings.

Now that we know the similarities between the utilities, I think you'll be interested to know the differences. These differences should help you decide where you might put some of your investment dollars to work.

Electric Utilities

Sales of electricity to industries amount to almost half of the utility business. This industrial business can fluctuate, especially in geographical areas sensitive to wide economic swings. Residential customers seem destined to consume more and more electricity, however, because of the wide variety of electrical appliances that are finding their way into the home. Commercial and industrial users, on the other hand, are finding more ways to conserve. All in all, electrical output is perhaps the most stable of all businesses and one that promises consistent although moderate growth in the future. Growth of air conditioning and the prospect of heating homes electrically (through use of the "heat pump") are all added benefits. Needless to say, rising energy costs are a detriment to future demands for both electricity and natural gas, but the costs have actually been moderating, reducing the pressure in recent years for conservation.

Natural Gas Utilities

Natural gas is a clean and efficient fuel that has achieved wide acceptance both in commercial and residential applications. Natural gas prices have fallen since 1980 as have the prices for crude oil and coal, the principal competing fuels. Lower prices, a less regulated operating environment, and the increased availability of natural gas have enabled natural gas utilities to compete more aggressively for customers. The increased competition, however, has put pressure on profit margins and earnings which in turn has helped accelerate the restructuring currently underway in the industry. Natural gas reserves are being depleted and, eventually, a tighter supply/ demand relationship should increase the industry's profitability, particularly if crude oil prices strengthen at the same time.

Telephone

The telephone business in general is more sensitive to economic cycles than the electricity business. The telephone industry has undergone tremendous change over the last decade with the split-up of AT&T and deregulation of parts of the business (equipment and long distance). Tremendous strides have been made in the technology of the telephone business and there are countless new fields of service that are already producing growth (digital services, mobile telephone, etc.). The courts, the F.C.C., and Congress are all moving the industry toward further deregulation except perhaps for local exchange services. This, of course, still provides the lion's share of revenues and profits for most telephone companies.

Water

Most cities own their own water facilities and the trend toward taking over private facilities continues. This is one utility that can (but seldom does) suffer from a shortage of its commodity.

WHAT TO CONSIDER IN BUYING UTILITY STOCKS

1. *The geographical area in which the utility operates.*

A utility operating in a fast-growing area has much better opportunity for growth than one in a stagnant or slow-growing region. Use recent population trends to estimate the kind of growth to expect in the future.

It is also important to consider an area's "background." Certain areas are dependent on heavy industry (machinery, steel, etc.), and business is subject to greater fluctuation because of this. For example, during the 1957–1958 recession Detroit Edison suffered from sharply lower industrial activity and reduced earnings in 1958, while the utility in my backyard, Pacific Gas and Electric (not dependent on heavy industry), showed increased profits for the year. Utilities that are very dependent on one industry are obviously riskier than those serving a diversified community.

2. *The attitude of the regulatory authorities.*

Public utility regulatory bodies can vary greatly in their philosophy from area to area. Some authorities are tough as nails on granting rate increases while others are extremely liberal. One of the reasons for the earlier rapid growth of utilities in Florida and Texas was the attitude of their governing bodies. Utilities in these states were consistently granted higher rates of return than those in other states, leading to somewhat better growth than companies operating under less favorable regulation.* In contrast, a state such as Oregon is well known

---

*Your first reaction might be that these higher profits are at the expense of the population, but liberal authorities claim that, in the long run, rate increases are to the existing population's benefit. After all, a utility that realizes its expansion will be profitable and it will do everything possible to promote growth in the region.

for its negative attitude toward private utilities. In 1960, for example, Portland General Electric was granted its first rate increase in eleven years. In more recent years such states as Louisiana, Kansas, Montana, Mississippi, and Wyoming have become known as "poor regulatory climate" areas. Utilities operating in these regions have to struggle to get adequate rate relief and, of course, their stockholders have suffered accordingly. Needless to say, it's of great benefit to stockholders to have the authorities on their side.

3. *The utility's past record of growth and future projections.*

As with industrial stocks, a utility company's past record of growth can give you a good indication of its future. Once again it's a matter of looking at a company's record of earnings per share over the *past* three to five years and then determining what has changed to alter this pattern either upward or downward over the *next* three to five years.

Naturally you will be especially attracted to those utilities whose records indicate consistent and rapid growth in the future.

4. *The quality of earnings of any company considered for investment.*

As mentioned on p. 265, many utilities' earnings are "overstated." Many book interest income on construction in progress, on the theory that they (the utility) had to borrow to build such facilities and such interest costs are nonrecurring (so when the facilities are completed, income will eventually offset such interest expenses). Utilities with heavy nuclear power involvement now present a quality question mark (forced plant shutdowns or abandonment negatively impact both book value and profits). *It is preferable to purchase utility or industrial common stocks that have the highest-quality reported earnings.*

5. *Energy sufficiency.*

It is preferable to own utilities that are energy-rich or energy-sufficient, as opposed to those that cannot control their fuel requirements as they would like.

6. *Environmental "purity."*

You certainly do not want polluters or "bad citizens."

7. *Strong balance sheets.*

Bond ratings provide a good insight into the financial strength of utilities. But you cannot rely on ratings alone because they are subject to change. Certainly you should prefer utilities that will retain high ratings and avoid those that are in fear of downgradings. And you do not want any more leverage (extent of bond borrowings) than can be afforded.

8. *Yield.*

In Chapter 21 I pointed out how high yield can limit your risk in a stock and how, in certain cases, high yield can signal that a stock should be bought for at least a temporary rise in price. I concluded, however, that yield is not as important if long-term growth of capital is your investment objective.

In the case of utility stocks, yield *is* often of major significance. This is because many utility stocks are bought by investors *who need income* and these people are naturally attracted by high yield. Many utility stock owners are widows or retired people who depend on their dividends to live; *many buy stocks on the basis of yield alone,* so we have to give this extra consideration when we analyze utility issues.

As with all stocks, correct timing of purchase can make a good deal of difference. It's true that you're not going to worry much how safe the $2.10 dividend for Southern California Edison is, but it's certainly to your benefit to buy the stock at 30 or 35 instead of 45, if you can. It's hard to generalize about exactly when utility stocks should be purchased, but there are two important factors to consider: (1) *the level and* (2) *trend of money rates* (that is, whether interest rates in the country are high or low at the time and whether they are going up or down in the near future).

Interest rates change. One year you get 9% on your bank savings account, and a few years later you get only 6%; one year you can buy U.S. government bonds that yield 10% or 12% and a year later you can get only 8% on the same bond. But why does it make so much difference to the utility stock buyer where interest rates are and which way they are trending?

The answer: *Because many utility stocks are bought for income, which puts them in strong competition with other income-producing securities for the investor's dollar.* For example, suppose U.S. government bonds are yielding 12% today and utility stocks are yielding 14%. Many investors who ordinarily put their money into government bonds might well be attracted instead to utility stocks, and thus it might be a good time to buy the utilities. Likewise, if the bonds are yielding 12% and the utilities 10% many investors might switch out of utilities into bonds and this might be an improper time to buy utilities. The *trend* of money rates is equally important. Suppose interest rates in the country begin to come down; perhaps business in general in the United States is suffering and the federal authorities try to stimulate it by lowering money rates. If you buy a utility stock today with a 12% yield and six months from now money rates have come down sharply, chances are that your utility purchase will be up in price. The figures would be something like this:

Buy a $100 stock paying $12 a year, for a yield of 12% when 12% is the "going rate" for income investors. Six months later the "going rate" is only 10%. The stock, still paying $12 a year, might sell at $120 to yield 10%.

$$(\$12 \div \$120 = .10 \text{ or } 10\%)$$

Thus your $100 stock has gone to $120—solely because of the change in money rates. The reverse is true when money rates trend higher. Therefore we can make the following generalization: *Utility stocks are an especially good buy if you think that interest rates in general are going lower,* or if existing yields on industrial stocks are low.*

9. *Price-earnings multiple.*

Earning power is important for utility stocks as it is for industrials and thus it is also important to compare the P/E multiples of utilities you are considering. *Dividends are paid out of a company's earnings; therefore the more earnings you have per dollar of market price, the more potential dividends you have.*

---

*Low interest rates have a double-barreled effect on utilities. Public utility companies, which rely on raising needed cash through the sale of bonds and other fixed-income securities, naturally save money when interest rates are low (their borrowing costs are lowered and this leads to increased profits).

Say you are comparing two utility stocks both of which sell for $50 per share. Company A pays out $5.50 per share in dividends for a yield of 11% ($5.50 ÷ $50 = .11 or 11%), while Company B only pays out $4.00 per share for a yield of 8% ($4.00 ÷ $50 = .08 or 8%). Is Company A a better buy with an 11% yield than Company B with an 8% yield? Not necessarily. Let's compare the earnings of these two:

Company A is earning $6.50 per share, which gives a P/E of 7.7 ($50 market price ÷ $6.50 earnings = 7.7). Company B is earning $8.00 per share, which gives a P/E of 6.2 ($50 market price ÷ $8.00 = 6.2).

On the basis of earnings, Company B is a better buy than Company A. Company A's yield is much higher because the company is paying out almost all its earnings in dividends to stockholders (85% of its $6.50 earnings paid out). In contrast, Company B is paying out only 50% of its $8.00 earnings directly to stockholders. If Company B were to pay out 85%, its dividend would be increased from $4.00 per share to $6.80, which would give a yield of 13.6%. Company B has chosen *not* to pay out 85%. It is probably retaining the bulk of its earnings for more expansion than Company A, and this expansion will no doubt lead to higher earnings *and higher dividends* to Company B stockholders in the future.

You can see how important earnings are. Like industrial stocks, *the utility stock with the most potential earning power is normally the best buy for you.*

GROWTH UTILITIES

For years Florida Power and Light, Texas Utilities, and other "growth utilities" were recommended to investors seeking capital growth. People were often amazed when a utility stock of any sort was suggested for dynamic gains. They would not have been amazed, however, if they had ever looked at the past records of companies such as those just mentioned. Here is what happened to these two companies over the 1950–1960 decade:

	FLORIDA POWER & LIGHT			TEXAS UTILITIES		
	Earnings per Share	Dividends per Share	Mean Market Price	Earnings per Share	Dividends per Share	Mean Market Price
1950	$ .61	$.32	5	$ .60	$.24	6⅛
1951	.62	.35	6⅛	.67	.34	7⅜
1952	.71	.37	7½	.78	.43	9⅞
1953	.77	.40	9	.83	.48	10¾
1954	.88	.44	12	.97	.52	14
1955	1.03	.51	16⅞	1.03	.58	17⅜
1956	1.29	.61	21¾	1.17	.64	19⅜
1957	1.49	.665	26	1.28	.72	22
1958	1.75	.76	36½	1.37	.80	27
1959	1.93	.865	49⅜	1.47	.88	34¾
1960	2.11	.97	60	1.56	.96	39¼

Indeed, the growth was both consistent and remarkable. And the performance of these two stocks in the market was equally remarkable. Both companies at that time passed the first three tests provided for you earlier in this chapter: they operated in fast-growing regions; they benefited from liberal regulatory commissions; they had good marks on the qualitative factors 4 through 7 and anticipated a continuation of their growth in the future.

Let's see how they stacked up, at the beginning of 1961, on tests 8 and 9, namely yield and P/E multiple:

	Market Price	Annual Dividend Rate	Yield (%)	Estimated Current Earnings	P/E Multiple
Florida Power & Light	65	$1.00	1.5	$2.15	30
Texas Utilities	45	1.04	2.3	1.63	28

Naturally, we have the benefit of hindsight here, so let's do a Compounding Growth Guide analysis of these two stocks as they might have been approached in 1961. First of all, let's see what the compound growth rates had been for the two companies.

Without going into the mathematics, here is how the recent past had stacked up:

Company	1955–1960 Annual Growth Rate (%)	1957–1960 (%)
Florida Power & Light	15½	12½
Texas Utilities	8½	7

An important lesson to consider here is the *most recent trend of events,* which in both cases shows some diminution of growth. Whereas, for example, FPL showed a 15½% annual growth rate from 1955 to 1960, the rate for the most recent three years was 12½%—and in the latest year (1960/1959) the rate had declined further to around 9%. In the case of TU, the five-year growth rate was 8½%, the three-year rate was 7%, and the latest year was only 6½%. Needless to say, these figures should have had a strong bearing on the all-important projected growth rate for the future. Granting some benefit of the doubt, however, let's assume that FPL qualified at that time as a 10% + growth company, and that TU promised about 7½% +.

Our next step would be to categorize the companies according to glamour. Since utilities lack the excitement of IBM or Hewlett-Packard or other glamour stocks (we reserve the Super Glamour category for areas and companies with more explosive profit possibilities), it would be logical to classify the slow-growth utilities as only Average Glamour stocks and the more rapid ones as Above-Average. Both FPL and TU were in the latter growth range. Looking to our guide (p. 201), we find that FPL (with assumed 10% growth) starts off with a P/E of 18–20 times and TU (with 7½%) with a P/E of around 18 times, under the 3½–5% prevailing interest rates during the early 1960s in the United States. Since both companies had recent institutional support, an additional 2–5 multiple would have resulted in a "buying area" of 20–25 times for FPL and 20–23 for TU.

Both of these assessments indicate that the two stocks were selling way above what our guide showed they deserved (the table on p. 272 shows a current 1961 multiple of 30 times for FPL versus our guide's 20–25 and a 28 P/E for TU versus our assessment of 20–23). Thus, despite the great past record of these utilities and notwithstanding their acceptance by the investment community, our guide pinpoints their "richness"—

both were selling way above what their combined growth rate–glamour image deserved.

This analysis does not refute the theory behind the purchase of growth stocks generally. In utilities, as well as in industrial stocks, investors can reap double-barreled rewards from ownership of the growth vehicle. They will not only end up with vastly superior capital appreciation, but *in the long run they will end up with more annual income from owning growth companies as opposed to those in the nongrowth or slow-growth category.*

Incidentally, our guide would have proved to be quite accurate. Some eight years later both FPL and TU were selling very little above their 1961 price—hardly the kind of performance you should be striving for. From 1969 to 1980, performance of the two was most discouraging, as was market action for all utilities. Interest rates had risen, leading to lower P/E's, and earnings turned decidedly cyclical. In the case of Texas Utilities, the deteriorating energy field, plus heavy overbuilding, has negatively affected both revenue/profit performance and the growth image of the region. For the 1980–1985 period earnings per share grew by only 6.5%/year for Texas Utilities. FPL's growth was 9.6% over the same period.

All stocks have their "right price," something our guide should help you with immensely. I think it only proper to close with the thought that utilities, which were once noncyclical and had consistent (though low) growth patterns, have developed decidedly cyclical tendencies. The problems reviewed in this chapter created costs that hampered earnings progress. The 1987 picture seems somewhat different. Ample capacity exists in the industry, cost pressures have subsided, and many utilities have strong (excess) cash flows. Conditions vary so widely from company to company that it is hard to generalize.

To conclude, utilities constitute a basically unattractive area for investment in the kind of rising-inflation environment experienced in the 1970–1980 decade, while disinflationary periods such as 1983–1986 are potentially very favorable.

PART X
Some Tax Advice for Investors

29

Ugh!

Perhaps you're thinking the letters "UGH" are a symbol for a secret stock that is going to be the IBM of tomorrow. So sorry! "Ugh!" is what people say when they start talking about income taxes. And that's what I'm going to talk about right now.

Not that I am an expert on taxes. "Only a fool is his own attorney," they say, and the same thing goes for the nonaccountant who thinks he can handle complicated tax problems by himself.

But I am familiar with tax items that concern the average investor and I want to explain certain aspects of today's tax law and particularly some ways you can save money.

DIVIDENDS

Very little discussion of dividends is necessary. At the present time you are exempt from income tax on the first $100 in domestic dividends you receive each year. If you are married, you and your spouse are entitled to $100 each for a total of $200.

Interestingly enough, there are a select number of stocks that pay dividends that are either partially or completely free from taxation. For years, a number of public utility stocks were able to pay out dividends that were either partially exempt or fully exempt from taxation, due to accounting peculiarities. Such is not the case today. Most companies in this position are resource companies (i.e., oil, natural gas, timber) organized as limited partnerships, from which dividends are considered a return of capital and are not operating income. (If oil reserves are not growing, sale of the commodity is only that of a "wasting asset" destined eventually to be drawn down to zero—something recognized by the I.R.S. and treated as a non-taxable return of capital. As an offset, the I.R.S. generally demands that shareholders reduce their cost basis by the amount of these dividends.)

Under the new tax law, capital gains and dividend income will both be taxed at the same rate (after Dec. 31, 1987). Since capital gains will lose their advantageous tax rate, investors may shift their preference to stocks that pay dividends and that offer higher yields. There are, however, important offsets to be considered. First, taxes have to be paid on dividend income each year and every year. This leaves you with less to reinvest and a lower (after-tax) return. In contrast, capital gains can be deferred, perhaps for many years; if so, the corresponding taxes can be deferred and your money can "compound" at a higher rate than if you had to pay taxes right along.

Secondly, the dividends you receive are still double taxed, once at the corporate level and once again when you pay your personal taxes. A *successful* company that retains the bulk of its earnings and can reinvest these funds into its business at high rates of return will probably achieve a far more advantageous outcome for its shareholders than one that funnels its profits out in dividends. A company that can grow faster can produce sharply higher capital gain opportunities (which, as mentioned, can be "tax-deferred").

REDUCING THE TAX BITE

I hope you'll have very few stock market losses in your lifetime, but let's be practical. In the stock market, as in all forms of investments, even the shrewdest of us will sometimes make mistakes and experience losses. While you will never make money by losing money, at least you can learn to take the fullest "advantage" of the losses you incur.

Our government is sympathetic about your losses—but

only to a limited extent. Uncle Sam will let you subtract any losses you incur during the year from your gains, dollar for dollar.

If you haven't taken any gains during the year, a loss still can be helpful by reducing the amount of normal income tax you have to pay. You see, each individual is allowed to take a $3,000 net loss (over and above gains taken) each year and use this to reduce the amount of income reported to Internal Revenue. Suppose your yearly taxable income is $30,750. As you know, the tax rate gets higher as your income grows; on the last $1,000 that hikes your income from $29,750 to $30,750, the rate is 28%. Thus by taking a $1,000 loss, which in this case lowers your income from $30,750 to $29,750, you are saving the 28% tax you would have to pay on this last $1,000, for a saving of $280. Incidentally, if you take a loss by selling a stock, you must wait thirty-one days to repurchase the same stock if you wish to deduct the loss on your income tax statement. If you buy it back *within thirty days,* Internal Revenue calls it a "wash sale" and forbids your utilizing the loss.

BENEFITING FROM OTHERS' LOSSES

Most Americans hate to deal with tax forms. I agree that these forms are a nuisance. If you *don't* fill out your form correctly, you go to *jail;* if you do fill it out right, you go to the *poorhouse!*

Most people are procrastinators at heart. They put off unpleasant tasks and decisions as long as possible. This applies to investors, too. They have a loss in a stock early in the year, yet wait till the very end of the year to sell the stock in order to establish a tax loss. Suddenly in November and December people comb through their stock lists to see where they can establish a loss that will "save" them some taxes. Naturally they sell the stocks that are down in price. All of a sudden a great deal of "tax-loss selling" occurs in certain depressed stocks. *This concentrated selling further depresses the market prices of these stocks— many times to bargain levels.* Therefore you should keep your eyes open in December for these artificially depressed issues.

ONE IMPORTANT WORD ABOUT LOSSES

Suppose you bought a stock at $50 and it's now selling at $45. You have a loss of $5 per share right now. Some people contend there is no such thing as a loss until a stock is sold. They insist they have suffered no loss on this $45 stock because they haven't sold it yet. After all, the stock might go back up to $50 and then they'd be even again. True, indeed. But the stock might never go back to $50—it might instead go down to $40 or $35.

Believe me when I say that if you bought a stock at $50 and it is now at $45, you have a loss of $5 whether you sell the stock or not. Which brings us to the point in mind! So many times I've heard people say, "I can't afford to sell that stock—I'd have to take a loss." This is incorrect investment thinking. If conditions have changed in the company or the industry since you bought the stock and *if the stock has lost its attraction, it should be sold regardless of what your cost is.* The smart thing to do is to admit your mistake and buy another stock that does look attractive. I'm sure you've heard that *the most successful investors are those who minimize their losses and maximize their gains.* This axiom recognizes the reality that losses are inevitable. If you fail to recognize your mistakes, you cannot abide by this good advice.

SPLITTING YOUR GAINS AND LOSSES

Tax planning can be important, and coordinating capital gains and losses with your anticipated other income can reap benefits. Let's assume we're in the month of December and that you have two stocks you are considering for sale—one for which you will have a $1,000 capital gain, and the other for which you will have a $1,000 loss. At first thought you might conclude that both stocks should be sold *this year* so that you incur no extra taxes (because the $1,000 loss offsets the $1,000 gain, thereby giving you no gain at all to report). While this seems logical, in practice it is not correct tax thinking. Instead, you might be able to save some important tax dollars by splitting your gain and loss into *separate* tax years. Here's the way it works if you are expecting your income of $28,750 to go up next year due to a $2,000 raise:

1. Sell the gain stock now. You will have a net $1,000 gain for the year and your taxable income will be increased to $29,750, leaving you still in the 15% bracket. Your $1,000 gain costs you only $150.
2. Wait till next year (only a few weeks away) to sell the loss stock. This reduces your $30,750 income to $29,750 and saves you the 28% tax on that last $1,000 of income.

Thus, by splitting your loss and gain into separate years, you have saved yourself $130 in taxes, as follows:

Tax *saved* by taking $1,000 loss next year:	$280
Capital gains tax to be paid on $1,000 gain this year:	$150
Tax Saving	$130

This strategy can be reversed—you can take loss *first* (this year) and take your gain the next year—if your earnings situation is reversed.

Incidentally, if you want to establish a capital gain (or capital loss) in one year, you can sell the stock right up to and including the very last day of the year. Trade date rather than settlement date determines the year of sale.

MORE INVESTMENT ADVICE ON TAXES

Now that you understand the importance of knowing something about taxes as they relate to your investments, paradoxically some good advice is not to let taxes overly influence *your investment judgment.* If you think a stock is greatly over-priced, then it is usually better to sell it, regardless of tax considerations.

If you own stock with an extremely low cost, you might be influenced in your investment decision by tax considerations. If, for example, your cost on ABC stock is $1 per share and it is now selling for $21 per share, you may think you are "locked in" to owning this stock because of taxes. After all, you will have to report a capital gain of $20 per share if you sell it, and the taxes on this gain may run up to $5.60 per share—which is a pretty big hunk. You have to be convinced that ABC stock is selling way too high at $21 before giving consideration to selling it. Or you have to have a new purchase in mind that looks exceptionally attractive to switch out of ABC.

The ABC case is the exception rather than the rule, however. Don't be afraid to pay some taxes if your investment judgment tells you a stock should be sold. Remember, unless you die owning a stock, you will eventually have to pay tax on your gain. In the ABC example, too often a person will refuse to sell, and argue that "after the $5.60 per share tax I am really receiving not $21.00 but only $15.40 a share for my stock." But all too often if the stock then proceeds to go down, the same person will sell it at a lower price—and then have to pay a tax that will net him far less than he would have received at the beginning.

PART XI

A Hard Look at Some Stock Market Theories

30

So You Want to Trade

"What I want is to make quick profits."

I wish I had a nickel for every time I've heard this expression over the years. Who doesn't want quick profits? I know I do. But *wanting* and *getting* are two different matters.

Perhaps you're disillusioned by my apparent pessimism about achieving quick gains in the stock market. After all, I am an investment adviser and therefore should know when the market is going up or down—specifically, I should know whether XYZ stock will go up or down 3 points over the next few weeks. Or should I?

My reply to people who assume that I know these answers is: "If I knew, I wouldn't be working—I'd be on the beach at Waikiki right now. And so would all the other investment experts in the world."

Don't misunderstand me. I'm in favor of quick profits and have made some fabulous gains for both my clients and myself in a fairly short time. But I think it only fair to say that there is a great deal of *luck* involved when price objectives on a stock are realized in a very short period.

Let's explore this! As you know, *stock prices go up when there are more buyers than sellers, and they go down when the pressure from sellers exceeds buying interest.* When you choose an attractive stock for the future, you are in essence saying, "I believe that this company's earnings will rise over the years" or "I believe the glamour status of this company will improve as time goes on," or "I expect the understated asset value to be recognized"—or a combination of these three statements. You conclude that these favorable fundamentals (understated asset value, increased earnings, and/or improved glamour status) will create more buyers for the stock than sellers and that the stock will therefore go up in price.

When you choose a stock for quick profits (say for a few weeks), it is another matter. Then you are saying, "I believe there will be more buyers than sellers in this stock *in the next few weeks.*" How can you know such a thing? How can you know what people all over the world are going to do with XYZ stock over a few weeks? To be truthful, you cannot.

Just when you're convinced that a mass of buying interest will build up in a stock over the near term, someone with a very large block of that stock may decide to sell. Perhaps a large institution has a block of one or two million shares and has to liquidate in these few weeks you are aiming for. Or imagine the innumerable news developments that could affect investor psychology, which in turn could affect the overall market and/ or the specific stock considered. Countless elements make it difficult to foretell what will happen to a stock (or the market in general) over a very short period of time.

If you don't think it's difficult to gauge where the market is going, try reading the sage comments in the periodic market letters published by most of the large brokerage houses. It's normal for these letters to hedge, but some are really absurd. Here's one that really caused me to chuckle one day:

> The market has had a sizable advance, one which indicates investors should take a cautious attitude. On the other hand, stocks appear on firm ground, because of improving earnings. As corporate earnings reports are released investor confidence should be strengthened, but the release of these reports may well invite profit-taking.

You tell me which way the market should go after reading this mumble-jumble from the mouth of a supposed expert!

There are, of course, self-proclaimed pundits who do not hedge their views and who are very definite about stock or market behavior over very short-term periods. Such conviction hardly makes them any more prescient than those who hedge— and for very good reasons.

Have you ever been to a gambling casino? How would you like to own one of the dice tables at one of these casinos? My guess is that you could retire in peace by owning just one. But suppose someone offered you ownership of one table for only an hour. Could you rest in peace with that? Certainly not! That one hour could be disastrous. Some lucky fellow might make twenty passes and the table might show a huge loss for this one hour. Still, over the years this table is certain to show a good profit because the percentages and statistics work in its favor. The same principle applies to stocks. Choose a good stock and the statistics will work in your favor as time goes by—but don't count on making a quick killing.

I hesitate to compare a gambling casino to the stock market, but when we talk about trading in and out of stocks *day in and day out*, the comparison is not so farfetched. Trading really is gambling, and I don't like to confuse it with investing for gains over a longer period of time.

There are many traders in the market—people who buy a stock one day and sell it the next for a small profit. This is about the toughest way to make a living I know of. *I wholeheartedly advise you against this kind of gambling.* I feel very strongly about this, so I think it only fair to tell you why:

1. You will pay a fortune in commissions to your broker. A broker should tell people who ask about day-to-day trading that "it will make *me rich, not you.*" I doubt whether your objective is to make your broker rich.
2. You are trading against professionals. There are hundreds of individuals on the floor of the exchanges who specialize in trading. They have the advantage of not paying commissions, so they can survive with very small profits every day. Their position on the exchange gives them a better "feel" for trends than you could ever hope for sitting in a brokerage office or wherever. In addition, you are at a time disadvantage; the professionals are on the spot and can act instantly. You are a minute or so away, and this can make a big difference (in the case of frequent "late tapes" you may be five, ten, or even thirty minutes behind them).

3. Trading involves making many decisions. It takes far more time than long-term investing and can detract from a person's everyday vocation.

4. Commissions and other execution costs (you may have to buy at the offer price on the specialist's book and ultimately sell at the bid price) make your breakeven point higher than you might think. For example, if the normal spread between bid and ask on a $30 stock is one-quarter of one point (25 cents) and if your commission is 30 cents per share to buy and the same to sell, your total cost (execution plus commissions) is 25 cents + 30 cents + 30 cents + 25 cents = $1.10 or almost 4% of the $30 stock price. This is the move upward you need to break even.

5. If short-term and long-term capital gains tax rates are ever differentiated again your (short term) trading gains will be subject to ordinary income tax. You simply won't benefit from an advantageous long-term capital gains tax rate if your scope is short-term.

6. You will *never have big winners*. Traders who are happy to make a few points will never own stocks that will double, triple, quadruple, etc.

Many people envy traders. They hear them brag about their fabulous turns in the market. But I ask you—do you suppose they would talk about their losses? No, indeed. Perhaps the best comment on the wisdom of trading was made by a man who had spent his whole working lifetime in the stock market. He said simply, "I know a lot of millionaire *investors*, but I *don't know one millionaire trader*." Another Wall Street expert explains in more statistical terms why heavy concentration on short-term timing is likely to be "hazardous to your *wealth!*" Using the forty years from 1945 to 1984 as his guide, he points out that big market surges are generally concentrated in bursts—and if you miss these bonanzas your probabilities for success diminish significantly. Missing even one of these surges dramatically reduces the benefits of owning equities at all. His statistical case is well supported, as is his conclusion that frequent jumping in and out of stocks is a most difficult and generally unrewarding strategy.

So now you know the way I feel about day-in and day-out trading. Still, there is a middle road between trading and long, long-term investing. Investors shouldn't have to wait a lifetime to realize worthwhile profits on their money. For the sensible, realistic investor I suggest the following:

1. Realize that your judgment will not be perfect and that you will have to take losses on occasions.
2. Buy stocks you "can sleep with." Don't buy junk.
3. Do not buy stock for small gains. Set your sights for good-sized profits.
4. Do not concern yourself after "the race is over." If you have decided on an investment philosophy of taking occasional profits, do not consider jumping off the nearest building if a stock goes way up after you have sold. It's part of your game.
5. Do not be impetuous and overeager to take down profits. Try to let them run.

CONCLUSION

Trading is gambling—not investing. The latter is both the easiest and the most profitable way of making money, so concentrate on it. You'll be glad you did!

31
Beating the Market

Human beings constantly strive to develop schemes that will make them money. Because the stock market itself is a vehicle for making money, you can imagine the number of schemes that have been invented to "beat the market."

Formerly there were plenty of illegal ways of moving stock prices to one's favor through manipulation. Fortunately the Securities Exchange Act of 1934 set up the Securities and Exchange Commission in the United States and most of these illegal practices are now a thing of the past.

Legal schemes, of course, remain, and every investor should be conscious of what they have to offer. Let's take a look at a few of the widely used stock market theories to see what merit they have.

THE DOW THEORY

The most widely published theory of all is the Dow theory. One Charles Henry Dow, who was the first editor of *The Wall Street Journal,* wrote some editorials in that paper from 1900 to 1902. These editorials were later interpreted by W. P. Hamilton and Robert Rhea to formulate the Dow theory.

Actually the originators of the theory did not contend that it would allow you to "beat the market." They suggested more modestly that it would tell you whether the stock market was in an overall upward trend (a bull market) or in an overall downward slide (a bear market). The originators were confident that their barometer could predict business conditions many months in advance. They were not interested in analyzing any of the economic indicators I discussed in Chapter 8. Instead, they contended that the action of the stock market itself would tell you where business was headed.

There are many skeptics of the Dow theory today, for the following reasons: a) the DJIA still consists of a mere thirty stocks; b) the thirty are different in both name and character from the original group; c) the original thesis of the theory was based heavily on the relationship between the DJIA and the Dow Jones Railroad Average, the latter of which ceased to exist in its earlier form on January 2, 1970; d) the Dow Jones Transportation Index, which replaced the Railroad Average, contains airline as well as rail issues; e) while the airlines, like the rails, are economically sensitive, they have certain important dissimilarities, too; and f) even the railroads are somewhat dissimilar from their earlier positions (some are considered more for either their natural resource ownership or for their breakup values than for their pure transportation services).

Like all theories, the Dow is subject to all sorts of interpretations and assessments. Also like all theories, it is sometimes right and sometimes wrong. It had a wonderful record in "predicting" a downfall in 1929. W. P. Hamilton published a now-famous editorial on October 25, 1929, entitled "A Turn in the Tide" in which he stated that the action of the averages on October 23 signaled the end of a long bull market and the beginning of a bear market. Had an investor sold all his holdings on October 23, he would have saved himself a fortune. He would already have seen the market on industrial stocks drop about 19%, but after October 23 it was to fall another 70% from its high to its low in 1932.

On the other hand, the Dow theory did not forecast the fantastic bull market that preceded the 1929 crash: the theory in early 1926 gave very bearish indications and the three and a half years that followed were the most profitable in history.

An objective appraisal of Hamilton's work was made by the economist Alfred Cowles III in 1933. Cowles studied Hamilton's editorials for the twenty-six-year period from 1904 to

1929. During this span Hamilton made ninety recommendations for a change in attitude toward the market (55% were
bullish, 16% bearish, and 29% doubtful). In retrospect, forty-
five of the ninety forecasts were correct and forty-five were
incorrect—an investor might have done as well by flipping a
coin. Cowles also concluded that an investor would have had a
better performance from outright ownership over these twenty-six years than from buying and selling on Hamilton's signals.

CHARTS

Many stock market students adhere to charts which depict
past individual stock and general market experience to predict
which way the market is going and the trend of individual
issues. There are countless charting systems, and most of them
attempt to correlate a relationship between market price action
and the volume of trading. The idea is that it is a sign of
strength when a stock advances on a large volume of shares
traded; conversely, when volume in the market or on one stock
enlarges as a stock declines, it shows that the pessimism is
mounting and that the trend is for lower prices.

In essence, the chartists contend that a study of a stock's
behavior not only tells you where a stock has been but also
where it is going. Say, for example, a stock has risen to $50 twice
in the last few months and each time the stock has backed down
from this $50 price. The second time it falls off from $50 the
chartists may conclude it has formed a "double top," concluding further that it will have a very difficult time going up
through this price in the near future.

Or a chartist might keep a trend line on a stock's behavior
just as you would on a company's sales trend, hoping he can
judge just where the stock is going.

Chartists have scores of terms to designate price action.
"Head-and-shoulders top," "dormant bottom," "scallop and
saucer," and "rounding top" are some of them. They all assume
it is possible to predict a stock's future by charts—*with little or no
regard for its fundamental values.* Pure chartists couldn't care less
about earnings, dividends, industry position, new products,

overall outlook. They assume instead that the charts will reflect these characteristics.

I can't help but think of charts and the position of the market way back on September 16, 1960. At that time the Dow Jones Industrial Average was hovering around the 600 level. The market had already retreated to this level three times and each time it had rallied upward— thus the 600 level was a "triple bottom." Chartists were saying that the market would meet tremendous support at this level. Why? Because business was getting better? Certainly not! Only because the charts told them so. What then should be so magic about 600 on the Dow Jones average? If people were becoming more pessimistic, the market would go lower regardless of "triple bottoms." It was only a matter of days until the magic number was pierced. This penetration below 600 caused many chartists to liquidate their holdings and this heavy selling forced the market lower still. By October 25, the average hit 566 and this proved to be the bottom of the decline—from which the market commenced a dramatic upsurge. In other words, the people who were frightened by the penetration of this ridiculous magic number sold out within 5% of what proved to be the market's low. The interesting thing is that most of these chartists had no idea what the outlook was for business, earnings, inflation, political climate, or other important considerations that affect and even determine the level of the stock market. All they were concerned with was the Dow Jones Industrial Average—and so they were completely fooled by its action.

Interestingly enough, a sharp decline in just *one* of the thirty stocks that made up the average might have caused the DJIA to go below 600. I ask you—should isolated declines like this speak for the whole market? Of course not.

Interpretation of charts is very much a personal affair. In a way, it's like abstract art. Take an abstract painting and show it to ten people and you'll get at least eight different interpretations of the meaning. Take one set of chart figures and show it to ten chartists and you're liable to get almost as many interpretations of which way the stock is going.

The trouble with most chart patterns is that they cause their followers to change their opinions so frequently. Chart services change like the wind. One day they put out a strong buy signal; two weeks later they see a change in the pattern and tell their clients to sell; then two weeks after that they tell them to buy again. The result is that the chartists' followers are forced in and out of the market time and time again. This is great for brokers' commissions, but not so great for the investor.

Another significant disadvantage to charting is what I've already mentioned about decisions made on the basis of the *chart alone*. Most buyers under this method have no idea *why* they are buying a company's stock, hardly a condition that fosters contentment or relaxation.

As you have no doubt gathered by now, it is the *way* in which charts are used (I should say "misused") that I object to. I admit that charts *can* be helpful. They can point out to the potential investor that "accumulation" is going on in a security—that supposedly knowledgeable people are quietly buying stock for investment purposes. (Or that "distribution," or concentrated selling, is being done by people who may know best what is really going on.) But upon discovering such accumulation, should one become a sheep and follow the action blindly? I say *no!* Never buy a stock "blind"—ignorant of the important facts I have stressed in this book. It's true that my insistence on sound reasoning may cause you to delay action and thus miss out on some winners, but this approach will help you avoid many more losers—and you should experience much better performance over the years. And no doubt you will sleep better at night because nothing is worse for the nerves than having no idea in the world why your stock is retreating.

I never buy a stock "blind" and I have *never* regretted sticking to this principle.

One further comment about the use of charts in common stock selection: I already mentioned a major thesis regarding charts, i.e., that they can be useful in pinpointing what "insiders" or other knowledgeable people are doing with their securities. There comes a point, however, when *too many* people are using charts—which is another way of saying that the chart no longer tells the tale. If, for example, a multitude of investors start basing their decisions on chart patterns, they begin to "feed" on one another. A chart may have bullish implications at the beginning, but as more and more chartists follow it, then there are simply more and more owners of the stock who really have *no* special information or reason for owning it. The buyers (or sellers, as the case may be) are perpetuating the chart pattern, and one day in the future, when the values start to tell, the chart will suddenly change from bullish to bearish (or vice versa) and one heck of a rush for the exits will commence. Then, with chartist support evaporating (as a matter of fact, just the opposite), a truly disastrous result can occur.

Therefore I implore you to be especially wary of charts in widespread use. In my first revision of *Primer,* I warned readers about the excessive use of charts in 1968. I stated that "the heavy charting of 1968 will be in large part responsible for some painful losses in lower quality issues sometime in the 1969–1970 period." Certainly this proved true.

BACK TO FUNDAMENTALS

Most great athletic coaches stress fundamentals. A football team that cannot block and tackle cannot be expected to win! After a disappointing loss the top coaches don't run helter-skelter looking for a magic play to beat next week's opponent— they put their athletes to work and cry, "Back to fundamentals!"

In buying stock you must be conscious of the fundamentals of potential earning power and positive cash flow to achieve success. If you forget your "blocking and tackling," you're asking for trouble. Whenever I think of charts versus fundamentals, I am reminded of a true story relayed to me of a woman who was very much involved in charting stocks in the 1920s. She was a master at it, and was making a handsome living from it. As she gained confidence in herself, she started selling some of the blue chip stocks she had owned for years and put the proceeds into stocks that looked good on the charts. One stock in particular had the most assuring chart pattern of any she had ever seen. That stock was Kolster Radio, which was then listed on the San Francisco Stock Exchange. Despite the fact that Kolster's fundamentals could hardly have encouraged anyone to buy it, the stock was zooming upward and was a chartist's dream. Higher and higher it went and by the end of 1928 Kolster was 73¼ and this lady chartist was up to her earrings in the stock. By January 1929, the trend of Kolster stock reversed itself and the bottom fell out suddenly. By May of the same year, the stock had plummeted to 25½. Then came a rally in June, but by October it was down to around 11 and by December it was $3. In January 1930 Kolster announced it was in receivership and went through bankruptcy proceedings. The worst part of this tragic story is that the lady had nothing left—no earning power, no dividends, no fundamentals on which she could at least hope for the future.

As you've gathered from both my earlier discussions and this illustration, I believe in buying value. This does not ensure you won't make an occasional mistake, but it does guarantee you won't end up with stock certificates that are useful only as wallpaper.

PART XII
Mutual Funds:
Pro and Con

32

Putting Your Dollars in Someone Else's Hands

About sixty years ago a group of business people decided that many investors wanted *someone else* to make their investment decisions for them. To accomplish this, they sold shares in *investment trusts*. The idea was simple: They would invest the money they received in stocks or bonds and each owner of the trust would share in any profits or losses the trust incurred.

The idea was indeed sound. The originators found that many people preferred to have experts do their thinking for them, consequently many dollars rolled in to buy these trusts.

Today investment trusts (or investment *companies*, as they are more commonly called) constitute a multibillion-dollar industry. Bond and stock mutual funds exist to meet practically every investment objective imaginable—utilizing practically every type of security available.

Investment trusts provide two major advantages for their owners: *professional management* and *diversification*. The first of these is obvious. The people who run the trusts and make the investment decisions are professionals who are expected to do a superior job. Most investment trusts likewise retain a large staff of experts, so owners have the advantage of the judgment of many versus the judgment of one (you!).

Diversification is another important advantage. When you buy shares of an investment trust, you are buying all the stocks or bonds they own; thus, you have your eggs spread around rather than all in one basket. It's interesting to note that there have been about 1,500 automobile manufacturers in the United States since 1920—and now there are only four (maybe three). If you had placed all your eggs in any one of the 1,496 that failed to survive, you'd have gone down the drain with them.

Investment trusts are *convenient* to own, too. If you had your own portfolio of twenty or thirty stocks, you'd be deluged with dividend checks from all the companies you owned (you could save part of the aggravation by keeping your securities in a broker "street name" account or in bank custody—but you may incur charges for this service). When you invest in a trust, which may own fifty or more different securities, you receive one check every three months (they lump all their dividends and interest received together for you).

There are a few other advantages. First, a trust supervises its investments constantly, whereas you as an individual owner might not have the time or inclination to do this religiously. Second, trust management is more flexible than the average individual. Professionals are more inclined to take profits on occasions, whereas individuals often "fall in love" with their stocks and lose their objectivity in appraising them. Third, because of their diversified holdings, trust shares are not as volatile—they do not move up and down as wildly—as most individual stocks do. Their owners are probably not as prone to panic in a declining market as they would be with the volatility of individual holdings. Of course, this relative lack of volatility is a two-sided coin; trust shares may not rise as fast in a good market, either. Many trusts are so widely diversified that they end up with only mediocre performance; a trust with fifty stocks, for example, may see twenty-five rise, ten fall, and fifteen remain unchanged on a strong day in the stock market.

Now for the *disadvantages*. Aside from mediocre performance, which may or may not apply, depending on the specific trust, the *major drawback of investment trusts is their costs of ownership*. All trusts charge a *management fee*, which generally runs at least ½ of 1% but which may run as high as around 1½% per year (and may average ¾ of 1% or more). In addition, fund shareholders are normally responsible for legal, accounting, and other trust expenses which, when combined with management fees, may bring total fees to the 1–2% per year levels. Now, 1–2% may not sound like much, but it is a sizable burden to overcome. Incidentally, these fees are charged against the income received by the trusts (the dividends and interest earned on the stocks and bonds held), thereby reducing the ordinary income paid to shareholders to the point where *trusts generally pay lower yields than can be obtained from owning comparable individual stocks or bonds outright.*

Another glaring criticism of trusts involves the large sales commissions charged to buy certain ones (to be discussed on pages 304–305).

Another drawback of the trusts involves their size. Most trusts (especially the mutual funds which continue to grow in size) accumulate large blocks of stocks. When these stocks are going *up* in price, the trusts have no problem in disposing of them, if they seek to do so. But what happens if the market is tumbling or if a company's business turns sour and its stock is being actively sold by the public? How can a trust with 400,000 or 500,000 or more shares get rid of them without driving the price down unmercifully? This problem was encountered in 1929 and in numerous subsequent periods of negative results, such as 1968–9, 1973–4, and in the first half of 1982.

There are two more facts you should know about investment trusts. The first involves a special kind of dividend usually distributed once a year—*a capital gain dividend.* This distribution comes from profits (not income) the trust takes during the year. Suppose, for example, your trust bought IBM a number of years ago and this year sells off some of the stock for a large gain. These profits are lumped together with others taken during the year, and after deducting losses taken, are paid out to you. As with any other capital gain, you have to pay tax on the profit. Capital gain dividends are bound to fluctuate with the market, the relative success of the individual trust, and the willingness of the trust management to make actual sales of certain securities. The dividends, therefore, can be sizable or they can be nothing. Some investors get very excited about the apparent total yield they receive when they add their regular investment income (the ordinary dividends from the trust) and the capital gain income together. Say you get a 3% yield from the regular dividends and then you get a capital gain dividend that, when related to the market price of the trust, amounts to another 12% yield. Total yield for the year looks like 15%, but I warn you not to think of it this way. First of all, capital gain distributions are likely to vary year-by-year. And second, the fact is that the capital gain dollars may only be a return of your own capital to you and thus should not be considered "true yield."

The bull market environment since late 1982 encouraged burgeoning growth in mutual fund sales, with bond funds literally running wild. For example, investors bought an astounding $71 billion of bond fund shares in 1985, and 1986 sales catapulted to $161 billion. Many fund managers, realizing the potential dangers of having their funds grow too large, countered by creating new funds! The total number of bond and stock funds increased from 460 to 1,100 over the 1982–1986 span, many of the new funds being offshoots of existing funds. In some cases you may find that "XYZ Fund" has started a follow-up fund called "XYZ II." This practice has created new assessment problems for investors, who might assume Fund II should duplicate Fund I's experience; worries about size might diminish, too, but of course any duplicate holdings in the two present the same liquidity problems as if they had been in one portfolio. Furthermore, Fund II may simply hold different stocks—but in the same industry groups as Fund I, thereby creating similar, though not identical, problems. If the fund manager attempts to solve this by using different portfolio managers in the two, then the XYZ II buyer may get an entirely different investment "look," perhaps not what attracted him to it in the first place.

A second question to be answered for you is: How does one judge management's performance in an investment trust? In an individual company you judge performance by the company's earnings record. *In an investment trust you judge performance by its growth in net asset value per share.*

Don't worry, you don't have to figure this net value; the trusts figure it for you and usually compute it once or twice a day. What they do is add the market values of all the securities held and divide the sum by the number of trust shares outstanding. This net asset value per share tells you how much each share would be worth if the trust were to liquidate completely. If management does a good job and buys stocks that go up in price, then the net asset value per share will go up. By noting the trend in net asset value per share (plus the income and capital gain dividends they pay out), you can judge management's performance. Incidentally, some investment services summarize the performance records of the trusts for you. The best known of these is the Wiesenberger service.

Time now to distinguish between the two basic types of investment trusts—the closed-end and the open-end.

CLOSED-END INVESTMENT TRUSTS

These are called closed-end because the *number of shares of the trust is limited.* Let's say a new closed-end trust is brought to market today. One million shares are to be sold at $10 per share. This one million shares is the total amount the trust is planning to issue. After issue, the trust can be bought or sold. It may be listed on one of the exchanges or may trade over-the-counter. Its price will no doubt be influenced by its net asset value per share at that time, but it may sell above this value (at a premium) or below it (at a discount). The resulting premiums or discounts, and to what degree, will depend on investor attitudes toward securities generally and on what people think of each trust's management. In other words, like other securities, it will sell at a price determined by supply and demand.

Remember, if and when you want to sell a closed-end trust, you have to depend on the market—you cannot require the trust to redeem the shares for you (as you will see, stockholders in an open-end trust do redeem their shares with the trust).

Closed-end trusts may differ in their philosophy and/or approach from open-end trusts. Closed-end trusts often can leverage themselves—they can borrow money to buy stocks. Likewise, they may or may not be limited in the kind of investments they can make (some are permitted to own large interests in privately-held companies that have no public market).

Some prominent examples of closed-end trusts are Adams Express, Lehman Corporation, and General American Investors, listed on the New York Stock Exchange, and Standard Shares, which is listed on the American Exchange.

OPEN-END TRUSTS—MUTUAL FUNDS

The number and size of mutual funds in this country has grown like Topsy. In 1950, for example, investors had $2.5 billion in funds investing in common stocks; by 1961, the figure exceeded $20 billion; by the year-end 1979 it had skyrocketed to over $50 billion, and by 1986 it was over $140 billion. This mushrooming can be attributed to the public's growing desire to put their dollars to work, to a rising stock market for most of this period, and to imaginative and aggressive sales efforts. This brings up a *major disadvantage of many mutual funds—the high selling commission involved.* Whereas the commission you pay to buy a stock on the New York Stock Exchange might be 1–2%, many mutuals have a "sales load" ranging anywhere from fractions of 1% to as high as 8½%. A person can buy $1,000 worth of stock on the exchange for a commission of $15.00 (you could buy a closed-end trust for this amount, too), while a similar purchase of a mutual fund *might* cost you $30, $50, or even $85.00. You can see why security salesmen eagerly seek mutual fund purchasers.

There are a few redeeming factors to consider, though. Of real importance is the fact that the sales load on a mutual fund normally covers your cost for *both buying and selling.* You may pay 3%, 5%, 8%, or whatever commission when you buy, but you may *pay no commission* (or, in some cases, only ½ of 1%) *if and when you sell the fund.* This, of course, is *not* true of the commission you pay to buy and sell an investment security on the exchange. You pay your 1–2% when you buy and another 1–2% when you sell. To be completely objective then, you should cut the mutual sales load in half in comparing it with other investments. On average you probably pay twice as much to buy the mutual fund, which is quite a premium to pay. And if you are the type of investor who almost never sells a stock (one who "buys and dies" with an issue), then you may be paying three or four times as much to purchase the mutual fund as you would if you bought a security on the stock exchange. All of this commission figuring is very approximate. With negotiated and discount rates now available, you may be able to buy and sell individual securities with lower rates than indicated, just as you may be able to find well-managed funds with very low sales fees or with *no* such fees (see page 308). Remember, however, that sales fees are only one part of your cost of owning funds; as indicated on pages 300–301, management fees and fund expenses must be considered, too.

Commission rates on funds, however, do drop sharply as the amount of purchase increases. Whereas the sales load might be 8½% on purchases up to $25,000, the rate might be about 7% over $25,000, 5% over $50,000—gradually working down to 1% on purchases over $500,000.

The financial section of newspapers list the prices of many mutual funds. These prices are shown like over-the-counter (unlisted) stocks—with a bid and an ask price. Here is how a typical quotation might appear:

	Bid	Ask
XYZ Mutual Fund	$10.00	$10.75

The bid price represents the net asset value per share of the fund. The ask price is the *net asset value plus the sales load.* In this case, the sales load is 7½%, or 75 cents, on a $10.00 net asset value for a total of $10.75. You buy mutual fund shares at the ask price; if and when you sell, you do so at the bid price.

As you can see, it's going to take time for you to break even after your purchase. It may take some time before XYZ net asset value rises to $10.75 per share—where you can get out without any loss. Thus *mutual funds with high sales loads should only be bought by long-term investors.* If you're investing money you might need in a year or two or even three, don't put the money into these funds. Also, be aware that some funds—called 12b-1 funds (named for the S.E.C. regulation that authorized them)—charge a certain percentage of your fund value annually in lieu of an up-front sales charge. These are obviously not no-load funds, so don't allow sales people to deceive you that they are.

On page 303, I explained that closed-end trusts have a limited number of shares outstanding and that a buyer or seller has to contend with market conditions of supply and demand. This is *not* the case in open-end trusts. They are called open-end because there is (normally) no limit to the number of shares they will sell. Open-end fund organizations are normally eager to sell as many shares as possible, and they stand ready to do so at the asset value plus sales commission. By the same token, mutuals must stand by to redeem their shares in cash at the asset value in unlimited amounts. This gives you a little protection, for even if the market goes down sharply, you know you can get the asset value as it stands on the day you redeem. In a closed-end trust, on the other hand, a sharply declining market might take the stock to a substantial discount from its asset value and you might have to settle for this if you want out.

You might be thinking now: Suppose a large number of mutual fund stockholders decided to redeem all at once. The mutual might have to sell many stocks very suddenly to raise cash for redemption, and these forced sales would tend to lower the asset value very sharply. Or perhaps the mutuals wouldn't be able to raise the cash right away at all. These are legitimate worries. Fortunately, redemptions of this type over the post–World War II period have not been that severe. But the risk, although not a high probability, does exist.

Types of Mutual Funds

There are many types of mutual funds. Some seek very aggressive capital gains and invest in growth stocks and some of the smaller companies that, while more speculative, could become the "IBMs of tomorrow." T. Rowe Price New American Growth, Fidelity Growth Company Fund, and Putnam's Investors are representative of these. Some funds have growth as a major objective, but take a more conservative approach—they concentrate mainly on already proven companies. Typical of these are Investment Company of America, Massachusetts Investors Trust, and Affiliated. Then you have funds whose major objective is to emphasize higher income while perhaps seeking more gradual gains over the years. Then there are "balanced funds," which own bonds and preferred stocks in addition to common stocks. Eaton Vance Investors and Wellington are good examples of these.

In addition, there are certain funds that concentrate on

specific industry groups, such as Chemical Fund. If you are enthusiastic about one segment of our economy but have a hard time making a choice of one stock in the group, you can achieve broad diversification by purchasing an industry fund.

How Have the Funds Performed?

The test of theory is performance. Countless inventors contemplated flying before the Wright brothers. The latter were heroes because their airplane didn't end up in a heap—it performed.

The same thing goes for mutual funds. The theory behind professional management, diversification, constant supervision, and flexibility is fine, but has it proved itself or has it ended up "in a heap"? The answer cannot be generalized because there are so many funds doing business; some have been quite successful and others have been unsuccessful. Just as in choosing individual stocks, you have to analyze the performance of the individual funds to determine whether they're worth considering.

Let's see, however, how an average of the funds performed from 1977–1986. Using the Wiesenberger compilation of mutual fund management results, which incidentally allows for both dividends and capital gain distributions made to shareholders but does *not* account for the sales charge made at the initial time of purchase, here is how a $1,000 investment would have grown from December 31, 1976, to December 31, 1986. Following are four broad categories of funds: (1) the large growth funds; (2) middle-of-the-road "growth and income" trusts; (3) funds that emphasize higher-income common stocks; and (4) very conservative balanced funds, which hold decent amounts of fixed-income securities along with common stocks. Repeating the fact that the sales load has not been deducted and thus the figures should be somewhat *lower*, here is how the mythical $1,000 would have looked after its ten-year life:

Categories:	(1)	(2)	(3)	(4)
	$3,727	$3,856	$3,625	$3,592

The annual compound returns ranged from 13.6% to 14.5%—certainly good numbers, but only in line with the S&P 500 Index annual return of 13.8%. Keep in mind, too, that the stock market had suffered an approximate 40% decline in the two years 1973–74, so fourteen-year results (from 1973–1986) are substantially lower than for the ten-year numbers.

Some funds did a lot better than these averages indicated—and some did a lot worse. The idea, of course, is to buy fund management that will outperform both the market and other funds.

You might have outperformed the statistics shown above by buying certain individual stocks. If you had put your money in certain big winners, you probably would have had far better success in much less time. But would you have bought these "stars"? And, just as important, would you have stayed with them, or would you have sold out for small gains?

One final, important, caveat. Just as in individual stocks, do *not* assume the past is any guarantee of the future. Be careful not to lose your objectivity because of a trust's magnificent recent performance. Its style of investing, perhaps its industry bias, may have just completed a dramatic move upward— resulting in exaggerated price levels. Or it may have produced its most favorable figures when it was considerably smaller in size, with little progress made as it became large. You certainly don't want to buy overvaluation or "undeserved" performance, so be sure to *investigate the reasons for past success. Be careful not to concentrate solely on the record itself.* (My recent book, *Investing with the Best,* is directed to clients of mutual funds and investment advisers; it provides further help in separating solid from less-solid performance numbers.)

OPEN-END NO-LOAD FUNDS

Another form of investment trust is the so-called no-load fund, which is the same as the mutual fund *with the exception that there is no sales charge to the buyer.* This vehicle is open-end in that it continuously offers shares and stands ready to redeem them whenever requested; and all transactions revolve around the trust's net asset value. Here, however, there is no sales charge to either buyer or seller. Thus, in the case of our example on p. 305, the $10 net asset value is the figure used for purchases and sales.

You are probably wondering why anyone would buy a mutual fund when he might find the same diversification and management without the significant sales load. Frankly, given comparable management, there is no reason to pay the load— unless the no-load trust charges a significantly higher annual management fee than the normal ¾ of 1% the mutuals generally charge or unless expenses are so high that your net cost is higher than comparable load funds. Aside from this possibility, the only reason an investor should choose a load over a no-load fund is the all-important management consideration. Good portfolio supervision and management can overcome the sales cost. If this stewardship is really superior in the mutual, the load should not stand in the way.

The burden of proof, however, is decidedly on the load funds to prove consistent superiority over no-load funds. Organizations such as the Vanguard Group of publicly-available no-load funds, along with many others, have compiled excellent records over the years. Given a continuation of such management, anyone considering investment trusts might heed the famous advertising slogan from the clothier Robert Hall: "Why pay for the overhead when you can't wear it."

CONCLUSIONS

When are funds suitable and preferable to direct ownership of individual securities? They seem most logical when: the investor does not have a great deal of time to study his investments; he doesn't have enough money to afford some diversification of stocks; he doesn't have an adviser who can guide him correctly; or he hasn't found an adviser who has his best interests at heart.

If you are in one of these categories, then you should consider investment trusts. Naturally, you should concentrate on superior management to offset the aforementioned additional costs. The right kind of "stewardship" can mean a lot to you and can overcome the additional costs fairly fast under the right conditions.

Mutual funds are ideal for periodic investment programs (i.e., monthly investment plans), to be discussed in Chapter 35.

PART XIII

Some Specific Help in Planning for the Future

33
The Four W's

Journalists are taught to emphasize certain facts in the first paragraph of a story. For one thing, they are taught to answer the "Four W's":

WHO (is involved in the story)?
WHAT (was the action which took place)?
WHERE (did the action occur)?
WHEN (did it happen)?

In the field of investments we have our own Four W's. Just as a journalist has to ask his basic W's, an investment adviser has to answer these:

WHO should invest in the stock market?
WHEN is a person ready to make the plunge?
WHAT is the investor's objective?
WHERE should the money be invested?

Let's look at the W's one by one.

WHO SHOULD INVEST IN THE STOCK MARKET?

There is room for *every* investor in the stock market. After all, there are as many types of stocks as there are types of investors, ranging from the most conservative to the most speculative.

313

So the market presents a potential "home" for everyone. There remains, though, the important question of just *when* a person is ready to take the plunge.

WHEN ARE YOU READY TO INVEST?

A good investment adviser should be able to tell you when you are ready to buy stocks. It goes without saying that you should have the basic necessities and a lot of luxuries you desire before you think of investing. After all, you need to live and enjoy life, and this should precede fortune building.

Please don't forget two necessities that you should certainly have before investing. First, be sure you have adequate *health insurance* for yourself and your family. If you've spent a few days in a hospital of late, you'll know the tremendous costs involved. I'm especially strong on so-called catastrophic health insurance, which protects you against the big expenses. Most families can afford bills that run to a *few hundred* dollars—it is the *thousands* that can create insurmountable problems. If you have normal health insurance *plus* the protection against catastrophe, you can be more relaxed about your investments and this is important.

A second necessity for most (not all) is *life insurance*. Some people call it "death insurance," and I suppose that's a more apropos title because life insurance is best bought for what it can do for your heirs *after* you're gone. Since we're all certain to die someday, "death insurance" is a basic part of our future planning.

But, how much life insurance should you carry? There is no one answer to this question. If you knew you were going to die tomorrow, you'd put all your dollars into life insurance and not one penny into stocks, real estate, or other investments. On the other hand, if you knew you were certain to live to be eighty, you'd put all your money into investments and not a penny into insurance. Some insurance salesmen stress the unpleasant possibility that you could be snuffed out tomorrow and therefore should carry large amounts of insurance to provide an adequate income for your family. To carry these amounts might cost you a small fortune in annual premiums and you'd be "insurance poor." As the saying goes, life insurance is a plan that keeps you poor all your life so you can die rich.

As with many other things in life, you are probably better off striking a happy medium in your life insurance buying. Have a program whereby you increase your coverage as time goes by and as you can better afford the premiums. Life is something of a gamble, and the best bet is that you will enjoy some years of good health and that you can buy progressively over the years.

Let me repeat: *No one* should think of investing in the market or real estate until he has adequate health and (for most) life insurance. In addition, almost every family should have a cash reserve—an emergency fund—before investing. Most home economists suggest that you put at least three months' salary into a savings-type account and never touch it. I heartily agree.

This advice will vary according to circumstances. For example, if you're a person with no dependents, you have little use for life insurance. Or if you know you're going to inherit a lot of money in ten or twenty years, you should protect yourself for now (through cheap term life insurance) instead of for the distant future. Or if your business will carry on regardless of your state of health, you require less life insurance and a smaller emergency fund than the next fellow.

WHAT IS YOUR OBJECTIVE IN INVESTING?

People invest their money for different reasons. Some want to get a higher return than they can obtain from bank interest so they can live better. Some want to see their money grow so they can drive Cadillacs instead of Chevrolets. And some (a large percentage) are looking ahead to retirement and invest so they can have security and comfort in their later years. In Chapter 35 I'll show you how to plan for the future, but now I just want to stress that it's important for your investment adviser to know what your objectives are.

There are two basic questions you should ask yourself and answer honestly. Then make sure your adviser knows the answers, too.

1. *How important is current income to you?*

Some people have a fixation about receiving a certain yield on their money and yet they never spend or use this income. As we've already seen, some of the most successful stock investments have been the growth companies, which generally pay low yields.

On the other hand, you may need additional income to live and higher dividends may be of great importance to you.

Determine which category you fit and let your broker (or counselor) know whether high dividends are necessary.

2. *How many years ahead are you looking for the major benefits of your investments?*

If your investment horizon is at least a few years—and preferably longer—you can consider equity investing. If not (if your time horizon is short), stick to fixed-income type investment vehicles.

WHERE SHOULD YOUR MONEY BE INVESTED?

You've satisfied yourself that you have adequate health and life insurance and an emergency fund; you've set your investment objectives and determined how important current income is to you and how far in the future you are looking for the real fruits of your investments. Now you're ready to pull the trigger!

Where should you put your money? Here again, there are a few questions you should ask yourself and then relate the answers to the person who's helping you with your investing decisions.

1. *When will you be investing again?*

If the capital you now have is all you expect to invest for quite a while, it's safer to stagger your purchases over a period of time—perhaps a few years. If instead you plan to invest sums consistently over the years, you don't have to worry about automatically spacing your investments.

2. *What is your personal temperament?*

Your investments are intended to make money for you, but it is extremely important that they also make you feel hopeful, reasonably relaxed, and confident. Alas, one important goal of having money is peace of mind. Attaining these positive attitudes is complicated by the inevitability of (hopefully only occasional) losses. Let's face it, some people are poor losers. It goes without saying that people who fall into this category should avoid volatile stocks, stocks that fluctuate wildly in the market. By the same token, aggressive investors who are looking for quick gains are not generally going to be happy with a slow-moving utility stock.

I recall an investor who owned conservative stocks, but who had become unhappy with her stable holdings and decided to put her next investment dollars into a growth stock. She did—and she bought a good one. A few days after she purchased her growth stock it had risen from 64 to 71. Her broker didn't hear from her. Then one day the stock dropped sharply from 71 back to 68½—a loss of 2½ points. That day the broker's phone did ring. She was concerned over the drop, even though she still had a 4½ point profit after only owning the stock ten days. The anxious calls continued for a few days until he finally advised her to sell the stock—on the basis that it was making her unhappy. She simply wasn't temperamentally equipped to own volatile stocks (even though she could afford losses) and the wide price movements were disturbing her. Living with a stock that bothers you is like living with a mate who makes you unhappy. So it's best to analyze a stock's "personality" before you "marry" it.

Decide how much risk you are willing to take when investing. I usually put it this way: Decide whether you want to *sleep well* or *eat well.* The "sleep well" stocks are ones that should have limited downside potential; they should be owned to provide you, not with spectacular gains, but with reasonable returns *and* peace of mind. Your "eat well" stocks are intended to put steak and caviar on the table.

> *Don't try for steak*
> *If it keeps you awake.*

Or, put another way:

> *Caviar's indeed a delicate dish,*
> *But the worrisome type should settle for fish.*

34
Stocks for People

I don't mean to imply by this title that there are stocks for animals as well as for human beings. But certain stocks have consistently met the different objectives of investors over the years. Every investment adviser has his own favorites. I have compiled a list of stocks that have proved rewarding for my clients in the past and that *I believe will continue to do well in the future.*

In presenting these securities I have separated them according to the individual's investment position. Determine under which category you fall and concentrate on those comments. I hope they will be helpful to you in shaping your investment decisions now and over the years. (Remember, though, that we are living in a changing society and the stock market changes accordingly. These stocks have to be reassessed according to outlook and according to market price at the time of your reading.)

Just one comment before starting. You will notice that I make reference in each case to the amount of fixed-income securities (bonds and preferred stocks) that are suitable for each portfolio. In our business we call this apportionment of fixed-income securities the amount of *balance* the investor wishes to achieve. The more conservative the investor's objectives, the more balance that person should build in. An elderly widow, for example, might have 50% or even more of her money in fixed-income securities (the other 50% in common stocks or in other equity investments such as real estate), in which case she would have a 50–50 balance. On the other hand, a young professional who has no need for immediate income and is looking twenty or thirty years away for the major benefits of his investment program might have *no* bonds or preferred stocks—and have *no balance* in the portfolio. *Balance refers solely to how the capital is divided between fixed-income securities and common stocks.*

We've talked about not having all your eggs in one stock; it is safer to have spread them around into different stocks. When we talk about *diversification*, we are talking about *how the common stocks are divided*. A certain percentage of the common stock portion of a portfolio might go into chemical stocks, a certain percentage into electrical equipment, foods, oil, utilities, and the like. This is diversification by industry. In addition, an investor may have some geographical diversification; in a large portfolio, for example, it is sometimes wise to have utility stocks from a few geographical locations (if you own utilities at all, that is); or the portfolio may seek international diversification by holding certain foreign securities.

While we're on the subject, let me warn you against *over*diversification. This is a common ill among investors. Many investors, thinking it is safer to keep diversifying and adding new companies to their portfolio, end up with a list of stocks as long as your arm. This ploy may provide very little safety; in fact, it can lead to dangerous consequences, because:

1. There are only so many companies that are truly deserving of investment and too often an investor ends up lowering standards merely to achieve diversification.
2. A long list of stocks is difficult to supervise. It's hard enough to keep current with ten or fifteen stocks, much less to have to keep up with fifty or sixty or more.
3. You pay greater brokerage commissions to buy many securities than you would if you concentrate on a lesser number.
4. You'll no doubt end up with very mediocre performance with too long a list. Even on a strong day in the market, you might see twenty stocks go up, ten go down, and ten remain unchanged.

5. Too much diversification can lead to laziness. When you concentrate on fewer issues, you take each more seriously and tend to analyze more efficiently. When you choose many, you are likely to be indiscriminate—and less efficient.

The most successful portfolios are those that concentrate to a degree rather than "buy the board" and try to own everything.

Now—on to stocks for people.

STOCKS FOR THE ULTRACONSERVATIVE

As for all the categories covered here, much will depend on just how much current income is needed. Fixed-income securities might account for as much as 50% of the list; 50% is conservative, however, and most advisers will put between 30% and 40% in bonds and place the remaining 60–70% in conservative common stocks such as the following:

Utilities such as Southern California Edison, Ameritech
Paper, with UnionCamp
Foods, such as Quaker Oats
Proprietary drugs, like American Home Products, Sterling
 Drug
Banking, such as Wells Fargo
Tobacco, like American Brands
Oil, such as Exxon or Chevron
Household, with Procter & Gamble
Retail trade, like Federated Department Stores
Also, a moderate amount might be invested in solid high-
 yielding industrial companies such as General Motors.

MIDDLE-OF-THE-ROAD OBJECTIVES OF GRADUAL GROWTH WITH GOOD SAFETY

This category is for those who have enough money to live on, but want a moderate current income to supplement their needs—and who need a feeling of security while planning for the future. If you won't retire for ten or twenty years, then I suggest little if any balance. Instead, I would choose the following common stocks:

Utilities, including Ameritech
Household, such as Procter & Gamble
Proprietary drugs, like American Home Products
Ethical drugs, such as Merck, Pfizer, Squibb, Bristol-Myers
Services, including Dun and Bradstreet, Marsh McLennan
Oil, including Amoco
Insurance: General Reinsurance
Electrical equipment: G.E., Emerson Electric
Forest products, like Georgia-Pacific
Banking: Wells Fargo
Tobacco: Philip Morris
Miscellaneous: MMM

AGGRESSIVE GROWTH

These suggestions are for people who are investing to build up capital. They have ample income and, as a matter of fact, would prefer not to add any more direct income; instead they want capital gains. They want their money in common stocks and are not attracted by fixed-income securities. These people should build up a foundation of growth stocks, such as:

Forest products, such as Boise Cascade
Office equipment and computers: IBM, Digital Equipment
Chemicals: Rohm & Haas
Energy: Royal Dutch
Drugs, like Johnson and Johnson, Merck, Pfizer, Squibb
Household: Tambrands, Noxell
Insurance: American International Group, Farmers Group
Hospital services, such as Community Psychiatric
Electronics, like Hewlett-Packard
Services: Marsh McLennan, Dun and Bradstreet, Kelly Services
Leisure time: Capital Cities Broadcasting, Gannett

HOW ABOUT THE KIDDIES?

Before we leave the subject of how to invest for different people, let's pause to consider what you might want to do for the younger set—for children, grandchildren, nephews, or others. Anyone making a gift to a child or having the responsibility for investing a child's money has good intentions, yet this is perhaps the least understood area of investment. Many grave errors have been made here.

Think, for example, of all the dollars that have flowed into annuities for children. Take little Junior, age three months. You don't want him to get his little mitts on any substantial money for eighteen or twenty-one years lest he squander it on a souped-up racing car with mink cushions. You want the money to grow so that it will pay for college or for furniture or a house. Putting money into an annuity is like putting it in the bank at 5–7% interest. You wouldn't consider that a good investment, I'm sure. I subscribe to the belief that money for children should be placed in stocks.

But which stocks? Amazingly, the first reaction of most parents is to put the money into the safest stock they can think of—with little regard for growth. My contention is that you should look instead to the solid growth companies. After all, even if the child is ten years of age, you are looking about ten years ahead and you want growth over this period. A child is an ideal growth investor because he has time and because he won't be reacting to the ups and downs of the market. If you believe in the growth of our country, then you must believe that a ten-year investment in a solid company in a good industry will achieve excellent results for your child. For this reason, I suggest you consult the stocks of either the middle-of-the-road or aggressive growth investor and put them in the safe deposit box for Junior.

35

How to Reach
That Pot of Gold

There are very few of us who don't dream a little. Our dreams, of course, take different forms. Some of us still see ourselves scoring the winning touchdown for dear old Peduka Sub Normal; others picture relaxing by the ol' fishing hole with not a care in the world; and still others dream of building mansions and owning yachts. Aside from scoring touchdowns and achieving very personal desires, many of our dreams have one thing in common: *they require money*.

Please don't misunderstand me. I know that money can't buy happiness and that countless joys and dreams are void of materialism. Yet it does take capital to live now and to retire later in life. Regardless of what you want for yourself now, it is important to build yourself a pot of gold at the end of your working years so that you can enjoy retirement. This involves *planning for the future,* and I hope to be able to help you do this.

"Planning for the future," I had a man growl to me, "is frustrating. You work and work and save your money all your life so that when you're old you can have the things *that only the young can enjoy.*" He had a good point, but it doesn't rule out the necessity for looking ahead and determining what you will need when you do retire.

Ask yourself how much *income you will need* when you stop working. Then look at how you will get this income. More often than not, people find that they haven't provided enough for themselves. And more often than not, they find out *too late* that they're short on capital.

Pick a monthly income figure out of the air. Assume you will need the equivalent of today's $1,000 per month to retire twenty years from now and live the way you want. But how much will be needed in 2006 to buy what $1,000 per month will buy you today? Needless to say, you need to account for inflation in your figuring. There's no way, however, of estimating cost of living increases very accurately for the future. From 1958 to 1966 inflation was a little under 1½% per year; since then the U.S. has experienced wide swings in the inflation rate, with certain years producing double-digit cost increases and others (particularly 1985–86) hovering in the 2–4% range. Let's assume a longer-term rate of 5% per year—a rate necessitating over $2,600 in year twenty to equate to today's $1,000 buying power.

Now that we've decided how much you'll need, we'd better see *where the money's going to come from.* Most of us are entitled to Social Security, and this might provide about $600 per month— the amount will no doubt be raised as time goes by. Let's assume that it is raised in line with inflation to about $1,600 per month by the year 2000 (I know this sounds astronomical, but the figure comes from tacking on the same 5% growth to our $600 base).

Next we should figure any other income you will be receiving at that time. Let's assume you will receive a pension from your company of about $500 per month when you retire.

Here's the way you stand right now:

In 2006, you will get:	$1,600	Social Security
	500	Pension
	$2,100	Total
In 2006, you will need:	$2,600	
You are lacking:	$ 500	per month

Unless inheritance promises to meet this requirement, you have to count on some form of investments to bring you that extra $500 per month in 2006. The logical question is: How much capital will you need in 2006 to give you an income of $500 per month, or $6,000 per year?

This is hard to answer because we don't know what kind of return after taxes we can count on from bonds, stocks, or real estate twenty years from now. But assuming an average after-tax return of 7% on your money, you will need almost $90,000 in assets to produce this $6,000 per year (7% of $90,000 = $6,300). Or you can turn over about $55,000–$60,000 in cash to a life insurance company and they'll guarantee to pay you $6,000 a year for the rest of your life (in this case, however, you will have no capital to leave to your heirs—the $55,000–$60,000 is no longer yours). Or you might find something that will net you 10% on your money and you'll need $60,000 (10% of $60,000 = $6,000).

Thus, depending on how you want to do it, you will need between $60,000 and $90,000 in 2006 to bring your income up to where you want it. Let's say that you need about $80,000 to live in the style to which you're accustomed twenty years from now.

Now the big question: How are you going to accumulate $80,000 in the next twenty years? The answer: through *saving*. Now don't run away. I, too, know that the number of people who are able to save $80,000 during their lives is small. But I also know that the reason so few are able to is that *they don't start early enough*.

You know that money compounds as it sits collecting a return. Take $100 and invest it at 6%; the first year your investment will grow to $106; the next year it will grow to $112.36. By the twelfth year it will be $201.22—it will have doubled. Thus the secret to accumulating capital is to start early and let your money compound itself.

Even though I know the figures, I never cease to be amazed at *how little a person has to save every year to accumulate a huge amount of money later in life*. To illustrate the point, here's a table that shows you *how much money you have to save each year to end up with $10,000 in fifteen, twenty, twenty-five, thirty, thirty-five, and forty years*.

	Yearly Saving That Will Produce $10,000—If Money Is Invested at a Compounding Rate of Return of			
Number of Years	6%	8%	10%	12%
40	$ 65	$ 40	$ 23	$ 13
35	90	60	37	23
30	133	90	61	41
25	182	135	102	75
20	272	220	175	139
15	430	370	315	268

The 6% column could represent money put in a bank savings account; the 8% column could represent net return from corporate bonds; and the 10% column should be achieved by putting your dollars into stocks or real estate. Naturally it's hard to generalize and predict just what rate of return (including both dividends and capital gains) you will get from stocks, but 6 to 10% after taxes is certainly an attainable range.

Now let's go back to your problem of amassing $80,000 over twenty years. The table tells how much you'll have to invest to accumulate *$10,000* in twenty years:

At   6%—$272 per year
At   8%—$220 per year
At 10%—$175 per year

Since we need $80,000, we have to multiply these figures by 8—which produces the following sums to be set aside (invested):

At   6%—$2,176
At   8%—$1,760
At 10%—$1,400

If you take the most conservative course and put all your money in the bank (ridiculous, of course, with low-risk Treasury and U.S. Government agencies' bonds yielding 7–9%), you will have to save $181 per month ($2,176 per year) to amass $80,000 in twenty years.

If your investments perform at the 10% rate, *you will only* *have to put aside $116 per month ($1,400 per year) to achieve your pot of gold.* Chances are you can save at least a portion of this amount and can count on a pretty good hunk of investment capital in 2006. The main thing is to *get started now* and let your investment snowball as time goes by.

If you're fortunate enough to have forty productive, saving years ahead of you, your pot of gold should be a cinch to reach. The table shows that you need set aside only $40 *per year* to accumulate $10,000 over forty years at the 8% rate of return. To amass $40,000, you will need four times as much, or $160 per year ($13.30 per month). I ask you—how many people cannot afford to do this?

The idea of investing money regularly in stocks has been widely publicized by both the New York Stock Exchange and the many mutual funds. The idea is simple. You send in your money periodically just as you would deposit money in a Christmas Club savings account in your local bank. Investing small amounts is "painless"—you will scarcely miss the money—and these small amounts can grow to large sums over the years.

Once people thought that stocks were only for the very rich, but the mutual funds have made a strong play for the small investor in recent years.

The funds have plans, which they usually call "periodic" or "cumulative" investment plans. Generally, there is an initial investment requirement of $300 or $500—after which you can invest in periodic installments as long as you contribute a minimum of around $300 per year. These plans normally call for automatic reinvestment of dividends (regular dividends at the fund's price with commission; capital gain distributions at net asset value without commission). Caution: some funds charge 4% for dividend reinvestment, an amount so excessive that it negates the very advantage of such reinvestment.

I recommend fund periodic investment programs because they are generally cheaper than buying small amounts of individual stocks outright. Investing up to $100 at one time on the exchange will generally entail a hefty commission; $200 at one time might cost 10%—and these are all "one-way" commissions (you have to pay another commission if and when you sell the stock). In contrast, you pay a commission generally only when you buy a fund—the 8% commission covers both buying and selling. *Unless you are investing over $200 at one time, it is normally as cheap or cheaper to buy the funds than it is to buy a stock on the New York Stock Exchange.* If you are investing less than $200, you may as well avail yourself of both the lower cost and the professional management provided by investment trusts—and this is where I believe the funds are most useful. They are ideal for a long-term periodic savings program and I strongly recommend them to anyone wanting to build a pot of gold.

DOLLAR AVERAGING

Periodic investment programs have many advantages. When you buy a stock at different intervals over a period of years, you will buy some at very low prices, some at high levels, and some in between. When you buy on a consistent basis, you are not trying to outguess the market—you are only trying to establish a reasonable average cost for yourself. As a matter of fact, a person engaged in systematic investing *actually benefits from declining prices* along the way. Say, for example, you have decided to invest $100 per month in a stock or an investment trust that sells at $10 per share. The first month your $100 buys you 10 shares. By the next month the stock has declined to $9, but is this drop cause to shed tears? Absolutely not. Just the opposite. Why? Because now your $100 buys you 11 1/10 shares of the same stock. You are getting more shares for the same amount of money. If the stock eventually sinks to $5, your $100 will buy you 20 shares. Now you are getting even more for your money. This is great—*provided that the stock eventually recovers and goes way up in price*. In other words, the problem of *timing is eliminated*—the only problem is selection of the right stock.

Many large investors, such as insurance companies and colleges, adhere to investing fixed amounts on a periodic program. In essence, they are saying, "We believe in the future of this company. We want to own the stock, and rather than try to pick out the low points (and maybe never get them), we aim for a reasonable average cost." They practice "dollar averaging," and this can be a wise policy for individuals as well as institutions. Dollar averaging forces you to buy your stock or stocks just when you might hesitate to do so—when the outlook for the market is gloomy and stock prices are low. This is, of course, precisely the time when you should be buying.

PART XIV

An Explosive Area for Profits

36

"Bikini" Stocks

Bikini bathing suits have been the rage of the beaches throughout the world for many years. The major reason for their popularity is, of course, that these small suits provide the male population with maximum exposure to feminine "pulchritude." The more curvaceous a woman is, the more she benefits from the small bathing suit. Of course these days, with more *men* wearing bikini briefs, women now have the same opportunities for "exposure" previously limited to only the male of the species.

It stands to reason that common stocks that provide maximum exposure to "pleasant things" will be popular, too. The more curvaceous a company is (with exciting products and developments), the more it benefits from "a small bathing suit"—in this case a *small amount of common stock outstanding*.

Consider, for example, a company that has a new product with dynamic possibilities. Assume this product has a sales potential of $10 million, on which the company should show a profit of $1 million. This $1 million may sound enticing, but everything is relative: to a very large company with 100 million shares outstanding, $1 million is peanuts (only 1 cent per share), whereas to a small organization with only 100,000 shares, $1 million amounts to a gigantic $10 per share.

Thus, you can see the possibilities that exist in a growing company with only a small number of shares on which to compute its earnings (a "small capitalization," as they say in investment circles). A company like General Electric, which has over 455 million shares, *has* to come up with *countless* new discoveries that will produce a large volume of sales and profits to keep earnings per share growing, while companies with only a few hundred thousand shares can grow rapidly with only one or two new developments. The experience of Mead Johnson and Company with its weight-reducing formula Metrecal was a perfect example, although it was short-lived. Mead Johnson had a little over 1¾ million shares outstanding (a relatively small capitalization) when it introduced Metrecal, and this one product was primarily responsible for the company's earnings ballooning from $3.02 per share in 1959 to $7.25 per share in 1960. This magnified effect was, in turn, responsible for Mead Johnson stock going from a low of 60 to a high of 164¾ during this one year.

Of course, there are two sides to the coin. Just as gains are magnified, so are losses. A small company that spends a great deal of money on a new development only to see it flop will experience large per share losses.

Still, because of the dramatic results that can be shown by small capitalization companies, investors should be willing to pay a premium to own the promising ones. But you do have to be particular about which bikini stocks you buy.

RESULTS OF FIRST-EDITION (*PRIMER*) BIKINIS

In the first printing of *Stock Market Primer* (1962) I compiled a list of eight bikini companies that had proved successful for me in the preceding years and that still appeared attractive. For the sake of example, I summed up the potential developments to which an investor had what I considered maximum exposure in each stock. Following is an *exact* reprint from the 1962 edition, showing my chosen "bikini" companies, the number of shares they had outstanding at that time, and the major developments that appeared to be the source of potential future excitement.

"BIKINI" STOCKS, 1962

Company	Shares Outstanding (No.)	Developments That Could Be Magnified
American District Telegraph	651,000	ADT, approximately 80%-owned by Grinnell Corp., is the nation's largest factor in the field of burglar and fire-alarm protection. Rising costs of employing round-the-clock watchmen plus constantly rising insurance rates (large discounts come from having efficient alarm systems) invite growing use of ADT services. Government has instituted antitrust suit against Grinnell; if ADT spins off to become a completely separate entity, its stock would become popular. True earnings hidden by heavy depreciation charges.
Dymo Industries	442,000	Company has a unique labeling tape (used in conjunction with its own machines) that could have wide application by both consumers and by industry.
Heli-Coil	698,000	Has patented fastening device with increased strength, which could open up unlimited markets for a wide variety of uses.
Interstate Hosts (now Host International)	841,000	Provides participation in the future of air travel without being subject to regulation by CAB. Provides restaurant, beverage, snack bar, gift shop, and newsstand services in many airports. Los Angeles airport (a major installation for Interstate) to be open completely in 1962.

Company	Shares Outstanding (No.)	Developments That Could Be Magnified
Masco Corp.	734,000	Masco manufactures the Delta faucet, one of the top selling one-lever faucets in the U.S. Delta has only one moving part and has been strongly merchandised by management. Trend in bathroom construction is toward the single-lever faucet.
Paddington Corp.	1,191,000	Exclusive distributor of J&B liquors, which have not yet been introduced into certain geographical areas (low saturation point).
Raychem Corp.	1,001,000	One of the few companies in the U.S. well advanced in the treatment of wire insulation and tubing by radiation. This method imparts certain qualities to materials (rubber, plastics, etc.) that add to temperature resistance, strength, etc.
Howard W. Sams	501,000	Leader in supplying technical diagrams of electronic equipment to repair and maintenance people. Recently bought Bobbs-Merrill, book publishers.

Just for the record, here is how these eight companies performed over the ensuing six years (all prices adjusted for subsequent splits, stock dividends, etc.):

Company	Sept. 1962 Price	Subsequent High	% Gain to High	1968 Year-End Price	% Gain to 1968
A.D.T.	12½	42	+237	39¾	+218
Dymo	18⅝	52⅛	+180	26½	+43
Heli-Coil	11½	39⅜	+251	23⅜	+103
Host Int.	3½	48	+1270	39	+1015
Masco	5½	48⅜	+780	41¼	+650
Paddington	23¾	45⅝	+84	40*	+68
Raychem	29½	323	+995	299	+915
Sams (Howard)	20	62	+210	58¼†	+190

*Merged into Charing Cross Importers, Ltd.
†Merged into International Telephone and Telegraph; price reflects 1968 value of ITT stock.

As you can see, the overall performance of these bikini equities was pretty dramatic. The eight stocks showed an *average gain of 400%—they quintupled in value*. Within the group, we find *two* that multiplied *over 10 times their September 1962 levels* (Host International and Raychem), one (Masco) that went up 7½ times, and two more (ADT and Sams) that about tripled. Their owners would have derived an even higher return if they had been able to sell near interim high points.

One further point should be stressed here—something that spells out the philosophy of many investors who seek out high-reward situations. Successful venture capitalists and special-situation stock buyers take the approach that a few big winners will achieve their goal. Realizing that it is difficult to predict exactly which individual stocks will succeed famously, they take a package approach and buy a handful (or so) of situations. Within the package, they hope to have selected a few like Hosts, Masco, and Raychem that will appreciate sufficiently to bring about a very high return. *Most important, this philosophy dictates holding on for the huge returns those several situations might produce*. As I hope you have already gleaned from your reading, the secret to success lies in thinking *BIG* and not being satisfied with small profits (if amassing large amounts of capital is your goal). Unless you absorb this philosophy, this chapter—or any other on common stock selection—will be of limited value to you.

Although the performance of these bikini stocks was dynamic, in many cases, the experience shown constitutes but a part of the story. So you can understand the approaches necessary to bikini selection, let me trace the reasoning and results of four of these companies—ones that I uncovered and recommended strongly to people many years ago.

Dymo was first brought to market in June 1960 at $9 per share. I knew absolutely nothing of this company at that time, but a few weeks later I saw its product in action and was impressed by it. I proceeded to study Dymo and found that it had many growth-company characteristics: management was aggressive, honest, able, and hard-working ("hungry," as we say in our business); its labeling machine was well engineered and the specialized Dymo tape had patent protection; the tape was expendable, meaning that repeat sales might be large; and competition was almost nonexistent.

Equally important was the fact that Dymo had less than 450,000 shares outstanding. At the time Dymo stock was selling for $14 per share, and I had only to ask the following question to conclude the stock was a great buy: Can Dymo some day soon earn $1 million? This question was so important to answer because with less than 450,000 shares outstanding, a net profit of $1 million meant per share earnings of over $2, which in turn suggested far higher prices for Dymo stock than the existing $14 per share (under P/E multiples common at that time).

My analysis concluded that Dymo had at least this earning potential in the near future, and it was on this basis that I became enthusiastic about this stock.

Before long the company had reached the $1 million level in earning power—and Dymo common stock soared to $120 per share. In a span of a few years the stock appreciated over eight times. The combination of a growing and profitable product and small capitalization had indeed produced spectacular results. Incidentally, Dymo is an example of a bikini company that required real flexibility. The company did not capitalize on its success as it should have; it failed to develop new products to complement its line—and, as was to be expected, competition soon appeared on the scene. Because of this, I changed my position on the stock (very luckily, near its high).

Another successful bikini stock of mine was Masco Corporation. In contrast to Dymo, which had just come on the market as a new issue and was trading over-the-counter, Masco had been publicly held for many years and was listed on the Detroit Stock Exchange. As with Dymo, I was attracted to Masco because of its product—the Delta one-lever faucet. I had learned that one-lever faucets were becoming the trend in certain types of new residential construction and modernization, and I soon discovered that Masco's Delta faucet was increasing its acceptance and popularity. Masco had engineered a quality product—one that had only one moving part (an important sales feature)—and had also developed strong merchandising. It was one of the top two manufacturers in its field.

I was amazed when I learned of Masco's growth record since it had introduced the Delta product in 1954 (the company had previously concentrated on serving the major auto manufacturers with auto parts—basically an unattractive business). Here's how the company's record looked in January 1961 when I first became interested in it:

Year	Earnings per Share
1956	$.06
1957	.15
1958	.17
1959	.48

You can imagine how amazed I was to find that Masco stock was selling at only $3.50 per share. Here was an ideal bikini stock— a well-managed company with a fine product line, increasing business, and only (*not* adjusted for subsequent splits) 367,000 shares outstanding—and it was selling for less than 7 times 1959 earnings (more than a year before).

My analysis (which, as in the case of Dymo, included contact with management) led me to believe that profits in the year just completed (1960) were higher than those of 1959, and that 1961 would show even better results. Some months later Masco reported 1960 net income of 65 cents per share. Yet the stock was still relatively unknown and was selling for a very reasonable $6 per share.

The rest of the story is certainly gratifying to me. Thanksgiving Day of 1961 (less than a year after my discovery of Masco) found Masco stock at (adjusted) $27 per share—or almost 8 times its worth in January. A little over four years later Masco had doubled again in price and was thus up about 16 times over its original "discovery" price. And today the stock is selling for over 400 times this original entry price.

The attraction of Host International should have been fairly obvious. As the description on page 335 indicates, the company had successful service operations located in airports that were certain to see increasing traffic over the years. In short, the thesis behind this bikini company was that it offered participation in the growth of air traffic without the vagaries of federal regulation.

Typical of so many bikini situations, Host International took a number of years to blossom and become fully appreciated. As a matter of fact, I lived with this stock for several years without finding any acceptance of its real worth. Once accepted, however, the stock found higher and higher evaluation by the investment community, which of course meant a higher and higher P/E multiple. At any rate, the stock multiplied more than elevenfold over the period 1962–1968.

Raychem was a company that had an unusual technological know-how in an area that held startling possibilities. It had a tremendous lead time on potential competitors—something that is hard to come by and is especially important in a bikini capitalization. Like Host International, Raychem took some time to develop. As a matter of fact, my research department published the "bible" on Raychem in July 1963 (some eighteen months after I completed the writing of *Primer*'s first edition) and the stock was actually lower then than before. A few years later, significant profits were experienced by the company and the combination of these figures and a real acceptance of Raychem by investors took the stock up to the $300 level (since then, the stock has been split the equivalent of 6-for-1 and its $103⅛ market price in 1986 was equal to around $620 on the original recommended price). Once again, concept plus earnings plus small number of shares outstanding brought unusual happiness to those who recognized bikini thinking.

SUBSEQUENT BIKINIS, 1976 AND 1980

In the last two revisions of *Primer* I submitted another set of bikini stocks—although then I used "larger bathing suits." I stated then that "I found it difficult to isolate a representative list of companies with extremely small capitalizations." This, I commented, brought up "an important investment point: that one should never 'strain' to produce investment ideas. If they come naturally after study, then they should be utilized; but if they do not, a person makes a mistake trying too hard."

I then listed seven companies of varying sizes in 1976 and then ten in 1980 that seemed to possess unusual prospects. Here are descriptions of these as they appeared in the two "Primer" editions, followed by performance of the stocks as of 1986:

"BIKINI" STOCKS, 1976

Company	No. of Shares Outstanding	Developments That Could Lead to Exceptional Growth
Beverage Management	1,713,000	Small but rapidly growing bottler and distributor of soft drinks. Opportunities for both geographical expansion and extension of product line.
Hanes Corp.	3,979,000	Company has built a strong consumer franchise through its L'Eggs division. Has recently survived entries in packaged hosiery and pantyhose from larger companies—none of which have been able to penetrate the L'Eggs market domination.
LA-Z-Boy Chair	4,643,000	The "Cadillac" of the little-known but rapidly growing reclining chair market. Very low saturation level of recliners in homes here and abroad. Unusual features of LA-Z-Boy chairs plus strong distribution. Now entering recliner-rocker and office furniture market.

Company	No. of Shares Outstanding	Developments That Could Lead to Exceptional Growth
Martin Processing	1,967,000	Possesses unusual know-how in the processing of nylon and polyester yarns for carpets. Ties in with trend toward multicolored tufted carpets.
Neutrogena	934,000	Company has successful skin-care product line, which it is now broadening. One successful new product could have strong impact on earnings, with existing small capitalization.
Pittway Corp.	3,259,000	Whereas part of Pittway's business is unexciting, more than 75% of earnings now come from Alarm Device Manufacturing Company—one of the most successful manufacturers of burglar, smoke-detection, and other security products. This business is growing very rapidly and has a very exciting future.
WD-40 Company	1,217,000	Admittedly a one-product company, but WD-40 has ever-growing uses as lubricant, rust preventive, etc. Still very low sales base and potential for significantly higher market saturation.

"BIKINI" STOCKS, 1980

Company	No. of Shares Outstanding	Developments That Could Lead to Exceptional Growth
Alpha Industries	2,511,000	Leader in millimeter technology, which will be used in "smart weaponry"—an important area of concentration in the future.
Chas. River Breeding Labs	2,641,000	Holds proprietary position in breeding, raising, and selling of animals for laboratory testing of all sorts.
Crawford & Co.	8,052,000	The country's leading independent adjuster of property and casualty claims and losses for insurance companies. An interesting service company, not well known in investment circles.
Moog Inc.	2,193,000	The world's leading producer of high-performance valves, which are critical to important and growing aerospace and industrial applications. One interesting way to invest in the future of industrial robots—rapidly increasing in usage here and abroad.

Company	No. of Shares Outstanding	Developments That Could Lead to Exceptional Growth
Pay'n Pak Stores	4,426,000	Fast-growing retailer in the home improvement (do-it-yourself) field. Located in fast-growing regions.
People's Drug Stores	3,689,000	A self-service drugstore chain; in good locations and with strong management (which owns a large share of the company).
Perini Corp.	3,363,000	A major contractor, but this is of little interest; company owns substantial real estate, which is undervalued on its balance sheet. Company is using its cash to repurchase its own shares.
Pinkerton's	2,360,000	Leading company in security services. Once a recognized growth company, it has gone through a flat period but seems to have made changes that promise renewed growth.
Trus Joist Corp.	3,600,000	Manufacturer of patented structural components for buildings. Large cost advantages make for interesting future for Trus Joist products.
Twin City Barge	1,604,000	Should participate in increasing barge business which facilitates grain shipments both domestically and overseas. (Barge shipment is cheaper than either truck or rail.)

Needless to say, there are risks in mentioning stocks in any publication where follow-up is impossible. An important investing trait is flexibility, which includes the need to reassess original judgments—which in turn includes the willingness to alter opinions and sell securities once favored. Further complications exist in Bikini-type lists because companies are sometimes bought out for cash, leading to imprecise performance results, especially when these buy-outs occur soon after publication. (This is exactly what occurred with Beverage Management and Hanes from the 1976 Bikini list and Pinkerton's and People's Drug from the 1980 edition.) With these caveats in mind, here is how the seventeen individual stocks and the two groupings fared from writing time through 1986:

1976 BIKINIS

Company	Average 1976 Price	Subsequent High Price	% Gain to High	Average 1986 Price	% Gain to 1986
Beverage Management	10⅝	25¾	+142	24 (a)	+126
Hanes	21½	61 (b)	+184	61 (b)	+184
LA-Z-Boy	18¾	72½	+287	62⅜	+233
Martin Processing	8½	27¾	+127	17⅝	+107
Neutrogena	1⅛	43½	+3767	34⅞	+3000
Pittway	35⅝	107½	+202	92¾	+160
WD-40	2⅞	33¼	+1057	27	+839
		AVERAGE	+824		+664

(a) Merged into Forstmann Little & Co. in January 1983 at $24 per share (cash) to Beverage shareholders.
(b) Merged into Consolidated Foods in January 1979 at $61 per share (cash) to Hanes.

1980 BIKINIS

Company	Average 1980 Price	Subsequent High Price	% Gain to High	Average 1986 Price	% Gain to 1986
Alpha Industries	$4\frac{3}{8}$	$28\frac{1}{8}$	+543	$9\frac{1}{2}$	+117
Chas. River Breeding	28	77	+175	$66\frac{1}{4}$(c)	+137
Crawford & Co.	$10\frac{1}{2}$	$26\frac{1}{4}$	+150	$22\frac{1}{8}$	+111
Moog Inc.	$13\frac{7}{8}$	$31\frac{7}{8}$(f)	+130	$16\frac{3}{4}$(f)	+21
Pay'n Pak Stores	$9\frac{7}{8}$	24	+143	$14\frac{3}{8}$	+46
People's Drug	$7\frac{5}{8}$	34(e)	+346	34(e)	+346
Perini	$18\frac{1}{2}$	$58\frac{1}{8}$(f)	+214	$43\frac{3}{4}$(f)	+343
Pinkerton's	39	$77\frac{1}{2}$(d)	+99	$77\frac{1}{2}$(d)	+99
Trus Joist	19	$36\frac{3}{4}$	+93	$30\frac{3}{8}$	+60
Twin City Barge	$11\frac{3}{4}$	17	+45	$\frac{7}{8}$	−93
		AVERAGE	+194		+119

(c) Merged into Bausch & Lomb in February of 1984; received $1\frac{3}{4}$ shares of B&L, market price 1986 $\$37\frac{3}{8}$.
(d) Acquired by American Brands in January of 1983 for $77.50 per share in cash.
(e) Acquired by Inasco Ltd. in May of 1984 for $34 per share in cash.
(f) Split into two separate companies in 1984; prices include both entities.

The 1976 Bikini list certainly performed well, averaging a 664% increase (23% per year compounded) for the seven stocks over the ten years, even after absorbing the penalty in the calculation resulting from the 1979 and 1983 buy-outs of Hanes and Beverage Management. Incidentally, the S&P 500 (with dividends, which were *not* included in the returns for the Bikinis) rose 130% over this same 1976–86 span or 8.7% per year compounded.

The 1980 edition didn't fare nearly as well. Six-year results averaged "only" 119%, or 14% per year compounded, versus 92% (11.5% per year compounded) for the S&P 500. While I obviously would have preferred the 1980 group to have been as stellar as prior editions, the experience serves as a good example for those of you contemplating investment in smaller-capitalization Bikini-type stocks.

Firstly, many of the best performers took time to develop. In the 1976 list, Martin Processing was an early disaster of sorts, Pittway was erratic in its upward progression, and LA-Z-Boy's success was very late in coming. Patience was required for all three.

Secondly, it is dangerous for investors to assume that

original recommendations will persist and/or that they are as valid any time in the future as they were at the beginning. Frankly, my enthusiasm for Martin Processing of the 1976 group waned well before it skyrocketed in price; fortunately, the same change of opinion by me occurred for Alpha Industries, Moog, and Twin City Barge well before they underperformed (in the case of Twin City, before it crumbled!). The lesson here is a repeat of the earlier plea for flexibility and the willingness to recognize mistakes and to do something about them.

With the necessary caveats that individual company progress, market prices, and opinions can change sharply between the time of this writing and when you read it, I hope it is worthwhile to submit a 1991 Bikini list for you. Remember, *the names are included as a learning tool, not as lasting investment recommendations.* I hope the exercise helps you to think in terms of *sound concepts and sound businesses which hopefully fit into the pattern for the future.* Here are ten "learning examples" for your critique and thought stimulation:

"BIKINI" STOCKS, 1991

Company	No. of Shares Outstanding	Development(s) Which Could Lead to Strong Growth
Baldwin Technology	17,056,000	One of the world's premier manufacturers of accessory equipment to the printing industry. Some products are consumables, most are proprietary capital equipment to increase efficiency and lower costs. Baldwin has purchased several (smaller) equipment suppliers. Synergies appear to be setting the stage for sharply higher profitability.

Company	No. of Shares Outstanding	Development(s) Which Could Lead to Strong Growth
Berkley (W.R.)	17,845,000	Insurance holding company concentrating in south and midwestern U.S. Property casualty is a tough business, but company is doing better than others—and the insurance cycle should recover soon.
Brady (W.H.) Co.	7,156,000	Leader in "surface" chemistry; new products aid labeling of hazardous chemicals and safety warnings (to conform to new federal laws).
Cabletron Systems	27,788,000	Manufacturer of computer interconnection products. Local area network systems are *the* future, and company is a leader in this field (including fiber optic systems).
Curtice-Burns Foods	8,874,000	Producer of wide range of food specialty goods, with strong regional brand acceptance.
DEP Corp.	5,686,000	Small manufacturer and marketer of personal care products; now expanding its product lines.
Diebold, Inc.	13,263,000	One of several manufacturers of ATM machines; plus point-of-sale and security products. IBM just became their main marketer in Europe (of ATM's). Bank consolidations mean fewer branches but more ATM's, since these machines should become useful way beyond cash withdrawals.

Company	No. of Shares Outstanding	Development(s) Which Could Lead to Strong Growth
Employee Benefit Plans	7,571,000	A leader in the design and servicing of health care plans and programs for employers. One way to offset the skyrocketing health costs that are becoming more an employers' responsibility.
Gibson (C.R.)	5,045,000	One of the nation's oldest producers of gift, stationery, and "memory" products; expanding product efforts.
Helene Curtis	9,679,000	Cosmetic company that has fought successfully against much larger competitors. Low labor factor; strong marketer and developer of new products. Excellent eventual acquisition candidate for larger company.
Loctite Corp.	36,400,000	Worldwide producer of many chemical specialties, with fairly unique markets. Fine long term record of earnings growth, yet company not that well known.
McGrath Rent Corp.	7,515,000	Fast-growing rental company specializing in modular buildings, now expanding into test and measurement instrument leasing/rental. Fine record, excellent management.
Waverly Press	4,038,000	Publisher of medical and scientific books and publications. Family-controlled business becoming slightly more aggressive.

In addition to the above, the Bikini thesis in 1991 can be extended to some large companies which have entered into so-called Leveraged Buyout plans—and which have securities trading in the marketplace that represent small interests in what are essentially privately owned enterprises. Contrary to my normal Bikini approach, these *are* big companies, and they carry significant debts on their balance sheets. Small pieces of some well-known names such as Holiday (Inns) Corp., Multimedia, FMC, Owens-Corning Fiberglas, and Revlon are, however, available for investors willing to assume the risks of highly leveraged entities.

PART XV
Do's and Don'ts in the Stock Market

37
Common Stock Commandments

The preceding pages have given you important fundamentals about investments and the stock market. In addition, I have provided rules in each chapter to improve your success in common stocks. Now I have some further comments that should be equally helpful to you. I call these "common stock commandments" and here they are:

1. *Do not make hasty, emotional decisions about buying and selling stocks.*

When you follow your emotions without stepping back for reflection, you are duplicating what the "masses" are doing, and this is not generally profitable. It is better to allow your emotions to return to normal, so that you can weigh the pros and cons objectively. Never allow yourself to be pressured into buying and selling securities by anyone. Hard-sell techniques hint there may be "stale merchandise on the shelf," and that's not what you want. If you're in doubt about buying or selling, my advice is to *do nothing*.

2. *If you are convinced that a company has dynamic growth prospects, do not sell it just because it looks temporarily too high.*

You may never be able to buy it back lower in price and you stand to miss a potential *big winner*—which is just what you should be looking for. Perhaps the gravest error I've seen made over the years is selling great companies with bright future prospects solely because they temporarily looked a few points too high.

3. *Do not fall in love with stocks to the point where you can no longer be objective in your appraisal of them.*

Stocks are different from human beings. You'd be foolish to think of your spouse all day the way he or she looks the first thing in the morning rather than under more normal circumstances. But you do have to scrutinize stocks and the companies they represent and think of their worst points; you have to reassess your feelings constantly and you must be brutal and unemotional in your appraisal.

4. *Do not concern yourself as much with the market in general as with the outlook for individual stocks.*

Oftentimes you will see a fine stock come down to an unquestionable bargain price, only to let your feeling about the general market dissuade you from buying it. As they say, it's not the stock market that counts, but the market for individual stocks. Buy a good value when it appears and do not let the general market sentiment unduly influence your decision.

5. *Forget about stock market "tips."*

If you learn to exercise good judgment, you won't have to rely on unreliable information. This is hardly an original point, but it's too often ignored. I'll never forget the day I was visited by a certain client at my office when I was Research Director for a brokerage firm. He wanted a recommendation on a good stock and I suggested he buy AMP, Inc., which looked very attractive to me. I related my reasoning to him about the industry, the company, and its apparent prospects, and I showed him all the facts and figures I had on the stock. I spent ten or fifteen minutes extolling the glowing outlook for this company, after which the client told me he would think about it and let me know. The next morning he called me and placed an order—for an entirely different stock, one of the "Happyjack Uranium" type. He explained he "had heard some very good things" about this stock and he wanted to own it. A year or so later his purchase was about half of his cost and he visited me again. This time he told me the "source" of his information: he had spent an hour at a very fancy cocktail lounge the evening of our original meeting and had overheard a very confidential conversation about this stock. A fine thing, I thought (and my client agreed). Here I had spent hours researching AMP, Inc. and had given him the benefits of these hours—and he turned around and disregarded this in favor of a hot tip he overheard between two strangers who had consumed an ample supply of martinis. This is such a common temptation that I can't resist warning you against following tips in the stock market.

6. *You get what you pay for in the stock market (as in everything else in life).*

Some people consider a $5 stock potentially attractive just because it's low in price. Nothing could be further from the truth. High-priced stocks usually provide far better value than low-priced stocks; they generally have more earnings, dividends—more value—behind them than the low-priced issues. Likewise, high-priced stocks go into "better hands" (many are purchased by longer-term holders), while the low-priced issues most often go into the hands of speculators and gamblers, who may be less informed and inclined to occasional panic selling. Also remember that high-priced stocks carry one potential that cheap stocks do not—they are all potential split candidates.

7. *Remember that stocks always look worst at the bottom of a bear market (when an air of gloom prevails) and best at the top of a bull market (when everybody is optimistic).*

Have strength and buy when things do look bleak and sell when they look too good to be true.

8. *Remember that you'll seldom—if ever—buy stocks right at the bottom or sell them right at the top.*

The stock market generally goes to extremes: when pessimism dominates, stocks go lower than they really should, on the basis of their fundamentals, and when optimism runs rampant, stocks go higher than they deserve to. Knowing this, don't expect your stocks to go up in price immediately after you buy them or to go down after you sell them, even though you are convinced that your analysis of their value is correct.

9.   *Do not buy stocks as you might store merchandise on sale.*

No doubt you've seen people scrapping and clamoring for goods on sale at stores like Macy's. They fight to buy this merchandise because of the reduced price and limited supply of the merchandise. Too often shoppers buy things they don't need or don't like, and then find they haven't made a "good buy" after all. *But they simply couldn't resist the urge to join others in competing for goods that are in limited supply.*

Actively traded common stocks are not in limited supply. Therefore, I advise you not to rush to buy as though the supply is going to dry up. If you've ever sat in a stock brokerage office and watched the "tape" (which shows stock transactions as they take place), you'll know what I mean. A certain stock might suddenly get active and start rising in price: one minute you see it at 35, a few seconds later it's 35½, then 36, 36¼, 36½, 37. By the time it has hit 37, it is human nature to feel an almost irresistible urge to buy the stock (regardless of its fundamentals of earnings, dividends, future outlook, etc.)—to get in on the gravy train, to join the rest of the flock who are clamoring to buy the stock as though it is "sale merchandise." Resist this urge. Only buy "goods" that seem rationally attractive and that meet your objectives.

10.   *There is no reason always to be in the stock market.*

After the stock market has had a long and sizable advance, it is prudent to take some profits. Too often, after selling, the money from the sale "burns a hole in the pocket" of the investor. It's like working in a candy shop: no matter how much willpower you have, after a few weeks the bonbons look awfully good. Go slowly—there are times when cash can be a valuable asset.

11.   *Seek professional advice for your investment.*

Find a broker or adviser who is honest and who you are convinced will have *your* best interests at heart. Make sure he knows your financial status, your objectives, and your temperament. If you don't know of a good broker or adviser, consult your bank or your friends and then go in and meet the person recommended to you. Take the same pains to find the best broker or adviser as you would to find the best doctor for yourself. With some bias I recommend again that you read *Investing with the Best,* which explains what to look for and what to look *out* for in your search for a superior investment manager.

12. *Take advantage of the research facilities your broker has to offer.*

Certainly you'll agree that *analysis is a better market tool than a dart.* The top brokerage firms spend millions of dollars every year to find the most attractive investments for their customers. Read the reports that are published—they will give you insight into the investment firm with whom you are dealing. Keep track of their performance over a period of years (performance over a few months may be deceiving, both because the general market may be against them and because you can't expect recommendations to bloom overnight).

13. *Remember that the public is generally wrong.*

The masses are not well informed about investments and the stock market. They have not disciplined themselves to make the right choices in the right industries at the right prices. They are moved mainly by their emotions, and history has proved them to be consistently wrong. If you don't believe this, I recommend that you read a book entitled *Extraordinary Popular Delusions and the Madness of Crowds,* written by Dr. Charles Mackay and published in 1841. The book is filled with concrete examples of the irrational behavior of human beings. Dr. Mackay's descriptions of the famous tulip mania in Holland in the 1630s and the famous South Sea Bubble about a century later are eye-opening, to say the least. Just in case your high school or college history is not vivid in your mind, let me tell you what happened in these two historical events.

Tulip bulbs in Holland in the early seventeenth century were originally sought by collectors and horticulturists, just as orchids and other rare flowers are sought today. As the prices of tulip bulbs rose in the 1630s, people commenced speculating in them. One thing led to another, prices rose further, and suddenly everyone from the downstairs maid to the chimney sweep was speculating in markets that had sprung up solely for trading in tulips. Higher and higher went the prices of tulips— till there was absolutely no relationship between price and the tulips' intrinsic value. As usual when a wide discrepancy exists between price and value, it was not long before prices came tumbling down. Fortunes that had been made speculating were quickly wiped out and the great majority suffered miserably from their emotional speculation.

In the eighteenth century similar speculation and failure occurred in shares of the English South Seas Company, and thereafter there were bursting "bubbles" in all types of stock companies set up for every conceivable venture. To illustrate how emotional and irrational people became, the records show that one company was able to sell its own shares to the public even though it stated that its objective was "to carry on an undertaking of great advantage but nobody is to know what it is."

Dr. Mackay wasn't alive to describe the almost unbelievable hysteria that overcame otherwise sensible people in our country in the late 1920s. In this (later) generation, we have witnessed boom-and-bust experience in uranium, boats, bowling, titanium, small business investment companies, technology fated to become obsolete, electronic games, and an absolute host of others that resulted in large losses for their emotional followers.

A wise investor should be wary of public overenthusiasm for anything. Don't *you* become "one of the herd." Resist the temptation to follow an exaggerated trend, no matter how assured it appears.

14.   *Beware of following stock market "fads."*

Remember the "sack" dresses that became the fad twenty years ago? Or mini-skirts approximately 15 years ago? Both fashions were ill-conceived from the very beginning (they didn't make sense in such a vanity-conscious nation as ours). Women who rushed to buy either sack outfits or mini-skirts found themselves with a useless wardrobe a short time later; and the retail stores that cluttered their racks with this merchandise suddenly found that their inventory was worth very little. This is but one of many examples of the fads in our country. Twenty-six years ago it was hula-hoops; twenty-two years ago it was trampoline centers; seventeen years ago it was "Batman," eight years ago it was CB radios, five years ago it was "PacMan"; three years ago it was Cabbage Patch dolls and next year it will be something else. As a general rule, if you get in early on a fad, you stand to make money. But if you come along anytime close to full recognition, you are asking for trouble.

The same thing goes for the stock market. Just like sack dresses, hula-hoops, trampolines, tulip bulbs, and the rest, the stock market occasionally develops fads for certain industries. In almost all cases a sudden rush to buy the fad stocks pushes them to truly unwarranted price levels. *When you buy at the height of popularity, you almost always pay prices that have little relationship to value.* As repeated so often, you are only asking for trouble when this situation exists, so remember to do some vacuum thinking and pay prices that correspond to the values emphasized in this book.

15. *Don't be so concerned with where a stock has already been; be concerned with where it is going.*

Many times I've heard people say, "It must be a bargain now—it's down 20 points from its high." Where a stock *has been* is history, it's "spilt milk." Investors may have bid up XYZ stock to $100 last year, but the outlook for the company may have changed entirely since then. Or it may have been emotional speculation (fad buying) that forced it up to an unreasonable price. *The important thing is what lies ahead, not what has already transpired,* and previous market prices have no bearing on the future.

16. *Take the time to supervise your stocks periodically.*

Needless to say, conditions constantly change. Don't shut yourself off from the outside world; take an objective look at your holdings periodically, with the thought of weeding out the "weak sisters" and adding stocks that have more potential. Your broker or adviser should be willing to make an analysis of your portfolio for you on a regular basis, and I encourage you to take advantage of this service.

17. *Concentrate on quality.*

While big profits are often made through buying and selling poor-quality common stocks, your success in the stock market is far, far more assured if you emphasize quality in your stock selections. Too many investors shy away from the top-notch companies in search of rags-to-riches performers. This approach is fine for a certain portion of your investment dollars; most people can afford an *occasional* "flyer." But a person who starts out looking for flyers usually ends up, not with just one or two, but with a host of poor-quality stocks—most of which turn out unsuccessful. These low-grade issues are certainly no foundation for a good portfolio; instead, the fine, well-managed companies should form the backbone. And don't for a minute think you can't make money without wild speculation—fabulous fortunes have been made over the years in such high-quality *non*speculative stocks as Abbott Laboratories, Bristol-Myers, Carnation, Coca-Cola, and the like. In other words, place your stress on the elite, not on the "cats and dogs" of the marketplace. "Remember," said one wise stock market philosopher, "if you sleep with dogs, you're bound to get fleas."

38
Final Financial Formulae

At the beginning of this book I discussed finding an effective formula for successful investing in the stock market. Unfortunately there is no pure mathematical formula that will solve all the problems of investing. You can't do as the mathematicians do and say $X = Y + Z^2 (4 \times Y^3)$ and be sure that X will be correct 100% of the time, but you should strive for a high batting average and the preceding pages have shown you how to lead the league in making successful purchases and sales of stocks.

Sometimes the simplest rules are the best. I could summarize all the sage advice that successful speculators and investors have passed down to us over the years in a simple, jocular rhyme:

Here's the money-making lullaby:
Buy stocks low and sell them high.

But of course that's oversimplification. There *is* one bit of sincere advice that will bring all that we have covered so far to a conclusion, and it can be stated in one significant word:

PATIENCE

Patience is often the secret to success in investing. Whether you own stocks or real estate or your own business, you cannot expect success to come overnight. Obviously, there may be times when some of the stocks you own are not moving up the way you would like. But remember, Rome wasn't built in a day. And patience is indeed an investment virtue. So don't be fidgety with your stocks. Don't be concerned with the day-to-day fluctuations that occur in the stock market. I always think of a statement made by one very successful investor. He contended that he made more money *by the seat of his pants than by his agile brain.* In other words:

If you believe in reasonable future growth of this country,
If you can locate the companies that will lead and share in this growth,
If you can isolate quality stocks representing top management and buy them at reasonable prices (i.e., buy value),
Then you should have patience and be willing to "sit" on the good stocks.

The result should be: real success in the stock market!

The preceding pages have given you the tools you need. I have provided the background and the hindsight necessary for success, plus the food for thought that prepares you to add foresight to hindsight. And I've supplied you with many basic rules that should keep you from making mistakes and a Compounding Growth Guide that enables you to judge a stock's fundamental value. In short, we've covered the bases and have both a solid defense against unnecessary losses and a potent offense for making sizable gains.

Appendix

How to Arrive at a Company's Annual Compound Growth Rate

The basis of our Compounding Growth Guide lies with the investor's appraisal of a company's future yearly rate of growth. The procedure involves:

1. Determination of a company's annual compound rate of growth over the *past* three to five years.
2. An analysis of whether this growth rate will increase or decrease over the *next* three to five years.
3. Allowance for the kind of institutional support a stock commands.
4. Conclusion of the "proper P/E," according to our guide.

Because the annual compound growth rate in the *past* and in the *future* is so important, I want to make it easy for you to be able to figure this rate. The mathematical formula for doing this is rather complicated, so I have done the figuring for you. The result is a very simple table for you to use.

All *you* have to do is figure what a company's *total increase in earnings per share* has been (or is projected to be) over a three to five year period, and then the table will tell you what the company's annual compound growth rate has been (or is projected to be). Your computation is very simple but, just for review, here is how total increase over a period of time (on a percentage basis) is computed:

First of all, subtract the earnings per share for the first year you are using (your base year) from the *last* year you are using. EXAMPLE: You are analyzing XYZ Company, which has had the following record over the last four years:

1986	$1.50
1985	1.37
1984	1.10
1983	1.15
1982	1.00

In this case, subtract the first year (the 1982 base year) from the last year (1986):

$$\$1.50 - \$1.00 = \$.50$$

Next divide this answer ($.50) by the base figure ($1.00):

$$\$.50 \div \$1.00 = .50 \text{ or } 50\%$$

This is the total percentage increase in earnings per share over the period you have chosen. XYZ's total growth from 1982–1986 was 50%.

Once you have arrived at this simple calculation of the percentage increase, it becomes only a matter of consulting the following table to determine the *yearly compound growth rate.* Simply:

1. Find the column in the horizontal A headings that delineates the number of years you have chosen for your growth calculation.
2. Glance down the vertical column from that point until you reach the approximate percentage figure that your calculations of growth have produced.
3. Look to the far left—to the vertical B figures—to determine what the compound *annual* rate of growth amounts to.

In our XYZ example above, you start by locating the "4 Yrs." column in A; then look down until you come to as close to 50% as you can (the 4 Yrs. column does not show 50 exactly but you can see that your answer lies between 46 and 52); look to the left to B and conclude that the 46% growth equals 10% per year compounded and 52% growth equals 11%. The answer, therefore, for XYZ annual growth from 1982–1986 is about 10⅔%.

Let me caution you about figuring growth rates. Be sure not to start with a year that is either greatly depressed or greatly inflated. Instead, choose a year that is more normal, or use the average of a few years as a base and compute growth from this.

COMPOUND GROWTH TABLE

B. Then the Compounded Annual Rate of Growth Is:

A. If Total Growth over the Below-Specified No. of Years Has Aggregated:

Rate of Growth	1 Yr.	2 Yrs.	3 Yrs.	4 Yrs.	5 Yrs.	6 Yrs.	7 Yrs.	8 Yrs.	9 Yrs.	10 Yrs.	15 Yrs.	20 Yrs.	25 Yrs.
1%	1%	2%	3%	4%	5%	6%	7%	8%	9%	10%	16%	22%	28%
2	2	4	6	8	10	13	15	17	19	22	35	49	64
3	3	6	9	13	16	19	23	27	30	34	56	81	109
4	4	8	12	17	22	26	32	37	42	48	80	119	167
5	5	10	16	22	28	34	41	48	55	63	108	165	239
6	6	12	19	26	34	42	50	59	69	79	140	221	330
7	7	14	22	31	40	50	61	72	84	97	176	287	440
8	8	17	26	36	47	59	71	85	100	116	217	366	590
9	9	19	29	41	54	68	83	99	117	137	264	461	760
10	10	21	33	46	61	77	95	114	136	159	318	573	980
11	11	23	37	52	68	87	108	130	156	184	378	710	1260
12	12	25	40	57	76	97	121	148	177	211	447	870	1600
13	13	28	44	63	84	108	135	166	200	239	525	1050	2020
14	14	30	48	69	93	119	150	185	225	271	614	1270	2550
15	15	32	52	75	101	131	166	206	252	305	714	1540	3190

16	16	35	56	81	110	144	183	228	280	341	830	1850	3990
17	17	37	60	87	119	157	200	251	311	381	950	2210	4970
18	18	39	64	94	129	170	218	276	343	428	1100	2640	6170
19	19	42	68	100	139	184	238	302	378	470	1260	3140	7640
20	20	44	73	107	149	199	258	330	416	519	1440	3730	9440
21	21	46	77	114	159	214	280	359	456	573			
22	22	49	82	121	170	230	302	390	498	630			
23	23	51	86	129	182	246	326	424	544	692			
24	24	54	91	137	193	264	351	459	593	760			
25	25	56	95	144	205	282	377	497	646	832			
26	26	59	100	150	219	300	404	535	700	908			
27	27	61	105	160	233	318	430	572	754	984			
28	28	64	110	170	242	340	462	622	825	1082			
29	29	67	115	176	258	360	492	665	888	1175			
30	30	69	120	186	271	383	528	716	961	1279			
31	31	72	125	195	286								
32	32	74	132	206	305								
33	33	77	136	215	318								
34	34	80	142	224	335								
35	35	82	147	234	350								
40	40	96	175	285	440								

Index

Abelson, Alan, 55
Accounts payable, 140
Accounts receivable, 137
Advance-decline ratio, 68
Advisory services, 55–56, 286
Aerospace industry, 244
Aggressive growth portfolio, 322
Airline industry, 245
Airplane industry, private, 231
Aluminum industry, 245
American Stock Exchange, 40, 70
Analyzing securities, 133–58
Annual reports, 170
Annuities, 10, 11
Arbitrage, 94–95
Arrearaged (accrued dividends), 20
Assets (balance sheet), 134, 137–39
"At-the-money," 112
Automobile industry, 61, 220, 246
Automotive parts industry, 246

Balance in a portfolio, 319–20
Balance of trade, 59
Balance sheets, 133–40, 176
  analysis of, 141–50
Bank deposits, statistics on, 57
Banks and banking:
  evaluating the industry, 246
  Federal Reserve Board, 55, 59, 62–64
Barron's, 46, 54, 55, 69
Bear markets, 71–72, 114, 355
"Bikini" stocks, 333–50
  1962 recommendations, 334–40
  1976 and 1980 recommendations, 341–48
  1987 list, 348–50
Bonds:
  corporate, *see* Corporate bonds
  interest rates, 20, 186, 187, 200, 201, 269, 270
  municipal, 8
  U.S. government, 5–7, 269–70
Book value per share, 143–44, 150, 176
Borrowing (corporate), 144–49, 198
Broadcasting industry, 247
Brokers, 27–32, 44–45, 46, 169, 356–57, 359
  commissions, 35, 48, 49, 287
Building industry, 61, 247
Bull Markets, 71–75, 114, 355

Business failures, 59
Business organization, forms of, 14–16
Business Week, 54
Buying stocks, *see* Investing; Market orders and transactions; Stock market theories

Call price, 20, 82
Calls, *see* Puts and calls
Capital gain dividend, 301–302
Capital gains tax, 100, 116, 278, 280–82, 288
Capitalization, companies with small, *see* "Bikini" stocks
Cash flow per share, 157–58
Central Market System, 33, 49
Charts, 292–95
Chemicals industry, 247
Chicago Options Market, 17
Children, investments for, 323
Cincinnati Stock Exchange, 40
Clean capitalization, 149
Closed-end investment trusts, 303, 306
Commissions, 35
  brokerage fees and, 35, 48, 49, 287, 320
  investment trust fees and, 300–301, 304–305, 328–29
Common stock, 13, 21
  "bikini" stock, 333–50
  commandments, 353–60
  dividends, *see* Dividends
  financial page information, 79–81
  outstanding, times present market values, 148
  portfolios, 319–24
  vs. preferred stock, 21–22
  quality, 355, 360
  splits, 73, 90–92, 355
  stock rights, 101–105, 110
  warrants, 106–109, 110
  yield, *see* Yield
  see also Price/earnings (P/E) multiples
Company approach theory, 168–75
Competition in an industry, 165–66
Compound growth rate, annual, 363–67
Compounding Growth Guide, 196–216, 240
  annual growth rate computation, 363–67
  examples, 203–15

368

Short covering, 36
Short selling, 35–38, 44, 68, 94, 95, 114–15, 116
Soft drinks industry, 257
Sole proprietorship, 14
Specialists, 27, 28, 30–32
Specialist's book, 31
Speculation, 69–70
Spreads, 118–19
Standard and Poor's advisory service, 55
Standard & Poor Stock Guide, 199
Steel industry, 62, 220, 258
Stock dividends, 99–100
Stock index futures, 123–25, 130
Stock index options, 119–23, 130
Stock market, 354–56
    bull and bear markets, 71–75, 114, 355
    economic indicators affecting the, 56–65
    fads, 358–59
    as forecaster of events, 53–54
    judging how it is doing, 66–70
    publications focusing on the, 54–56
    tips, 354–55
Stock market theories, 290–96
Stock rights, 101–105, 110
Stocks, *see* Common stock; Preferred stock
Stop-buy orders, 38–39, 44
Stop-sell orders, 38, 39, 44
Straddles, 118–19
Strike price, 112
Survey of Current Business, 55

Takeovers, 144
Taxes, 277–82
    capital gains, 100, 116, 178, 280–82, 288
    capital losses, 279–81
    cash dividends and, 177, 277–78
    partnership vs. corporation, 16–17
    sole proprietorship, 14
    stock dividends and, 100
Telephone stocks, 266

Temperament, personal, 317–18
    portfolio recommendations and, 319–22
Tender offer, 144
Textiles industry, 258
Third Market, 48, 49
Tobacco industry, 359
Tokyo Stock Exchange, 25, 26
Total return, 178
Traders and trading, 285–89
Trading department, 44
Treasury bills, bonds, and notes, 5, 8
Trucking industry, 259

Ultraconservative portfolio, 321
Underwriters, 101
Unfilled orders, manufacturer's, 57–58
U.S. Department of Commerce, 45
U.S. government:
    agencies, securities of, 8
    securities, 5–7, 19, 269–70
Universal life insurance, 10–11
Unlisted stock, 43–47
Utilities stocks, 61, 263–74, 277
    characteristics of, 263–65
    considerations in buying, 267–71
    growth, 271–74

Value Line, 55, 199
Vending machine stocks, 227–28
Volatility of stock's price, 198
Volume of trading, 68, 80

Wall Street Journal, 46, 54
Warrants, 106–109, 110
Waste management industry, 259
Water utilities, 267
Wholesale price levels, 62
Wiesenberger service, 303, 307
William O'Neill service, 199

Yield, 68–69, 177–80, 236
    on utilities stocks, 269–70
Yield to maturity (bond), 86